P9-DEP-396

inside

women's college basketball

Anatomy of a Season

Richard Kent

TAYLOR TRADE PUBLISHING

DALLAS, TEXAS

Copyright © 2000 by Richard Kent
All rights reserved

No part of this book may be reproduced in any form or by any means—including
photocopying and electronic reproduction—without written permission from the
publisher.

Book design by Mark McGarry
Set in Monotype Dante

Published by Taylor Publishing Company
1550 West Mockingbird Lane
Dallas, Texas 75235
www.taylorpub.com

Library of Congress Cataloging-in-Publication Data
Kent, Richard G.
   Inside women's college basketball / Richard Kent.
      p. cm.
  Includes index.
  ISBN 0-87833-188-3 (cloth)
     1. Basketball for women—United States. 2. National Collegiate Athletic
Association. I. Title.
GV886 .K48 2000
796.323'63'0820973—dc21   00-042589

10 9 8 7 6 5 4 3 2 1

Printed in the United States of America

*To every woman who has ever played
or dreamed of playing college basketball.*

contents

acknowledgments

A lot of events needed to coalesce to turn this book from a dream into a reality. Rutgers University, my beloved alma mater, needed to win the AIAW National Championship in none other than Philadelphia in 1982 to pique my interest in women's basketball. My friend, Chris Dailey, the captain of the aforesaid Rutgers team, needed to move on as an assistant from Rutgers to Cornell and then take a major coaching gamble at the University of Connecticut under a brash former Virginia assistant to whom she introduced me, Geno Auriemma. Connecticut, a school that in the mid-80s had to give away tickets to put 50 people in the stands, now a scant 10 years later had to turn away crowds in excess of 10,000 who wanted to watch a dream team led by Player of the Year, Rebecca Lobo, win a National Championship.

With those events as the background, I started the "Big East Women's Basketball Report" with my friend Paul Jaffe, a college basketball fanatic but a virtual stranger to the glorious women's game. That publication never could have started without the financial support given by Bob's Stores out of Meriden, Connecticut, and specifically the confidence entrusted in Paul and me first by Ellen Ornato and then by Joan Ahlquist of Bob's. Without them, none of this would ever have happened and most importantly, this year-long project—or more appropriately described as this labor of love— needed the expert writing of my coauthors: Kate Smith of the *Newark Star Ledger,* Mike DiMauro of the *New London Day,* Rachel McLoughlin of the *Connecticut Post,* Karin Crompton, a veteran Connecticut sportswriter, and Don Harrison, a Connecticut freelance writer and twice Connecticut Sportswriter of the Year. I especially want to thank Kate and Rachel for going above and beyond the call.

I want to give special thanks to a number of people throughout the college basketball world who helped me with this project. Kevin McConnell and Marla Rodriguez of Rutgers were helpful right from the start. So were Ann Wheelwright of Boston College and head coach Ed Swanson of Sacred Heart University. I also cannot ignore the help throughout the season given to me by Tammy Donovan of the Big East Conference. During the tournament, I got valuable insights from Josh Krulewitz, Jay Bilas, and Doris Burke of ESPN.

Sue Donahue of the NCAA was extremely helpful, and I also wish to acknowledge the invaluable assistance of my assistant, Jennifer Mengold.

I would like to thank my wife Lisa and my daughters Lindsay and Sarah; and all of the people at Taylor Publishing, including but not limited to Mike Emmerich, Jennifer Thomas, and Delia Guzman.

To all of these people and many more, I would like to say a resounding "Thanks."

foreword

By Vivian Stringer

The 2000 season was one of the most memorable of my 28-year career, which spans three decades and three different programs. The season was special, not because everything went perfectly or that we "sailed" through the season on cloud nine. What made this season special was the fact that we completed something we set out to do nearly five years ago. When I came to Rutgers from the University of Iowa, where we had just assembled the nation's number-one recruiting class, I said that Rutgers, the State University of New Jersey, would be the "Jewel of the East." Most people wrote off the statement as either arrogant or silly. Truthfully, it was simply a declaration of what we wanted to build at Rutgers. I believe that in order to reach great heights, you must set your sight at the top and state your goals boldly. And that's what we did. To those outside the program, we looked silly in the first two years. Then, in the third year we went to the NCAA Tournament Sweet Sixteen; the following year, we advanced to the Elite Eight. In 2000 we knew that we had all of the elements necessary to go one step further...to the Final Four in Philadelphia. So, once again, we declared our goals boldly and publicly on our media guide cover. The cover says "Destination Philadelphia 2000 Final Four."

Did we know we would be in the Final Four? No. But we believed we could be and continued to believe that even during our losses to George Washington, Villanova, and others. We had eight losses, the most of anyone in the Final Four, but we believed we could be there. The season really was about staying true to our mission no matter what. It's a great lesson to learn for life, not just for basketball.

During the season, we saw glimpses of why we believed we belonged in the Final Four. Early in the season, we defeated a very good Texas team that coincidentally was my 600th career victory. Although the numbers have never been important to me, it was very special to achieve that milestone with one of the icons of the game, Jody Conradt, present. More than the wins, when I reflect on the number of games I have coached, it is mind boggling. However, I am pleased to think of all the young ladies' lives I have touched and how many women have been positively influenced by the game of basketball. Right after the Texas win, we came back with a big victory over UCLA, ranked No. 6 at the time. I thought we did a good job of adjusting to the different style of game and executing what we needed to do to win. I was encouraged by our effort and execution in this game.

Another game that gave us reason to believe was the Notre Dame game. I thought Notre Dame was one of the best teams in the country with their incredibly balanced attack. They could hurt you inside and outside and had players who could get the job done at every position. We knew we needed to play a near perfect game to beat them. It was good to see that we had learned from our earlier defeat. They beat us pretty good at our place; but we made some adjustments, and that meant to me that we were finally comfortable enough with all of the elements of the game to be able to change on a dime.

The greatest victory of the season was, of course, our last. Defeating Georgia to get to the Final Four was really inspiring because once again I saw our players' will to win overcome every obstacle. Georgia had de-molished North Carolina in the West Regional semifinal game and looked like world beaters with their inside-outside game. We knew that we had to play well, execute our defense, and remain extremely focused. We did all of those things.

It was also a special season because the biggest event in women's bas-ketball returned to where it all began, Philadelphia. I remember when three or four coaches got together in Philadelphia to create a group that would give women's basketball a voice in the NCAA. It's now called the WBCA and has a membership of approximately 4,500. It was good for me to return to where so much of my career took place, right outside Philadelphia at a small school called Cheyney State. A tiny school with no budget, we advanced to the first-ever NCAA Final Four in 1982. While it was a great honor to play in the first-ever NCAA Final Four, I knew then that the time would come when a small school like Cheyney, which I love dearly, would no longer be able to compete with the bigger schools with large budgets. Women's basketball has progressed so far from the early days. I saw this day coming, but I don't think I ever imagined it quite like it was actually being there and being a part of it. At the 2000 Final Four we drew the largest crowd to see a women's basketball game in the state of Pennsylvania, not to mention the national television audience on ESPN. There was incredible media attention and wild fan support. The games were intense with high-level athletes competing well. This was what I dreamed of back then. This dream too became a reality.

People are excited about the game; just look at the success of the WNBA. There have been women's pro leagues before, but none has en-joyed the level of popularity that the current women have. That people are writing books about women's basketball is another measure of just how far we have come.

I would like to thank the author of this book, Richard Kent, who has been one of the most dedicated observers of the women's game I have met since coming back East. He follows the game very closely, attending many of our games as well as any nationally significant game played. Richard publishes the "Big East Women's Basketball Reports," which are always informative and full of interviews and features that we would probably not be aware of otherwise. His dedication is such that he finds time to do all of these things in service of women's basketball while maintaining a demanding full-time job as a lawyer. Many times, he will be in court all day, at basketball games by night, and running a basketball all-star game on the weekend. His boys and girls high school all-star games are great ways for those kids to show off their talents and get to play against great competition. A Rutgers graduate, he also has hosted many events that allow me, my staff, and the student-athletes the opportunity to meet so many of the distinguished and loyal Scarlet Knight fans. For all of these contributions, and for this book, we thank him.

introduction

Suffice it to say that April, May, and June are my least favorite months of the year. Most especially in 1999. I am a college basketball junkie, and those are the months which directly follow the end of the season. There are obviously no summer league games taking place, and October 15, the start of practice, seems very far away.

I have never had such wild expectations for a women's basketball season as I had anticipating the start of the 1999–2000 season and specifically the expectation of a fabulous end of March and early April in nearby Philadelphia, the site of the Final Four. I am a big-time Rutgers fan and live in the state of Connecticut. Right smack in the middle of that behemoth called Huskymania. I am also an admirer of the Tennessee program and specifically of head coach Pat Summitt, whom I consider to be the best coach in the game, and her star junior, Tamika Catchings, whom I consider to be the best current college player.

I am fully aware of the coaching abilities of Andy Landers at Georgia, Leon Barmore at Louisiana Tech, Rene Portland at Penn State, Wendy Larry at Old Dominion, Theresa Grentz of Illinois and a former Rutgers coach, and Gail Goestenkors of Duke. I knew that all of those teams would contend along with Connecticut, Tennessee, and Rutgers for a national championship.

Sure, my alma mater Rutgers had won an AIAW National Championship in 1982, but it had never gone further than the Elite Eight in the NCAA. I thought in the spring of 1999 that 2000 would be the year that the Scarlet Knights would finally find themselves in the Promised Land.

I knew that UConn would once again be a dominant program, not only in the Big East, but nationally. There was no finer motivator in the country than head coach Geno Auriemma, and UConn had going into the season more depth than any other team in the country. They also had a big question mark at point guard. Would Sue Bird, former National High School Player of the Year out of powerhouse Christ the King in New York, revert to her earlier freshman form or would she be debilitated by her December 1998 season-ending knee injury? I knew that Bird would be the key to the team and that if she came out healthy and hungry the Huskies would surely be the team to beat.

Tennessee had talent and a great coach in Summitt, but it would be the first season in four years without their dominant player, the greatest woman to ever play college basketball, Chamique Holdsclaw. How would they respond to life after Chamique? Would Catchings and Semeka Randall be able to fill the void created by the departure of such a superstar? That question remained to be answered.

Towards the end of the spring I came up with the idea of putting together a book about this much-anticipated season. A book that would not only chronicle Connecticut, Tennessee, and Rutgers, but would also deal with the plethora of national powerhouse and not so powerful teams that those three teams would encounter throughout the season. I then decided that the national scene, and specifically recruiting, along with some of the unique personalities in the game, such as KC Jones, had to be dealt with in some depth. With a player of the caliber of Diana Taurasi ready to start her senior year in Chino, California, and about to undergo a recruiting battle, the likes of which we have not often seen in women's college basketball, I knew full well the significance of covering the national scene.

I then started to think about tiny Sacred Heart University right in my backyard and positioned to enter the Division I ranks. Would coach Ed Swanson and his team, just recently accepted by the NEC, fall flat on their faces? Would they have a mediocre season or would they really shine despite all of the bright lights shining on the Connecticut program? That of course all remained to be seen. But I truly believed that the Sacred Heart story was an interesting one and should be told. And I'm glad that it was.

I next set out to find some of the best writers around. Since I had covered women's college basketball for nearly a decade, I knew most of the writers. Finding the best writers was one of the easiest tasks. Convincing them to take on such a project within the context of the demands of acting as beat writers was more difficult. It was there that I used my skills of persuasion, honed in law school and in the courtroom, to convince such superstars of the writing profession as Kate Smith from the *Newark Star Ledger*, Rachel McLoughlin of the *Connecticut Post*, Mike DiMauro of the *New London Day*, and Karin Crompton to join me. They all ultimately did. All of the readers of this book are better off for that decision.

Since Sacred Heart didn't really have a beat writer, I thought long and hard about whom I should recruit. It then dawned on me that Don Harrison, nationally recognized sportswriter and twice decorated as Connecticut Sportswriter of the Year was close to the program and might be available. He was indeed interested, and I had all of my writers. I decided that I personally would concentrate on the postseason, which included the postseason conference tournaments and the three-week frenzy known as March Madness. The NCAA Tournament.

Next was to arrive at a workable and readable format, which would blend the writing strengths and abilities of each of these writers. Connecticut, Rutgers, and Tennessee were clearly going to be featured. Interestingly enough, they were all traveling to Europe in the summer. Each NCAA Division I school is permitted to make a summer trip every four years. This was the season for all three of those programs. It was decided that the European trips would be covered and that the most critical games and story lines, as they developed throughout the season, would also be dealt with in depth. We knew going into the season that a key injury to one of three or four players on any one of those teams early on in the season could kill their title hopes long before the tournament ever began. Fortunately for all three schools, that didn't happen this season.

And indeed what a ride it was for Connecticut, Tennessee, and Rutgers, and on a different level for Sacred Heart. The three former programs all made it to the Final Four in Philadelphia.

For UConn, it was an easy ride. Bird turned out to be the real deal and Shea Ralph performed in a way which belied her two almost career-ending anterior cruciate ligament injuries.

Tennessee had a slightly more difficult run, especially in the tough SEC Conference, but also emerged virtually unscathed in Philadelphia.

For Rutgers, as Coach Stringer tells us in her preface, it was a seesaw ride. The Scarlet Knights were ranked No. 1 preseason by influential *Street & Smith's* magazine, yet proceeded to get blown out in their opener against relatively unheralded North Carolina State. They lost to teams like Villanova and George Washington during the season and narrowly escaped a major upset at Syracuse. On the flip side, they defeated Texas, Old Dominion, and UCLA at home during the season and nearly upset No. 1 UConn, narrowly falling 49–45 in Piscataway. They had a heart-stopping semifinal Big East win over Notre Dame and a thrilling eight-point win over Georgia in the West Regional final in, of all places, Portland, Oregon.

For Rutgers, the ride to Philadelphia was probably both the most difficult and the most gratifying, and for that reason we have decided to open with the Scarlet Knights.

chapter one

rutgers

Preseason

Goosebumps crept up Shawnetta Stewart's arms as she recounted the dream. The vision was so clear it was almost real. There she was, playing in the NCAA Final Four, climbing a ladder and cutting down the net.

It was a recurring dream for Stewart, a senior forward on the Rutgers women's basketball team. And it always gave her chills.

"I see myself there every night," she said. "Last year, we thought we saw the light, but we really didn't. It was still cloudy. This year, we really see ourselves there. The picture is clearer now.

"We wanted it in the same way, but experience is the key. Purdue (the 1999 national champion) had that experience. They had been to that level and lost. Last year was just their year. This year, we have that key experience. Truly, this year we're ready to take it a step further."

No one had higher expectations for the Rutgers women's basketball team than the players. It seemed like Rutgers' year. In 1998, it shocked many by upsetting Iowa State to earn a spot in the NCAA Sweet Sixteen, where it lost to eventual-champion Tennessee. In 1999, the team made it to the Elite Eight, where it lost to eventual-champion Purdue. With just one key player lost—starting guard Tomora Young—the Final Four was a natural progression.

The pundits agreed. Rutgers was ranked in the Top 5 by every major preseason poll. *Street & Smith's* magazine rated it the No. 1 team in the country, the first preseason No. 1 ranking coach C. Vivian Stringer had ever received in 27 years of coaching and two Final Four appearances.

"I think they're going to make the Final Four in Philadelphia," said Clay Kallem of *Street & Smith's.* "When you make preseason predictions, you throw darts at the wall and hope you get it right. But with this team, they can only be better than last year.

"You have to have all five positions filled to win a national championship. Rutgers has all those pieces, where when you look at Tennessee, Georgia, and UConn, there's a piece missing. Maybe they can make up for it with athleticism, but maybe they can't."

Doug Herakovich, editor of the *Women's Basketball Journal,* said Rutgers was one of several teams with championship potential. "It's hard to find a weakness with them," said Herakovich, whose publication ranked Rutgers third behind UConn and Tennessee. "They have the kind of talent and the kind of coach that should make them a serious contender.

"The field is a little more open this year. There doesn't seem to be one or two teams that are in the race. There are six or seven teams. If Rutgers gets a few breaks and stays healthy, they should be in there."

Rutgers and the area media preferred to focus on the *Street & Smith's* ranking. After *Street & Smith's* poll was released, hordes swarmed the Rutgers Athletic Center (RAC). Papers and television stations that had never regularly covered Rutgers were scrambling for player interviews and showing up for press conferences that, in the past, had been attended by just a few media members.

The team's annual media day was nothing short of a zoo. After Stringer addressed the crowd, the press was let loose on the players. The team sat autographing posters—getting a jump start for its annual Meet the Team Knight—while reporters traveled in a pack trying to find out who the key players were.

Tasha Pointer, Rutgers' junior point guard, was the crowd favorite. Pointer and Stewart were both named preseason candidates for the Naismith Player of the Year award. And Pointer was the reason *Street & Smith's* rated Rutgers ahead of Tennessee and Connecticut.

"Maybe Rutgers doesn't have the individual brilliance of (UConn's) Svetlana Abrosimova or (Tennessee's) Tamika Catchings, but it's got a point guard who's gone through the fire," Kallem said. "UConn is loaded, but I'm not sure Sue Bird is the answer."

This Rutgers team was known for its swagger. Some called it arrogance. The players thought of it as confidence. They were their own biggest supporters. And they had no doubt about the season. "What do you mean, 'If Rutgers doesn't make it to the Final Four?'" Pointer said when asked whether anything short of Philadelphia would be a disappointment.

Like many teams in the Big East, Rutgers did a summer tour of Europe. It came back focused and unified. The time away gave the players a chance to focus simply on the team and where it wanted to be come March.

"We have all the ingredients," junior forward Linda Miles said. "We have a long bench and team unity. The only thing that can stop us now is ourselves."

The Omen

In retrospect, it should have been an omen. Something is bound to go wrong when no one agrees to play your team in the most prestigious invitation-only event in women's college basketball.

While half of the State Farm Tip-Off Classic—the half featuring host Tennessee and Louisiana Tech—was set, the other half—the one featuring Rutgers—struggled to find a willing and eligible team. Not an easy task when your search begins in August after most schools' schedules were at the printers in July.

Rutgers was supposed to play Oregon, but that didn't pan out when Oregon tangled itself in an NCAA rules violation. Oregon agreed to play in the Tip-Off Classic after having committed itself to another NCAA-sanctioned game. When it realized the error—teams are allowed just one NCAA-sanctioned event per year—Oregon backed out.

Rumors flew over who would take its place. North Carolina State took the offer. While not the first choice, North Carolina State certainly was not a bad choice. It turned out to be an appropriate one for a classic that prides itself on inviting elite teams. Sure North Carolina State started the season ranked No. 20, which doesn't exactly qualify as cream of the crop. But what do the experts know? The team turned out to be one of the surprise success stories of the season, at least until center Summer Erb got injured toward the end of the regular season.

In all the scrambling to find a replacement, communication between Rutgers and the tournament organizers seemed to break down a bit. Rutgers was just about the last to know who its opponent would be. And to the players, it didn't seem to matter. Players always say it doesn't matter. But it does. The Rutgers team that arrives at UConn games isn't the same one that shows up at Walsh Gymnasium in South Orange to play Seton Hall. And the Rutgers team that arrived in Knoxville for the nationally televised season opener was ready to play a No. 20 team. Problem was, North Carolina State had been terribly underrated.

It turned out that the first game of the women's basketball season left Rutgers coach C. Vivian Stringer with one question: "Why?"

Why was Rutgers ranked in the top five in all the major preseason polls?

In its first opportunity to prove itself a national power, Rutgers, which was ranked No. 4 by the Associated Press, failed to play like a Top 5 team and only occasionally played like a Top 25 team.

The Tip-Off Classic is restricted to elite teams, and the invitation to play signified that Rutgers had gained national respect. But when it lost to

No. 20 North Carolina State 68–55 on national television, Rutgers lost a lot of that respect.

"NC State is probably wondering how we were ranked so well," Stringer said. "I'm left wondering that myself. It's like, we thought we'd play a little bit and shake NC State down. You can't come here that way."

Rutgers fell apart on multiple levels and failed to execute fundamentals. It held Summer Erb, the 1999 Atlantic Coast Conference Player of the Year, to eight points, but let a pair of freshmen—Terah James and Kaayla Chones—tear through its defense.

"We didn't execute correctly, didn't play aggressive defense, and we didn't pick up the intensity," point guard Tasha Pointer said. "It was the little things that hurt us.

"We had mental errors more than anything. We went over things a million times in preparation for the game, but we still had mental breakdowns. That's when turnovers occur. If we had been a little more patient and allowed the game to come to us, then some of those unforced turnovers would never have happened."

Stringer wasn't surprised by the loss. She could sense in practice that her team wasn't ready. "I've been very upset because we haven't been playing well," she said. "I told (Temple men's coach John Chaney) last night that if we played the way we've been playing the last 10 days, we're going to lose this game."

Repercussions

There were 12 long days to think about the loss and to break down the breakdowns against North Carolina State. It seemed like an eternity for Rutgers, which had dropped to No. 8 in the polls and was eager to prove itself.

There was more than a week of wrenching four-hour practices to pay for the embarrassment of collapsing on national television and to ensure that the same mistakes would not be repeated.

And just when it seemed the team had learned its lesson, Stringer decided it had not. Rather, some of them had not.

Stringer pulled Tasha Pointer, Shawnetta Stewart, and Usha Gilmore from the starting lineup, giving them seven minutes to study their opponent before putting them in against Northeastern in the Rutgers Coca-Cola Classic on Thanksgiving weekend.

Stringer was furious after the season-opening loss, in which the three started with junior center Tammy Sutton-Brown and sophomore forward Davalyn Cunningham. Sutton-Brown sprained her ankle between games. Cunningham, at 6'0" the tallest healthy Rutgers player, stayed in the starting lineup. She was joined by junior forward Linda Miles and three first-time starters, sophomore guard Christina Fowler, freshman guard Mauri Horton, and junior point guard Karlita Washington, a junior college transfer in her first season at Rutgers.

Stringer said the lineup change was "not totally" a result of the North Carolina State game. She said the change saved the veteran starters for the long run and gave them time to study their opponents. She also wanted her second-string players to gain more experience.

Stringer later said that the lineup change was based on who made the greatest effort and played with the most intensity during practice. It's a system she used while coaching at Iowa, she said. Stringer equated her plan to a relay race. She sends out a group to set the pace and stay close to opponents. Then she sends in the ringers.

"We stay with you, but then our burners are right behind," she said. "You know how psychologically damaging it can be when they don't recognize Tasha Pointer or Shawnetta Stewart out there? They see Mauri Horton, a freshman, or Karlita Washington. And they're like, 'Who's so-and-so?' That's devastating.

"Then they see this other group coming in. And that group is pumped up, and they're just waiting to put even more pressure on you. I'm playing the game, the mind side of it right now."

It also played mind games with the players, who knew they had to earn minutes on the court. "It elevates everyone's level of play," Miles said. "You don't own a starting position. So it makes you constantly work hard so you can go out there and start. And if you don't start, you want to be able to contribute somehow. No one is promised anything within her system. If you get out and bust your butt in practice every day, you're going to get to set the tone. That's what she's looking for, a tone-setting team."

Stringer also may have gotten the only team in the country that brought Naismith Player of the Year candidates off the bench.

Familiar Form

Rutgers showed its first signs of championship form against Wisconsin. After giving up the lead with three minutes to play, Rutgers stayed composed to come from behind and beat No. 25 Wisconsin 63–61 on a basket and free throw by Tasha Pointer in the Rutgers Coca-Cola Classic on November 28.

"We all just had confidence in one another," Pointer said. "While things seemed like they were going bad and looking bad, the leaders on the team were out there saying everything was okay. We believed that we could do it."

After Rutgers lost to North Carolina State in the season opener, many questioned its high ranking. And when Rutgers allowed Wisconsin to go on a 19–4 run and take a 59–53 lead with 3:06 remaining, it seemed like those same questions would resurface. But Rutgers would not allow the late-game drought to spoil 30 minutes of hard work and its chance at redemption.

"We're hurt and we're down," Rutgers coach C. Vivian Stringer said. "We felt bad when we lost to North Carolina State (in the season opener). And this was a team that threatened everything that we're working toward. I told them this would be one of about four games that define us. Where is our character? Where is our heart?"

Character and heart drove Rutgers in the final two minutes of play.

Jen Clemente suited up for the first time in almost a year. She had red-shirted the year before with a blood clot on her lungs and strained her foot before the first exhibition game this season. She told Stringer she could only give two minutes of playing time. During those two, she hit two free throws to spark the team. Christina Fowler, who averaged only five minutes last season, hit a free throw then intercepted a pass and scored a layup to bring Rutgers within a point, 59–58, with 1:32 remaining.

Freshman Kourtney Walton sank two free throws to give Rutgers a 60–59 lead with 1:19 to play.

After Tamara Moore hit a layup to give Wisconsin a 61–60 lead with 51 seconds on the clock, Pointer hit a layup with 37 seconds left and sank the front end of a one-and-one with 28 seconds left to give Rutgers the victory.

"They knew the play we were going to run," Pointer said. "And I thought my girl was going to overplay me. In the past I would have gone through with the play. But now that I'm in my wiser days, I knew she had to foul me or I'd hit the shot. Then I just played by reaction. I reacted to what she gave me."

For the second straight game, Stringer started Fowler, Mauri Horton, and Karlita Washington and left Usha Gilmore, Pointer, and Shawnetta Stewart on the bench.

"In the four years that I've been here, that was the greatest team effort I've seen," Stringer said. "We used just about everyone here. Everyone gave what they could."

Back to Square One

With Pointer and Stewart on the bench, Rutgers struggled through a game against Wisconsin, eventually displaying some championship form to pull out a victory. It also managed a victory at Ohio State.

But the system failed against George Washington.

Just about everything went wrong on that trip, starting with the bus ride to Washington. Rutgers has a regular driver, Danny LeSane. He's been driving the Rutgers bus for seven years. He knows the East Coast circuit, having driven the team to Georgetown plenty of times and having given tours of the capital city to private groups.

The bus company assigned a new driver to the team for the George Washington game. The trip became legendary for its stories of whiplash and the five and a half hours it took to make the three-hour drive. It was a fiasco.

So was the game.

It was Rutgers' most pathetic display of the season. George Washington was without a field goal for the final 18 minutes of the first half, shot 13 percent from the field in the first half and 29 percent for the game, yet still won 63–58.

It was, in Stringer's words, "a basketball phenomenon."

All aspects of Rutgers' game fell apart. Shawnetta Stewart had been struggling from the outside and made just four of 18 shots. No one's outside shots were falling, and it wasn't until the final minutes that Tasha Pointer started driving the lane for some points. But by then, the damage was done.

"You'd think we'd be smart enough to realize that when we're not hitting, we need to drive or pass it inside," Stringer said. "We didn't even think in terms of attacking. Any time you don't reach double digits in assists, something is wrong."

Something was wrong.

"This is not the team you saw last year," Stewart said.

It certainly wasn't. The team that made it to the Elite Eight had intensity and offensive firepower. This team couldn't score. It made a habit of holding teams without a field goal but couldn't take advantage of the scoring opportunities it created.

Only Stewart could score consistently from three-point range. And no one could fill the void while Stewart struggled.

Looking at the team, many wondered what had happened in the eight months since the NCAA Tournament. The team lost just two players, only one of whom—Tomora Young—had any impact. No one realized just how much of an impact Young had. No one expected the team would miss her as much as it did.

Young, a shooting guard, gave the team balance on the perimeter. Though her shooting wasn't always hot, opponents had to worry about her. "She was capable of scoring 20 points any night," Stringer said.

Without Young, it became easy for opponents to concentrate on Stewart. They could risk three-pointers to other Rutgers players because chances were they wouldn't make them. Young could, so the defense had to split up and cover both wing players.

Stringer brought in freshmen Mauri Horton and Kourtney Walton to fill the void on the perimeter, but they had not worked out as well as Stringer had hoped early on. Walton had bouts of homesickness. But more than that, they had few opportunities to develop. They saw limited minutes because Rutgers never got big enough leads.

Rutgers' inside game wasn't productive either. For the George Washington game, centers Tammy Sutton-Brown and Jen Clemente were just returning from injuries. Center Coko Eggleston was recovering from knee surgery. Davalyn Cunningham, a 6'0" sophomore power forward, was filling in at center. She did fine, but clearly was not at her natural position. Rutgers needed height. It needed 6'4" Sutton-Brown to become the player she was a year earlier.

Rutgers seemed to have hit the bottom. And not even Coach Stringer was sure what could be done to revive her team. "Somehow I've got to get us better prepared," she said. "It's my job to show our team how to find another way to get it done. Bite, kick, holler, scream, anything you can to figure out a way to win."

Approaching a Milestone

Little was said about the milestone. As Stringer approached victory No. 600, she and her team kept it low-key. Stringer redirected questions about it. She didn't allow her players to talk about it. There were too many other pressures weighing down Rutgers in December. Stringer wasn't about to let a personal achievement be one of them.

"I would like the team to just forget about it and play," Stringer said. "I'd feel much better if I could see us in one game play like I know we can. I'm hesitant to put that pressure on them. I'd rather just get it over with."

But it was a hard subject to avoid. The media was alerted before the first game of the season that she was approaching the plateau and every new copy of pregame notes had an updated countdown. At first everyone had figured the victory would come on the road against George Washington. After all, she needed only five to reach 600, and it was quietly assumed that Rutgers would win its first five games. But after losing to North Carolina State and George Washington, the target date was knocked to mid-December.

Everyone knew it was coming. And even though Stringer tried to shield her players from pressure, they put it on themselves. They knew they had screwed up, losing unnecessarily to George Washington. They knew the milestone should have been reached against Pittsburgh. And they blamed themselves for not bringing it to Stringer sooner.

"We were really upset at ourselves that we were not able to get it to her against Pitt," Rutgers guard Usha Gilmore said. "We were very disappointed after that game. We're trying to get on track and start playing the basketball we know how to play, the basketball that she taught us how to play. We're struggling a little bit, but we've been all working individually to get better. We're going to try to make it work against Texas. Everybody's working real hard to stay focused and get really intense.

We're very excited about this number coming up to 600. We're trying to get her what she deserves."

They knew they'd eventually get her to the milestone. They just wanted to do it immediately. The bond between Stringer and her players is impenetrable. As much as they want to succeed for themselves, they want to succeed for her. She's like the mother they don't want to disappoint. You can sense that from talking to them.

"She has the ability to get the best out of people, whether it's defensively, offensively, mentally, or emotionally," Tasha Pointer said. "She helps them improve their skills. Some players come in and they're mediocre, some players you've never heard of. She makes nobodies, somebodies. She makes people who were all-state coming out of high school into All-Americans.

"I know she's a role model because of what she goes through every day. She's teaching us the game of life, how to stay focused, how to be committed to one role. Even if things are going wrong one day, don't lose sight of the bigger picture. Even when she's having down days, you could never tell in practice because she's still coaching, still giving us energy and expecting us to be the best.

"Every time she raises her voice—which she's done a lot more this season—it's hard on her because that's not her coaching style. Everyone sees Coach Stringer teaching, but how often do you see her yell? She has a light voice. She's not one of those coaches that's trying to embarrass me. She takes into consideration that each player wants to do her best. She provides us with motivation, makes us believe that we're probably better than what we are. I think any great coach would do that. It's not like it's a lie. Every day she doesn't feed us red roses and tell us we're the best, or have us believe that we can play with anybody, but we're always prepared for the game.

"I've never seen her outcoached. She's outcoached everybody we've played. Because our coach struggles daily and has struggled throughout her life, I think we're just an extension of her. We go through adversity, but that only makes us stronger, only makes us better, makes the team progress."

■

The outside pressure arrived about game No. 599, against Pitt on December 8. There were 10 days before the target date and media began to swarm at the Rutgers Athletic Center. The weekly press conference doubled in size, with television cameras setting up to capture Stringer's thoughts and feelings.

There wasn't much to capture at first. But a day or two before the Texas game, she started to think about the upcoming game and its meaning. "I would like this game to just return us to ourselves," she said. "And when I do remember it, I want to remember it not as No. 600, but as the game that became the turning point for us."

As she approached a milestone that spoke as much to longevity as to success, she looked back on a career that had been as memorable for its losses as for its successes. "It makes me smile and be proud," she said. "I like the idea that I know what it was like when there was nothing. I can sit back and say, I remember when...."

Coach Stringer

Stringer walked through the underground corridor, an unfamiliar white noise enveloping her as she approached the University of Iowa basketball court. She emerged from the tunnel unable to hear anything but the overpowering hum of the crowd, which had descended upon the arena like a swarm of black-and-gold bumblebees.

The arena is shaped like a bowl, with the court sunk at its base. Windows wrap around all 360 degrees of the building, though you never would have known on that particular day. Bodies were lined 15 deep around the lobby-level rim of the bowl, blocking the sun from sneaking through the glass walls.

At that moment, Stringer knew the outcome of the upcoming game was irrelevant. All that mattered was impressing the 22,157 fans who were there to witness the first women's basketball sellout in Iowa history.

"I was scared to play because I wanted our team to make them proud," Stringer said. "I just wanted to have a good showing and show that women's basketball is exciting."

Stringer, then in her third year as Iowa's head coach, cried after that game. Not because her team lost to Ohio State on that February day, but because, a week after she had verbalized her dream of selling out the arena, it had come true.

Now nearing the end of 1999, of the 784 games Stringer had coached in her 27-year career, 599 were victories. But when asked for her five most memorable games, Stringer told stories about three losses—including the one to Ohio State—and just two victories. She doesn't always measure success by the won-lost column.

On December 18, Stringer attempted victory No. 600 against Texas. She aimed to join Jody Conradt of Texas and Pat Summitt of Tennessee as the only Division I women's basketball coaches to win 600 games. Unlike Conradt and Summitt, both of whom achieved more than 700 victories at one school, Stringer earned her victories by coaching at three Division I schools.

Stringer is one of the most successful coaches in the history of women's basketball. She is the only coach to bring three different programs to the NCAA Tournament and the only one to bring two programs—Pennsylvania's Cheyney State and Iowa—to the Final Four. But to her peers and players, she is more than just a great coach. She is a role model, a pioneer, a teacher, and an advocate.

"She's a professor of basketball, not just a coach," said Hall of Famer Nancy Lieberman-Cline, who played for Stringer when she coached the U.S. National Team in 1989 and is now the coach of the WNBA's Detroit

Shock. "Her depth knows no limits. She has changed the way women's basketball is played because of her teaching and the way she interacts with players. She treats them like family. She's a joy to be around, a great sharer of information.

"She may have 600 wins on the court, but she has about 6,000 off the court in people's lives. She doesn't even know how many people's lives she's affected. She's a Hall of Famer waiting to happen."

When Stringer started coaching at Cheyney State in 1971, she was younger than some of her players and shorter than most of them. Recently graduated from Slippery Rock State College, she spent mornings playing pickup ball with her players, then showered and headed back to the gym to conduct practice.

John Chaney was the men's coach at Cheyney back in those days. They held joint practices, took turns lecturing, and spent endless hours philosophizing and developing lessons.

"She's someone who's spent all of her life being not only a great teacher but also a great student," Chaney said. "She's one of the greatest coaches in the country, man or woman. She's something special."

> I remember our first near-perfect game at Cheyney. It was against Immaculata, and they had won a couple of national championships. It came down to the last shot. I still remember the newspaper the next day. It had all these pictures of the ball at every spot in its arc. In the final one, it showed the ball hitting the net. In the background, you could see the clock down to nothing. We played near perfect, but it wasn't meant to be.

In her 12 years at Cheyney, Stringer built an NCAA Division I program at a Division II school. She burned out car after car, spending her own money traveling the country recruiting players for a school that couldn't afford to fly her, for a school that couldn't afford scholarships.

"It's difficult to recruit youngsters with a suitcase full of financial aid forms when someone else walks in with scholarship papers," Chaney said. "But Vivian would tell these parents that they shouldn't take the scholarships but should pay for their child to go to Cheyney because of her. She'd say, 'I'm going to take care of your child. I'll make sure she graduates.'"

Stringer built a national powerhouse out of a veritable poorhouse. Chaney remembers school administrators hoping the team would lose in the 1982 NCAA Tournament. It couldn't afford to send the team around the country, Chaney said. That was the first year Stringer brought a team to the Final Four. Cheyney lost to Louisiana Tech in the national championship.

> In the regional final, I overheard people from the NCAA saying they couldn't believe we were going to win. They couldn't even pronounce Cheyney. They had decided who would be in the Final Four. But we had a determination, a fire in our eyes.
>
> That La Tech game was special. It makes you cry because we had sophomores out there, they were babies. And they had 12,000 or 13,000 people cheering against them. All they had were themselves.

Eleven seasons later Stringer brought her second team, Iowa, to the Final Four. It was one of the most difficult years of her life. Her husband died of a heart attack on Thanksgiving Day, her daughter was in the hospital in Philadelphia for six months, and Stringer was traveling between the Midwest and the East Coast after every game.

Her team got a tough draw in the 1993 NCAA Tournament. It needed to hurdle Auburn and Tennessee to get to the Final Four. It cleared both.

"Vivian certainly has been a great role model, leader, and spokeswoman for the game," Pat Summitt said. "And she's been very successful, whether at Cheyney, Iowa, or now Rutgers. She's certainly well respected for her ability to recruit and coach. I have great respect for her."

> I remember that Tennessee game because it was a game we weren't supposed to win. They were running such complicated plays, but we didn't have time to prepare for them. We had Auburn the night before. But instead of my players being like, woe is me, they were like, bring them on.

Stringer's most successful teams share the ability to excel when no one expects them to. They also buy into the same thing: Stringer.

Rutgers guard Usha Gilmore had given a verbal commitment to South Carolina when Rutgers assistant coach Jolette Law called her. Gilmore had never heard of Rutgers, but she had known of Stringer since seventh grade. Gilmore had seen a television program about Stringer. Her mother told the young player that she would one day play for Stringer. Gilmore had forgotten about that until Law told Gilmore that Stringer had taken over as Rutgers' head coach. Then Law put Stringer on the phone.

"I said, 'Hold on for a minute,'" Gilmore recalled. "Then I ran into my parents' bedroom to tell my mom that Coach Stringer called me. I was starstruck."

Gilmore was part of Stringer's first recruiting class at Rutgers. In her sophomore year, 1998, Rutgers shocked plenty of people by advancing to the Sweet Sixteen with a victory over heavily favored Iowa State. It was one of Stringer's greatest coaching memories.

> We had a bunch of freshmen and sophomores on the court. In the final seconds, we had Tasha Pointer shooting a one-and-one, Linda Miles grabbing a rebound, and Tammy Sutton-Brown blocking a shot. That was the game against all odds.

Stringer's 600th victory, a 68–64 triumph over Texas on December 18, will go down with those other memorable ones.

Nothing touches her more than the triumph of the human spirit. So when her team scrapped up its every last resource to overcome a three-point deficit and a season of disappointment, Stringer could think of no more appropriate way to earn her 600th career victory. And finally, she showed how much it meant to her.

> I think that the human spirit prevailed tonight. We had the attitude that we won't be satisfied if we don't come out victorious or don't play to our potential.
> This was the perfect game—to see the great struggle, the great

intensity, the spirit of those whose lives I've been able to touch. What's special was the way that this game was won. It symbolizes us. They weren't going to be denied. It was about finding a way in life and not waiting for someone to give it to us.

I'm glad we played a team like Texas. We wanted to play a great team with a great coach, because only in that situation could we find out what our character is all about. With all of the pressures of today on the line, it was good to see what this team is made of. We're not going to disappoint ourselves.

This win represents so many of the young women at Cheyney and so many of the women at Iowa. It was a struggle. With the intensity and spirit of the way we played, I am truly grateful.

I know that this was a great, great win because of how it was done and what we had to overcome to get there. It's early in the season and we're at the point where we want to start. We want to declare to ourselves that we're back. I thank this team, which showed me how to be down but not out.

Stringer avoided a Gatorade shower after earning the victory. Instead, her players hoisted the petite coach on their shoulders and presented her with a bouquet of red and white roses. The Rutgers cheerleaders held up a congratulatory banner, and Rutgers athletic director Robert Mulcahy gave Stringer a commemorative poster and an inscribed basketball. The fans waved signs that proclaimed "600" and Pointer and LaTana Lillard gave Stringer a Rutgers jersey with the most appropriate number—600. Her three children—David, Janine, and Justin—were there.

The only thing missing, Stringer said, was her husband, the late William D. Stringer, who had died on Thanksgiving Day, 1993. "If my husband were here it would be more special," she said. "He was there for all my games."

It wasn't just about Stringer. It was about the team. And it was about the sport.

"I congratulate Vivian. She is a wonderful ambassador for this game," Conradt said. "Of course, I would have liked to delay it for one game. We were hoping Rutgers might get over-emotional because of the importance of this day for their coach, but they held it together and Vivian deserves this. She has built three nationally ranked teams, two of which reached the Final Four. I don't think any women's coach has been able to do that. And I don't think anyone will be able do that for a long time."

It was the night the players turned things around, both mentally and in their game. It was the first night since the season opener that Shawnetta Stewart and Tasha Pointer reappeared in the starting lineup. It was the game when Stewart emerged from her slump, scoring 23 points while being matched up against Texas' All-American, Edwina Brown.

"We wanted to win for Coach Stringer, but we had to prove something to ourselves too," Stewart said. "We've been struggling, and tonight was the game we had to prove to ourselves that we could win."

Coming off the bench for five games, Stewart averaged just 8.6 points per game. In the two games that she started, she averaged 19 points.

"Shawnetta has had to carry a tremendous burden," Stringer said. "Everyone in the world is watching her and Tasha. She's not playing the way she's going to. But her legs were lighter, and she was playing with less of a burden."

The Test

The deadline for Rutgers was December 21, 1999. There was no question that the turnaround would happen then or never. There had been so much struggle, too much struggle thus far. Confidence was waning, morale was weakening. No one knew what was wrong with the team— not the players, not the coaches, and certainly not the fans.

After 28 years of coaching, Stringer had become a master mind reader, able to sift through emotions and thoughts without a word being spoken. But this team stumped her like no other. They listened but didn't hear. They cut up in practice, yapping on the sidelines while others scrimmaged. They forced her to add new elements—yelling and cussing—to practice. She lost her voice and sometimes felt as if she were losing her mind.

This is what a *Street & Smith's* preseason No. 1 team practices like? This is what it plays like?

She knew her team would change. It had to change. Ask Shawnetta Stewart why she chose Rutgers. She'll tell you it was because of Stringer. You'll get the same response from Usha Gilmore, who along with Stewart was in Stringer's first Rutgers recruiting class.

They chose Stringer, but more than that they chose her dream. Stringer was the rainbow leading them to a pot of gold. That's not what they knew; it's what they believed. Stringer had a dream of a national championship team, and she sold them on it. The juniors and seniors were chasing that dream. That's why Stringer knew that they would come around. If a nationally ranked high school player—as each of these women was—is willing to put her faith and her career into a coach and a dream, you can guarantee that she'll fight for the dream.

Rutgers knew its dream hinged, in a sense, on December 21. That day would either put them over the hump mentally or confirm what many already were saying, that Rutgers was overrated.

The threat, the doubt, the urgency—they all collided in one day. The season came down to, or seemed to come down to, one game against No. 6 UCLA.

Rutgers had slipped to No. 15 in the nation, a far cry from the preseason rankings that pegged it as a Top 5 program. Those same preseason polls had also placed UCLA in the Top 5, but unlike Rutgers, the Bruins had managed to stay in that vicinity.

UCLA had been struggling. Senior center Maylana Martin, who had been among the Top 10 preseason candidates for Naismith Player of the Year, had nagging back pain. Erica Gomez, the team's senior point guard and the school's all-time assists leader, injured her shoulder over the summer and was recovering from surgery. Gomez was scheduled to return for the start of PAC 10 play in January. But anyone who knew her knew she would be back before that.

On the day of her surgery, Gomez' father, Lorenzo, predicted his daughter would be back for the Rutgers matchup. "That's the game she's aiming for," he said. "She wants to return for Rutgers."

Gomez grew up in Keyport, New Jersey, a mere half hour from Rutgers. She attended St. John Vianney High School, a powerhouse in New Jersey high school basketball, and led it to three straight state titles. And since she went West, she hadn't been home to play.

"I was pushing myself to get back for this," Gomez said. "I wanted to get to play at home. But more than that, I wanted us to win."

Gomez returned to play Cal State-Fullerton on December 17, a warm-up for her New Jersey homecoming.

Her early return could present big problems for Rutgers, which wasn't accustomed to point guards who could go assist for assist with Tasha Pointer. Gomez, UCLA's all-team leader in assists, had that potential. She's the kind of player who can send a bounce pass from half-court to the middle of the key. And she can do it with alarming accuracy.

Earning Credibility

Sometimes teams have to lose something before they know what they've got. Take a lead, for example. Or a Top 10 ranking.

It had been a long time since Rutgers had been an underdog. But that's really where the team excels. They were the dreamers, after all. They were the ones whose decision to play for Rutgers was based on little more than confidence in their ability to build a powerhouse. This was the team that shocked Iowa State in the second round of the 1998 NCAA Tournament and marched into Nashville believing it would stop Tennessee, then a two-time and defending national champion, in the Sweet Sixteen.

This was a team that fed off others' doubt. It reveled in the opportunity to prove someone or something wrong, whether doubting critics or national polls. The contest with UCLA was the vehicle to do that.

Individually and collectively, it was a breakout game. Playing with something to prove, Shawnetta Stewart scored 28 points and had 12 rebounds to lead Rutgers to a 72–46 victory over UCLA. Unfortunately for Rutgers, it was the first night of winter break, so the upset was witnessed by a paltry crowd of 1,812 at the Rutgers Athletic Center.

The victory gave Rutgers what it longed for all season—credibility. Rutgers finally proved itself against an elite team. It had beaten Wisconsin and Texas, both ranked No. 25 at the time, but it had not been tested by a Top 10 team. "We wanted to send a message to ourselves and the country," Stewart said. "We wanted to show that we can play with anyone."

Rutgers didn't just play with UCLA, it played around it, holding one of the nation's best offensive teams to barely half its average of 81 points. Rutgers brought out the worst in UCLA, forcing 26 turnovers and holding the Bruins to their lowest point total of the season. "It was a big thing for us to do that to them," Rutgers forward Linda Miles said. "They're one of the nation's leading scorers. So it's exciting to hold that team down."

"It's not just UCLA, it's anybody," Stewart said. "We want to hold everyone under 50 points."

All five of UCLA's starting players averaged double digits, but only Martin (19 points) was able to break that barrier against Rutgers. UCLA was scoreless for nine minutes of the first half and did not score a field goal in the final 6:56.

"Rutgers makes you rush shots," UCLA coach Kathy Olivier said. "We tried to do too much on every possession."

In her homecoming debut, Gomez gave her team the best and worst gift. She gave UCLA its only lead, 33–32, on a three-point play with 15:39 to play. And that lead inspired Rutgers to a 20–7 run that wreaked havoc on her team. "It was like a flashback," Stewart said. "It was the same feeling we had when we first got to Rutgers. We came out with such intensity."

For Stewart, too, it was a breakout game. She'd finally, truly come out of her slump, scoring a season-high 28 points, earning two steals, and a team-high six assists. And she couldn't have selected a better time. "Shy came back in the nick of time," Stringer said. "We're counting on her."

To be a top team, Rutgers needed her. She was their shooter. She was one of their leaders. She was the closest Rutgers had to a total package, as needed for All-American and Player of the Year consideration. Without her, the Final Four would remain just a dream.

But against UCLA, Stewart returned. And after UCLA, the Rutgers of preseason expectations was resurrected...or so everyone thought.

Tammy Arrives

Rutgers got past USC, Massachusetts, and Miami without a problem. It struggled slightly against intrastate rival Seton Hall, letting Seton Hall tie the game in the second half before winning by 20.

Tammy Sutton-Brown led the way, showing her old form against Seton Hall. With a 67 percent field goal percentage, Sutton-Brown had been Rutgers' most reliable shooter the previous season. But she was averaging just 36 percent from the field this season.

Her confidence was shaken, but she knew the cure. She just needed the ball to drop. She needed to feel herself hold the ball high over her 6'4" head, muscle by her defender, drop-step in the key, and bank a shot into the basket. And she needed to do it early in a game.

That was always her shot. That's when she knew she was dangerous. That's when she felt like one of the best centers in the Big East. That shot and that confidence had eluded Sutton-Brown early in the season, but she reclaimed them both at Seton Hall, scoring a game- and season-high 18 points in the 65–45 victory.

"I'm back on track," Sutton-Brown said. "And as long as I keep on going forward, I'll be fine."

After Seton Hall had tied the score 29–29 in the opening minutes of the second half, Sutton-Brown scored the go-ahead layup and sparked an 11–0 run that Seton Hall couldn't overcome.

"We want to try to go to Tammy any time we can," Stringer said. "That decision was made at the beginning of the year. Like Shawnetta in the beginning of the year, Tammy's been struggling.

"She's been looking good in practice, seems to be a lot more comfortable. Her timing is there, and she's making cuts with a great deal of confidence. All things concerning levels of confidence rest on the individual themselves. But only through work and persistence can you find out what you can do to get it. You can't hope to come out of a slump. You can't hope to not drop the ball anymore. You can't hope for timing. You have to play your way out of it.

"Tammy has got to come aggressive, come to the ball aggressive. My intention is to get her to be the player she's capable of being. It's not like 'What happened to Tammy?' Tammy has it. She never lost it. She can do it and turn it on when her mind allows her to turn it on. Tammy has to break out of this like Shawnetta had to break through the shooting problems she had."

The difference for Sutton-Brown came less than 20 seconds after tip-off, when she scored a little bunny shot—her specialty—on her first attempt. The basket sent Rutgers on a 10-0 run, which she closed out on her second attempt.

"In any game, after the first couple shots go in, you feel more confident," Sutton-Brown said. "So I felt really good after that."

On the Team Bus

Meet Danny LeSane.

LeSane has driven buses since the Nixon administration, and for the last seven years he has shuttled the Rutgers women's basketball team around the East Coast.

There was that one time in December when someone else drove the team to Washington, but don't bring up that nightmare. He's heard about it ever since. Suffice to say, no one gets whiplash when Danny drives, and everyone was grateful to have him back for the Georgetown trip.

It was about 11 A.M. when he pulled up to the Rutgers Athletic Center in the red-and-black Scarlet Knight mobile. With a sword-wielding knight plastered on the side and "Get Into the Game" splashed across the front, it's kind of hard to miss.

LeSane was early, as usual. The team wasn't leaving until 2, at least that's what the schedule said, but everyone knew that would never happen. That was okay. The more time watching practice, the better.

"I always try to watch an hour or so of practice," LeSane said. "I'm part of the team. Everyone around here knows me."

They really do.

The team ended practice with a huddle exactly at 1. One minute later, they broke from the huddle with a shout of "Synergy," a phrase they picked up during their summer tour through Europe.

The players had an hour to shower and haul their bags out to the bus. You could tell who needed time to primp: they were the last ones out, like Tammy Sutton-Brown.

As far as luggage, there was a system, Danny said. The bus has three storage compartments. By the time the players were showered, he had each one open.

"Coaches' bags always go here," he said, pointing to the compartment closest to the front of the bus. "Players' bags go in the other two. I've got them trained. Everyone knows where to put their stuff."

Danny was just outside or on the bus to greet everyone. He got a hug from Karlita Washington. She owed him one from the Seton Hall trip, when he drove all the way back from Exit 8 on the turnpike to return a bag she left on the bus.

Players loaded their own bags, tossing them haphazardly into a pile. The system worked against Shauntai Hall. She was the first on the bus, so her bags were at the bottom. It wouldn't have been so bad except she always felt like she'd forgotten something, so she had to dig out her bag and double-check for sneakers and her uniform. All there.

Getting to the bus quickly was key. The good seats went fast. Stringer always got the front seat. Tasha Pointer took the back one. The standing order from Blimpie's—a staple of road trips—took up two seats. Everyone else grabbed a sub and filled in where they could.

Managers were in charge of entertainment, which meant a pretrip trip to Blockbuster. Maria Martin got the job. Her choice of *Entrapment*—the Sean-Connery-meets-Catherine-Zeta-Jones action flick—didn't go over too well. "We saw that last year," came a shout from the back. Too bad.

One monitor was on the fritz and seemed to respond only to Stringer, who gave it a fist to the side, a la Fonzie. It worked.

About a half hour into the ride, everything went silent. Assistant coach Jolette Law folded herself into a seat and sacked out with the pillow and blanket she brought from home. Half the team seemed to have brought pillows—Davalyn Cunningham's pillow case was made from a Rutgers T-shirt—and about half the team slept. Feet flew everywhere, over the backs of seats, into the aisle, across the aisle.

Pointer and Washington started a card game. Sutton-Brown leafed through *Glamour.* Usha Gilmore did a little singing. Larry Lawlor, the assistant coach, read the sports section. And Big Man, aka Mark Peterson, the team's 6'9" academic advisor, declared himself King Tetris after setting a new high score on his Gameboy.

Christina Fowler wasn't impressed. She could do better, at least that's what she told Big Man. The trash talking started but didn't last long. That's not why Christina had ventured to the front of the bus, a good three-quarters of an aisle from her seat. She had other things to worry about. She was on a reconnaissance mission, searching for notebook paper. After all, she couldn't play hangman without paper.

The movie was over. Almost everyone was awake. The bus got loud.

Linda Miles argued the merits of a team massage therapist. "We'd be re-freshed," she said.

Traffic got heavy. A wall of brake lights forced the bus to stop, prompting Usha to sing Boyz II Men's "End of the Road."

LeSane had been silent the whole trip. But now he was on the mike, getting ready to give a tour. His dad was a truck driver and musician. His brothers got the musical talent. He inherited the love of driving. He's been crisscrossing the country with tours for so many years that it doesn't matter if the team's in Boston or Washington, he knows something about everywhere.

"That's my job," he said. "That's what I do. And I love what I do, so I want to be the best at it."

The tour ended when the bus stopped at the hotel. Everyone waited while Coach Lawlor checked in. Danny hopped off and started unloading bags.

Coach Stringer was mad because some people were talking during Danny's tour. "When you have somebody who knows, be smart and drain them of information," she said. "Take advantage of him. He's a good man who was trying to explain.

"I know everybody here loves Danny. Seriously, I do know that. And I know that no one was trying to show disrespect. But it's high time that you don't allow anyone to guess about anything. You express exactly how you feel.

"Now, would you like to say thank you to Danny?"

"Thank you, Danny," the team said in unison.

But he wasn't on the bus.

"Okay, he's not here. That was ignorant, wasn't it?" Stringer joked, breaking the tension.

When LeSane climbed back aboard, he was greeted with another collective thank-you.

Room assignments were announced and keys distributed. Washington was just saying how she'd never roomed with Shawnetta Stewart. Now they were paired together for the night. Talk about coincidence.

Everyone was anxious to get off. Pointer jumped on Kourtney Walton's back for a ride down the aisle. Walton was not having it. She shook off her junior captain.

It was time to mess with Coach Law. Walton walked by and touched her foot. She and Coach Law engaged in a battle of who got the last touch. Walton did a touch-and-run, escaping victorious. Pointer did the same thing, though both she and Coach Law claimed victory.

The luggage was lined up. Bags were grabbed. Rutgers had finished a typical bus ride.

The Oversight

With top-ranked Connecticut looming two days away, Rutgers didn't want to worry about Villanova. "It's hard, because we can't wait to play UConn, but we have a policy of focusing on one game at a time," Rutgers guard Karlita Washington said. "We've got to have the same intensity against Villanova that we'll have against UConn."

As much of a nuisance as the Villanova game was, it was a nuisance that Rutgers couldn't afford to overlook. "I know that's what coaches are expected to say, take it one game at a time," Stringer said. "But I think that this is the worst situation. I'm glad that my assistant isn't responsible for this kind of scheduling because he or she would be fired. I don't appreciate it. The game means too much to me. Both games do.

"I'd like to basically forget about Villanova and get on to Connecticut. Let's not kid each other, we've got one doggone day to get to Connecticut. And the fear is that you step over Villanova—especially with them shooting the ball as well as they do from three-point range and being as dangerous as they are—and focus on Connecticut. And if we take our eyes off of Villanova, we're going to lose."

Rutgers took its eyes off of Villanova.

After Shawnetta Stewart made a three-pointer with less than one second remaining in regulation to force overtime, Rutgers gave up a four-point lead and allowed itself to get beaten on free throws, 66–65, before the third-largest crowd in Rutgers women's basketball history—6,362—on its home court.

Villanova had nothing to lose, and it showed in its game. "I thought we had a 10 percent chance of winning this," Villanova coach Harry Perretta said. "I felt that their strengths were our weaknesses—their pressure defense against our inexperienced ball handlers."

But Rutgers was the team that looked inexperienced. "We played like freshmen," Stringer said. "We were anxious, not as calm as we'd like to be."

The loss left Rutgers asking one question: How can we beat top-ranked Connecticut when we can't even beat Villanova?

"We played like (garbage) tonight. There's nothing we can do about it now," Stewart said. "We've got to get this loss out of our minds and go up (to UConn) and play."

Rutgers shot 37 percent from the field and 63 percent from the free throw line, numbers that wouldn't stand against UConn.

"I know about Connecticut, they know about Connecticut, we know about Connecticut," Stringer said. "If Connecticut can take us by 50, they will. I don't think I'll have to say anything (to my team). We have to play with pride and play in a survival mode."

A Team in Limbo

Long after the fans had abandoned the Rutgers Athletic Center, the Rutgers women's basketball team remained in its locker room. One question hung in the air: What's wrong with us?

That's what the players tried to figure out in an emergency team meeting after losing to Villanova. "At this point in the season, it's not about what the coaches say to us," sophomore guard Christina Fowler said. "They've given us the X's and O's. They've given us the knowledge, the inspiration, the encouragement.

"That meeting was about talking to each other and finding out what each of us brings to the table. It was about looking each other in the face and recommitting to each other."

And it was about refocusing.

As Rutgers ventured into its toughest game of the regular season against top-ranked Connecticut at the Hartford Civic Center, it had no time to dwell on its loss to unranked Villanova.

At the team's five-hour practice the day before the UConn game, it didn't. There was no yelling. There was no talk of Villanova. It was practice as usual, which, for the past week, had meant preparing for UConn.

All the preparation in the world didn't guarantee victory, though. At least not for this Rutgers team. "Our coaches have worked so hard to prepare us," Tasha Pointer said. "It's unbelievable how hard they've worked. And it's unbelievable how fast we've screwed it up."

Despite losing to two unranked teams—Villanova and George Washington—Rutgers still believed it had a shot at beating 14–0 UConn.

"Our one testimony is that we've been there before, we know what it's like to win," Pointer said. "Our greatest competition is within ourselves. If we can control ourselves, we've got a chance to win. We know we can do it."

Rutgers certainly had the incentive. No team excites and motivates it like UConn. In many ways, UConn is what Rutgers aspires to be. It's a perennial power, a Big East tournament champion and an NCAA champion.

But Rutgers and UConn were not rivals. Not yet. "Rivalries come when teams share wins and losses," UConn coach Geno Auriemma said haughtily. "It hasn't come to that with Rutgers.

"If you're talking about in our league, in terms of having to win the Big East championship, we feel like we're the team to beat because for the last six years we've won the league. Until somebody beats us, we're it."

Since joining the Big East in 1995, Rutgers had beaten UConn once in eight games. Its only victory was in 1997–98. In their one meeting in the 1998–99 season, UConn won 56–55, despite being without four players.

Rutgers acknowledged that UConn still reigned. "I don't think you can win a game once in four years, especially if you play them two times a year, and say we've got a rivalry," Stringer said. "I hardly think so. I respect myself more. I consider a rivalry something where you cannot—in no way, shape, or form—begin to predict its outcome.

"It's a foregone conclusion…that if you were going out to Las Vegas, you'd bet the house on Connecticut. So let's be real about this. On the other hand, I would say that if Tennessee and Connecticut were playing, you would probably fill in a couple of 'If Tennessee can do this or Tennessee can do that.' That's a rivalry. It would be fair to say that we are still working to earn the respect. We're not there. We're trying to get there.

"But I don't worry about the word 'rivalry.' I'll tell you what I'd like to earn, and that's one more point than they do."

Even though Rutgers held the top-ranked team in the nation to its season-low point total, it didn't leave the Hartford Civic Center satisfied with its 65–50 loss before a sellout crowd of 16,294.

The postgame interview wasn't pretty. The players were on the defensive and Stringer had little to say. "We came here to win a game," Usha Gilmore said, "not to say that they beat us by only 15."

It was a game of missed opportunity for Rutgers, which had a 21–12 lead with five minutes left in the first half before allowing UConn to end the half with 17 unanswered points. That run was the turning point of the game. UConn took a 29–21 halftime lead and extended the margin from there.

"I think we created a situation where maybe if we could have cut out six minutes, seven minutes…it would have been a much better game," Stringer said. "I thought we played as capable as we could right now. We just didn't do a lot of things. But we're just not consistent with our game yet."

The game affirmed UConn's dominance in the Big East. Huskies coach Geno Auriemma reminded his team of its importance before the game. "No one's done more for this conference than Connecticut basketball," Auriemma told them. "No one's done more in our league, ever, than we have. No one's brought our league to the level that it is, and nobody's had a hand in it more than we have. There's a price to pay for that. It means everybody who comes into your building wants a piece of that."

For 17 minutes, Rutgers looked as if it might get a piece of that. Defensively, it outplayed UConn. But its offense caused its demise. Rutgers simply did not have the scoring power to beat a team of UConn's caliber.

The Scarlet Knights shot 27 percent in the first half (9-for-33) and 32 percent for the game (21-for-65). UConn, while having its second-worst shooting game of the season, still fared better, averaging 38 percent from the field.

"Defense is what makes us tick," Stewart said. "Once we get that going, we're okay. But when we had defensive breakdowns, it slowed our offense."

Rutgers built an 18–11 lead on seven points by Sutton-Brown and six by Gilmore. It then missed seven shots and was scoreless for four and a half minutes before Fowler converted a three-point play for Rutgers' final points with 5:06 left in the half.

UConn also struggled, making just four of 16 shots from the floor, missing half of its free throws, and going without a field goal for seven of the opening 17 minutes. The difference was that UConn's offense eventually kicked in.

Midterm Evaluation

At the start of the season, no one questioned where Rutgers would spend the first weekend in April. Surely, Rutgers would be in Philadelphia, realizing its dream of playing in the Final Four of the NCAA Tournament. That's what all the polls predicted, and that's what Rutgers and its fans bought into.

But at midseason, coming off back-to-back Big East losses to Villanova and top-ranked Connecticut, Rutgers already had four losses, as many as it had at the end of the 1998–99 regular season.

It was time to ask: Is Rutgers still on track?

"No, we're not," Stringer said. "We can get on track, but we have to practice and do everything else with a sense of urgency."

Urgency was a word Stringer used a lot. And it was a feeling that was starting to sink in for her players.

"We have to adopt a 'the time is now' attitude," Christina Fowler said. "We're halfway through the season, and we have to get it together. We can't take a day off, mentally, from practice. We can't put off extra conditioning until tomorrow. We've got to do it now. It has to come from ourselves. Everybody on this team has the will to win, but the will to work to win is something that makes championship teams."

Time was Rutgers' worst enemy at that point. It was late in the season to lack focus and consistency. It was also late to lack offensive firepower.

"You can't just show up two games before it's the Final Four—shazam!" Stringer said. "You can't do that. You've got to find your game. And you've got to do it enough times that in a crucial situation, it becomes second nature and you come to expect it.

"If you say so-and-so really looked good last night, the fact that you have to comment on it says that it's outstanding and it's different than what you're used to seeing.

"I would much rather, if you don't mind, have you show me what you can do now (instead of during the postseason). It's like when you're dead, do you really need the flowers? Or would you like some candy and flowers now? You know what will happen, at the end we'll say, 'Dag, we were just peaking. Dag, we could have had this.'"

Fowler said the UConn game—particularly the 15 minutes in which Rutgers dominated—showed the team what it could do. The last 25 minutes showed Rutgers what it needed to work on.

"We realized for the first part of the game that we can play with the best team in the country," Fowler said. "We can compete. We executed our offense and defense and showed we can stick with anybody. We have the potential to be the best, but that's still potential. That game has given us more drive to keep working. But mostly it showed us how much we have to improve. We lost control. Now, it's about being able to play 40 minutes and stay in control. A five-minute breakdown against a team as good as Connecticut is too much."

This was not the Rutgers that people expected to see by January, but the players still thought the Final Four was a possibility. "There were some unexpected bumps in the trail, and we've gone through trials that weren't expected on such a veteran team," Fowler said. "Mentally, we realize that we have a lot to work on still. But just as the potential was there in the beginning of the season, it continues to be there."

Picking Up the Pieces

There's a certain amount of cruelty in sending a team to play the worst team in the conference directly after playing the best team in the conference. But someone has to do it. This time it was Rutgers, which followed its UConn loss with a road trip to West Virginia.

The timing and situation could not have been worse. Rutgers struggled to pump itself to battle the only team that hadn't won a conference game.

The trip was a mental and emotional letdown. Rutgers went from playing in a packed Hartford Civic Center to playing before 483 in the Morgantown High School gym.

West Virginia's coliseum was closed that season because of asbestos, so the team borrowed the high school gym. For a team that's accustomed to having fans behind the baskets, it was a little disconcerting to be shooting five feet from the wall.

But it was fitting that the game was played in a high school gym, because it looked like a high school game. Stringer had taught the team a new offensive set the day before, but the team hadn't quite mastered it. So Rutgers struggled to move the ball.

But the Scarlet Knights waited until the final two minutes to take the final lead on two free throws by Davalyn Cunningham. "It's very disheartening to not have the lead so late in the game," Tasha Pointer said. "It's devastating because we're not babies out there. If it were freshmen and sophomores out there, you could understand and expect that. But we're experienced players. You'd think we would have learned by now."

The 55–49 victory was painful to watch, and the Rutgers women were the first to admit it. "We beat ourselves, if anything," Tammy Sutton-Brown said. "We know they're the worst team in the Big East. And we're supposed to be at the top near Connecticut. We expect more from ourselves."

Granted, West Virginia was having a good game. But still, this was a game Rutgers, then No. 11 in the polls, should have won by 20 points. UConn, after all, had beaten West Virginia by 40 points, 75–35.

There was little satisfaction in the victory for Rutgers, but West Virginia left the game pumped. "These girls showed they can play with one of the best teams in the country," West Virginia coach Alexis Basil said of her team. "There's no excuse for us not to do this again."

Rutgers turned over the ball 18 times in the first half. And while the Scarlet Knights floundered, tossing up junk shots that occasionally fell, West Virginia's Mandy Ronay equaled her career high in three-pointers (three) within the first four minutes. By the end of the half, Ronay had five three-pointers for 15 points, two points shy of Rutgers' point total at the half.

"We have to take pride in our offense," Sutton-Brown said. "We have great defense. But we have to develop a more offensive mentality, especially in the first five minutes. That's something we didn't do today, get out there and spread the margin in the opening minutes."

Crunch Month

The most important stretch of the regular season was also the most difficult for Rutgers. Players gather around television sets in March, anxious for ESPN's Robin Roberts to reveal their fate on Selection Sunday. But teams usually determine their fate in February.

"The last 10 games are very important," said Bernadette McGlade, chair of the NCAA women's basketball selections committee. "We want to see what kind of trend a team is on, whether it's on an upswing or a downswing."

February schedules are filled primarily with intraconference competition. For teams in weaker conferences, the final month is an easy ride. For Rutgers, it wasn't.

The Big East was among the most powerful, with four teams ranked in the Top 25. Rutgers played four ranked opponents in the first seven games of February, including top-ranked UConn, then No. 5 Notre Dame, and then No. 18 Boston College. It started the month with a non-conference game against then No. 16 Old Dominion.

Rutgers, then No. 10, knew the Old Dominion outcome could affect more than just its won-lost column. It could affect where the team played in the NCAA Tournament.

And it knew the NCAA selection committee—the 10-member group that chooses and seeds the 64 teams for the NCAA Tournament—was watching closely. Every member has a satellite dish. Every member is expected to watch as many games as possible. Any member could have been watching Rutgers play Old Dominion. If they weren't, they would surely be looking for the result.

It was still premature to predict whether Rutgers would earn one of the top 16 seeds, which would allow it to host the first two rounds of the tournament. "They're ahead of the middle of the pack," said Sue Tyler, the athletic director at Maine and a third-year member of the NCAA selections committee. "But they have some things to put together before the end of the season. They're a strong team. Their conference play will be important. The remainder of their schedule is very strong, which probably won't make or break them. I expect they'll play well."

Rutgers had to play well, starting immediately. Old Dominion was one of those teams that didn't get much respect, despite its national ranking and high RPI standing. Coach Wendy Larry, who had been signed to a new five-year contract days before the Rutgers game, had built a strong and consistent program at the Virginia school. But the Colonial Athletic Conference was weak, which allowed Old Dominion to stack up victories.

After the way her team had been playing, Stringer wouldn't underestimate any opponent. She hoped her players wouldn't either.

"I hope that we understand the significance of this Old Dominion game," she said. "I think that if we're going to prove ourselves to be getting stronger as we get into the last part of the season, we need to demonstrate that we can get the win. There's no question in my mind what we need to do. I couldn't ask for a better schedule. We need to demonstrate that we're developed, we're ready to play, and we can handle our opponents."

■

The clock read 40 seconds.

The scoreboard read 53–50, with Rutgers leading and the ball in the trailing team's possession.

Shawnetta Stewart read her opponent's eyes.

And what the forward saw gave away her opponent's game plan.

"I was just reading the person with the ball's eyes, and I could tell that was the pass she was looking for," Stewart said. "So I just stuck my hand out there."

Stewart intercepted a pass with 40 seconds remaining to squelch Old Dominion's attempt to tie the game. She then made four free throws in the final 21 seconds, leading Rutgers to a 58–50 victory over Old Dominion.

It was Rutgers' biggest victory in more than a month.

"We played better tonight, and we've been practicing better," Stringer said. "We have a lot of important games coming up. The schedule will really test us, and we'll know at the end of that whether we're tournament-ready."

The victory was also important for the players' confidence as they prepared for the three remaining ranked opponents. "We're ready for the challenge," Stewart said. "We're looking forward to the next couple of games. Playing a ranked team tonight, we take this as a valuable win."

It wasn't an easy one, though. Rutgers had trailed most of the first half but used a late spurt to take a 25–21 lead at halftime. It was three points away from a tie game with a minute left.

Stewart's steal and free throws, along with a free throw from Tasha Pointer, secured the victory.

Putting Stewart on the foul line was not the Monarchs' preference.

"I know how important Stewart is to this basketball team. I know how important Pointer is to this basketball team," Larry said. "I thought defensively we did some really fine things against a great backcourt. But when (Stewart) had to step up to the line and knock down shots, she did. It was unfortunate that she was the one that we had to put on the line."

Rutgers never seemed fazed during Old Dominion's comeback, which came slowly over the final seven and a half minutes of the game. "I think a team of our caliber should be able to come out and win in games such as this," Stewart said. "We knew they were going to come back. Coach told us they weren't going to go down easily."

Center Lucienne Berthieu scored seven of the final 11 points for Old Dominion. But while Berthieu came up big at the end, her performance was hindered by foul trouble.

Berthieu and Tammy Sutton-Brown battled in the paint. Berthieu had picked up two fouls in the first five minutes of play and finished with four.

Sutton-Brown worked around the 6'2" Berthieu and her replacements, all of whom were smaller than 6'4" Sutton-Brown.

"She was huge in more than one way," Larry said. "She about had her way with us."

The Reunion

Marianna Freeman knew the butterflies would pass. She knew her nerves would settle.

And when the Syracuse women's basketball coach looked to the opposite bench, she would see only an opponent, not the woman who recruited her, shepherded her through college, taught her how to coach, and became one of her closest friends.

No, when Syracuse played at Rutgers, Freeman and Stringer would simply be coaching opponents. At least for 40 minutes.

"I still get butterflies, and I'm nervous, but I look forward to playing her," said Freeman, who played for Stringer at Cheyney State and coached with her at Iowa.

"I think about it before the game. But when we start playing, it's just like any other game. She becomes another opponent for that 40 minutes. When it's over, she becomes Vivian Stringer—my friend, mentor, and college coach."

Their relationship had started with a question: "Hey, Slim, do you play basketball?"

Freeman and her twin sister were at a college fair when an admissions counselor from Cheyney asked the question during their junior year of high school.

It happened that Freeman did play basketball. She averaged 24 points per game and was an All-American at Delaware's Smyrna High School.

The admissions counselor said she would be in touch, but the next call came from Stringer, then the head women's basketball coach at Cheyney.

Freeman liked Stringer immediately. But she knew she couldn't go to

Cheyney unless the coach passed inspection by her grandmother, who raised Freeman, her sister, and her brother.

"My grandmother had a great feeling for people," Freeman said. "When Vivian left, and I remember this exactly, she said, 'That's where you'll go. She is a very warm lady, and I know that she'll take care of you.'

"That did it for me. My grandmother was rarely wrong."

And she wasn't wrong about Stringer. "Vivian's love was tough love," said Freeman, who played for Stringer from 1975 through 1979. "You have to care about her to handle the way she pushes you, because she's a very driven person. But she's real."

■

While the reunion aspect was nice, both coaches dreaded the game. It was a no-win situation. As much as Stringer wanted to win, she didn't want to win at Freeman's expense. And she did, every time they had played since Stringer took the Rutgers job in 1995.

After the Old Dominion game, Stringer had a feeling her team was ready to break out. She hoped it would happen against someone other than Freeman.

Of course, the game that she desperately wanted to be respectable turned into a 40-minute circus, staged live before the third-largest crowd in the history of the women's basketball team—6,419.

Karlita Washington trailed her opponent like a Patriot missile, sprinting the length of the court and swatting a breakaway layup into the stands.

The crowd went crazy. Washington's Rutgers teammates, including an injured Tasha Pointer, jumped up from their seats. Shawnetta Stewart literally fainted on the sidelines.

At the end of the show—Usha Gilmore equated it to "The Bold and the Beautiful" but Stringer preferred "The Young and the Restless"—Rutgers won 77–41. At the time, it was a season-high in points for Rutgers.

With Pointer sidelined after spraining her left ankle in practice the night before, Washington filled in at point guard. The junior, who had transferred to Rutgers from a junior college, scored a season- and game-high 19 points, grabbed a team-high six rebounds, and had two steals, two assists, and a block. "My confidence is at another level now," Washington said.

The 5'9" Washington's block of a Jaime James layup caused an eruption on the sidelines. Stewart jumped from her seat and collapsed on the floor, fainting from a combination of dehydration and excitement. No one knew what happened, not even the teammates standing beside her.

"I thought that she was celebrating, laying there like, 'Did y'all see that?'" Gilmore said. "I was saying, 'Shy, get up. We're going to get in trouble; get off the court.'"

Play didn't stop, so Gilmore and Pointer dragged Stewart, who was partially on the court, to the sideline. Stewart came to and started laughing from embarrassment.

"She was a little dehydrated, probably hadn't eaten properly and just got excited," Stringer said.

Some wondered how Washington would perform in her first start. The performance impressed Pointer, who knew how difficult it was to memorize Rutgers' 31 offensive plays, its many defensive plays, and each player's role.

"It's hard to control the tempo of the game when you're just trying to remember the plays and get everyone else involved," Pointer said. "I'm proud of her because it's rough when everyone out there is used to me playing the point. A lot of people haven't given her a fair chance running the point. Once you get used to something—like a sneaker—you don't want to get a new pair."

Everything clicked against Syracuse. The team shot 50 percent from the field and 50 percent from three-point range.

"It was good to see us play offensively as well as we did," Stringer said. "It was good to see everyone step up, in particular Karlita, who has had signs of brilliance and at times been shaky. I think she can do the same things we saw today against the best competition. She's an outstanding guard, and that is what we were hoping for.

"We know that she's a scorer. We recruited her as a scoring point guard. Maybe it was good that Tasha had her street clothes on, because (Washington) knew we couldn't pull her and she was in there for the long haul."

Measuring Sticks

All games were not created equal.

It's diplomatic to say that every regular-season game is equally important, but it's not true.

Some games simply have more meaning, like a rematch with Connecticut. Or meetings with Notre Dame and Boston College.

Talk about measuring sticks. For a Rutgers team that had had its eye on the Final Four since practice began October 15, these were the types of games that would go a long way in establishing how long their March Madness would last.

Look back on every successful team, every champion, and you can point to several steps along the way where it gained the confidence needed to be a champion. Rutgers had that chance in an 11-day span—with all three games in the friendly confines of the Rutgers Athletic Center.

Of course, it all started with a game against UConn.

"We've known all season how we can play, and this game is the perfect opportunity to show people," Christina Fowler said. "Winning this game would definitely help us with our ranking. But more than anything, we're playing for our pride, for ourselves.

"The rankings mean a lot, but I know this is about personal pride, about playing the way we can play. Along with that come the rankings and respect."

Not to mention adding even more juice to the momentum Rutgers had gained with its two-game winning streak. At that point in the season, when the NCAA selection committee was looking closely for signs of improvement, victories were crucial.

"It would mean a lot for us, a team that's been struggling throughout the year," Tasha Pointer said of defeating UConn. "At the same time, it means a lot to say there's more than one team in the Big East, more than just UConn.

"When I first came to Rutgers, the only team anyone talked about was Connecticut. But now in the same breath as UConn, you have to mention Notre Dame, Boston College, and Rutgers. We've changed the air of the Big East Conference. Now you can look at the Big East and know that more than one team will represent the conference in the NCAA Tournament."

But there was still a disparity. UConn had won six straight Big East titles and hadn't lost a conference game all season.

"Connecticut is a great team that rebounds and plays every second," Stringer said. "They are never done until the lights are out. It would be major for us to beat them. It would help tremendously with our confidence. We've begun to play better, but we can't know how good we are going to be until we get a measure. It's a chance to see what the best is.

"We need to have shots drop that haven't been dropping. We're going to have to play great defense. We're going to have to be on, and Connecticut is going to have to be off.

"But being the competitors that we are, we're going to have to ignore what makes reasonable and sound sense about what should happen and be that team that overcomes the odds. That's one thing that we do like. We like to be down because that gives us somewhere to go—up. Connecticut is as high as you can go."

Emotion is a powerful factor when UConn and Rutgers meet. Some call them rivals. Others call them enemies. But somehow when they play, the stakes always seem high.

This was Rutgers' chance to finally hit its stride. The team had derailed from its expected track, getting itself into a jam with four early losses. It had come close to losing several others.

But now it had a chance to show it was worthy of the high preseason expectations, that it was, as every major preseason poll predicted, a Top 5 pick.

And if anyone could help Rutgers prove it, it was Connecticut. "There is definitely something about us and UConn," Fowler said. "I think it's just that the best brings out the best. The competitiveness we have with each other in practice is just magnified when we go against other competition. Just knowing that they're No. 1 brings up the intensity and the energy level.

"Our team is going to take that intensity, take that burning fire and say, 'We want to be No. 1. We're good enough to be there.'"

■

Save the pep talk about good losses. Rutgers has heard it and doesn't buy it.

Yes, Rutgers limited all but one UConn player to single digits. And, yes, Rutgers gave UConn its closest conference match of the year.

But when the Scarlet Knights walked off the court after a 49–45 loss, even though it was to the nation's top-ranked team, close was not good enough.

"We're not a team that looks for moral victories," Tasha Pointer said. "There's nothing moral about hanging in there, then losing. This season is urgent. You can't say this loss wasn't that bad. A loss is a loss, and if you have enough of them when it's all over, you're not invited to the dance."

The toughest part was that it didn't have to be a loss in front of the women's-record 8,579 fans. The Scarlet Knights led 33–28 with 15 minutes to play. They were tied at 40 with 6:43 to play.

After UConn went on an 8–0 run that set Rutgers back 48–40, Usha

Gilmore banked a three-pointer and Shawnetta Stewart had a baseline jumper to make it a 48–45 game with 2:26 to go.

On Rutgers' next possession, Gilmore had a shot blocked by UConn's Kelly Schumacher. Rutgers got the ball back but then turned it over on a shot-clock violation with 1:30 left.

After a UConn turnover and missed shots by Gilmore and Stewart, Rutgers sent UConn's Asjha Jones to the line. Jones made the second of two free throws with 23 seconds remaining to put the game out of reach.

"A lot of writers in New Jersey think we're arrogant," UConn coach Geno Auriemma said. "That's what I've heard. I know they think we talk too much. But we can back it up. When we show up, we come to play.

"These games are great because we know how bad they want to beat us. Vivian Stringer is probably sitting there saying, 'There's not a whole lot we did wrong, except lose the game.'"

That's exactly what Stringer was thinking. While her players were disappointed, Stringer was encouraged by their performance.

"I was very proud of my team," she said. "I think they worked every second of the game. Sometimes shots fall, sometimes they don't. I don't think anyone took shots out of rotation.

"I thought the team stayed focused for 40 minutes. And contrary to the score, I'm encouraged as long as we continue to really and truly believe in ourselves."

Rutgers, which led by as many as 11 and took a 26–20 lead at halftime, gave up 11 points to Abrosimova, but held the rest of UConn's roster to single digits. It held UConn to its lowest scoring game since 1993. It was UConn's narrowest margin of victory for the season.

"We pretty much kept them in check," Stewart said. "We were confident going into the last 10 minutes.

"'This is the No. 1 team in the country, and we always play them real well. We know we belong in Philadelphia, and this game is not going to stop us. We're going to keep on pushing.'"

Here for the Long Haul

It had been just about a year since rumors flew of Stringer's possible departure. Some said she was headed to Maryland. Others said she was looking at the WNBA.

But on February 18, the day before Rutgers' game against Notre Dame, Stringer made it known that she wasn't going anywhere for a long time by signing a three-year contract extension that secured her through the 2004–05 season and made her the highest-paid coach at Rutgers.

"I consider Vivian to be the top coach in the country," Rutgers athletic director Robert Mulcahy said after announcing the deal. "Her record has demonstrated that, and certainly I felt that she should be paid on a par with the top coaches in the country. That's what I tried to do here."

Under the terms of the agreement, Stringer's base salary increases from $150,000 to $175,000 per year. Her total package is worth $400,000 per year, which includes compensation for camps, public relations and promotions, and expenses incurred for the cost of living in New Jersey.

In her 28-year career, Stringer (617–188) has collected three national coach of the year awards and has earned a reputation for building national powers. But she said that her days of building programs are over and that she likely will finish her career at Rutgers.

"The fair statement would be to say that I do not intend to ever build a program again in my life," Stringer said. "The fair statement is that I want to see us through to a national championship. It's always tough starting a program, and I'm happy here. I'm happy at our university. I'm happy in this part of the country. And it would be fair to say that I do not intend to coach again. You never say never, but I don't anticipate that I will."

Mulcahy said he studied the salaries of the nation's top coaches—including Tennessee's Pat Summitt—to arrive at a fair figure for Stringer. Summitt, whose total earnings package is undisclosed, also makes a base salary of $175,000.

When Stringer arrived at Rutgers in 1995, she was reportedly the highest-paid women's basketball coach in the country with a package worth $300,000. She was also the highest-paid coach at the university, and she brought with her promises of greatness.

"In coming to Rutgers, I've had a vision, continue to have that vision, and have every reason to believe that we're going to achieve our goal," Stringer said. "I have nothing but great feelings about my position here and the success that we're going to continue to have."

Her original seven-year contract, signed in 1995 and due to expire at the end of the 2001–02 season, contained a provision that it would be reevaluated at the end of the 1999–2000 season. Stringer and Mulcahy had been discussing the contract's terms throughout the season.

"I just felt that the time to announce it was at this particular time in the season," Mulcahy said. "We've seen how well the season's gone, and we're looking at the balance of the season. I wanted to do it before people looked at the end result and before they judged the tournament. It's based upon what I had seen as progress in the last three years.

"One of the core beliefs I have is that for a program to be successful it has to have the right leader there for a significant period of time in order to build consistency. We have that with Vivian."

The Silent Assassin

Sometimes the most dangerous people are the ones you already know, the ones no one suspects. And yet, when you look closely, all the signs are there.

Rutgers sensed a killer in its presence. Unlike so many other teams, it saw the signs.

While all the Big East hoopla swirled around UConn, Notre Dame had been quietly assassinating every conference opponent that crossed its schedule. Its next target was Rutgers.

"We're sneaking up on a lot of teams," Notre Dame coach Muffet

Muffet McGraw is the head coach of Notre Dame. Here, she reflects on her career and the Fighting Irish's surprising 1999–2000 season.

Growing up in West Chester, Pennsylvania, a small suburb of Philadelphia, I found myself living in an area where women's basketball was played at the highest level in the nation.

Muffet McGraw

First West Chester State, then tiny Immaculata College, I watched as our local heroes were crowned national champions in the AIAW. As I sat in the stands and watched games along with a much smaller but enthusiastic group of supporters, my dream of winning a national championship began to take form.

Despite my admiration for Cathy Rush and her mighty Mac champions, and despite the thrill of seeing her in the stands at one of my high school games, I found that repeating as champion of Immaculata was not as alluring as playing the underdog trying to unseat the perennial champion. And so I went off to St. Joseph's University and played for two former Immaculata stars, Theresa Grentz and Rene Portland. While my dream of winning a national championship never came to fruition, I had the opportunity to be a pioneer that ended up fifth in the nation my senior year.

For me, Philadelphia will always be where women's basketball was born. There are many coaches in the country like myself whose coaching roots stretch back to Philly. After a number of stops on my coaching resume, all in the Philadelphia area, I found a home at the University of Notre Dame. After joining the Big East Conference, our program catapulted onto the national scene. With a Final Four appearance in 1997, Cinderella had finally become a regular guest at the ball. The 1999–2000 season began with a vision of hope and a dream of taking my team home to Philly.

With a first-team All-American in Ruth Riley at center, a talented and healthy point guard named Niele Ivey, and a promising rookie, Alicia Ratay, there was much reason for optimism in South Bend. Our focus was preparing for March, and after an early-season loss to Purdue, we won a school-record 20 consecutive games. The highlight of the streak was a late February win at Rutgers after being down by six with 24 seconds to play. Alicia Ratay hit back-to-back three-pointers to send the game into overtime. She set a Big East record going 7-for-7 from the three-point line in that win.

After a disappointing semifinal loss in the Big East tournament, preparation for the "real" season began. Selection Sunday came, and for the first time in the program's history, we hosted the first and second rounds as the No. 2 seed in the Mideast region.

Wearing green uniforms to celebrate our St. Patrick's Day date with San Diego, we played with focus and intensity and advanced to the second round against George Washington. We played the best game of the season that night and the luck of the Irish had us back in the Sweet Sixteen. I was halfway home.

Three Big East teams made the Sweet Sixteen—each of us in a different region. Thoughts of the Big East dominating the Final Four raced through the conference.

The Mideast regional was in Memphis, and our first opponent was Texas Tech. We had beaten the Lady Raiders on their home floor two years before in Lubbock, Texas. We knew that revenge would be on their mind, and it turned out to be a very powerful motivator for them. After jumping out to an early lead, Ruth Riley was called for a succession of fouls, and suddenly the tables were turned.

We were down by four with four minutes to go, but this time there would be no late-game heroics by the Irish. Our dream of getting back to the Final Four was shattered. I think that left a part of me in Memphis that day. Even as I watched the tears from our seniors and saw the frustration and disappointment in my players' eyes, I knew that there would be another chance for them to play in the Final Four, but for me, the dream of a triumphant return to Philly was over.

As I arrived in Philadelphia and met with friends and family, the desolation of that last game still haunted me. But after being congratulated for a job well done, it suddenly hit me. We had a very successful season, and making it to the Sweet Sixteen was a great accomplishment. I also realized that the number of coaches who have never been to the Final Four far outweigh those fortunate few who have. I have been blessed with many good things in my life, and coaching at Notre Dame is certainly one of them.

It was great to see two Big East teams in the Final Four, and to have the national champion in our league proves that the league is one of the best conferences in the country. Maybe next year, the luck of the Irish will prevail and there will be three Big East teams in the Final Four. Congratulations to Connecticut and to the city of Philadelphia. You threw a great party, and even though I wasn't one of the four honored guests, I felt like one of the hosts. As always, I'm proud to call Philly home.

McGraw said. "People are surprised by how many of our players can hurt them."

What most people seemed to forget was that Notre Dame was ranked No. 5 in the country and No. 1 in the conference. That's right, No. 1, as in ahead of UConn, if only because it played one more game.

Yet Notre Dame simply hadn't gotten the respect and attention of UConn or even, to some degree, of Rutgers.

"Maybe it's because they have such great football prominence, but people can't seem to take them seriously with basketball," Stringer said. "Muffet McGraw has done a great job. They're not No. 5 for nothing. We know that we struggled last year with them."

The year before Rutgers had struggled and lost to them in the Big East tournament, yet somehow came away with a higher seed in the NCAA Tournament.

After point guard Niele Ivey tore her anterior cruciate ligament in the victory over Rutgers, the selections committee robbed the Irish of a top 16 seed and home-court advantage for the first two rounds of the 1999 NCAA Tournament. Rutgers got a No. 3 seed. Notre Dame got a No. 5 one and was shipped to Baton Rouge, Louisiana, where it lost to Louisiana State University in the second round. The Irish hadn't forgotten the slight.

"If I were a coach, I would forever remind my players that we will never give the NCAA a chance to do that again," Stringer said. "And when they consider Rutgers, they can say, 'You know, Rutgers took your spot. They got the higher seed.'

"Their coach has a right to be somewhat offended. Notre Dame is a great team, and yet people always talk about Connecticut."

Let UConn have the spotlight, McGraw said. Her team was perfectly happy with its perfect 12–0 conference record. It had taken advantage of its time in the shadow. While UConn got the much-deserved glory, Notre Dame capitalized on being a bit underestimated. Consequently, its record had swelled to 22–3 when it got to Rutgers.

"Teams come in intent on shutting down Ruth Riley," McGraw said. "Then they're surprised by the others who have stepped up."

Riley, a 6'5" All-American center, was the obvious threat. But she wasn't alone. Notre Dame had a trio of unstoppable guards in seniors Niele Ivey, Danielle Green, and Alicia Ratay, the most overachieving freshman in the country.

"Our key has been balance," McGraw said. "Last year we were so dependent on Ruth; we lived and died by how she played. But now you can't look at any one player and say you have to shut her down."

A Stunning Loss

Shawnetta Stewart fiddled with her shoelaces while the band played the alma mater. She didn't relace them. She didn't quite tie them. She simply bent over and distracted herself by rearranging a couple of strings.

Then she stopped. And she hung there, head dropped and arms hanging. She had nothing left physically, mentally, or emotionally.

Stewart had brought No. 8 Rutgers back from a 19-point deficit. She had single-handedly given Rutgers a lead with three three-point baskets in a two minute span.

And, after 45 minutes of pouring every last ounce of herself into the game, she knew it was not enough. Rutgers had lost, 78–74, in overtime to No. 5 Notre Dame, unable to hold a six-point lead with 25 seconds remaining in regulation.

All that was left for Stewart to do was retire to her private world of disappointment while 5,397 people surrounded her at the Rutgers Athletic Center.

"This is our toughest loss, even though we lost to (top-ranked) UConn twice," Stewart said. "We had a chance to knock out a team that's ranked. So, this is a very tough loss at this point in the season."

A victory over Notre Dame would have been huge for Rutgers when the selections committee seeded teams for the NCAA Tournament. And it would have all but assured the Scarlet Knights a top-three seed at the Big East tournament, securing a first-round bye and almost guaranteeing that it wouldn't face UConn until the championship game.

Rutgers was left with no choice but to beat top 20 Boston College in a battle for the No. 3 seed.

And yet, it didn't have to come to that. And Rutgers knew it.

"It was silent in the locker room," Stewart said. "It was the same feeling after the Connecticut game. You have a game, and you let it slip out of your hands."

With Rutgers trailing by eight, Stewart hit three consecutive baseline three-pointers to give Rutgers its first lead, 52–51, with 8:18 to play. When her coach was asked about the importance of the shots, Stewart jumped in, "It doesn't matter. We lost the game." Rutgers led 65–59 with 25 seconds to play. That's when Notre Dame freshman Alicia Ratay scored back-to-back three-pointers, including the game-tying one with 3.9 seconds left in regulation.

"I was there," said Karlita Washington, one of three Rutgers players guarding Ratay on the shot. "It was a tough shot."

"I saw nails on the ball," Stringer said. "What more could you ask for except a block?"

Some thought Stringer could have asked for a foul, instead of letting Ratay take the shot.

In overtime, Ratay made two free throws to put Notre Dame ahead 76–74, and Niele Ivey sealed the victory on two free throws with 6.3 seconds left.

"I think we've been stunned by Connecticut and Notre Dame," Stringer said. "I think we felt comfortable and confident that we had that game."

Rutgers made the most remarkable run of its season to tie the game. It had fallen behind by 19 points before ending the first half with a 12–3 run to cut the deficit to 32–22 at the break.

"I give Muffet McGraw a lot of credit because she has a great team,"

Stringer said. "But I give my team as much if not more. We had every reason to sit down.

"So, I'm not completely at a loss or devastated to the point where I would say, 'Poor Rutgers, we keep coming in second.' You have to remember that we keep coming in second to Connecticut and Notre Dame. Is Connecticut that good? Is Notre Dame that good? If so, then we are getting better. Even in a loss, we scored, and we haven't done that in quite some time."

Backs to the Wall

Rutgers was flirting with the fourth seed in the Big East tournament, and the only way to avoid it was by beating Boston College. The Scarlet Knights, ranked No. 8, needed no reminders of the game's importance.

"This has been on our minds since we dropped two games that were within our reach, against Notre Dame and Connecticut," Davalyn Cunningham said. "We really are fighting for this position."

At stake was the third seed in the 13-team Big East tournament, a highly coveted position because the top three seeds receive first-round byes.

That's no big deal for the first round, which Rutgers would likely win without much struggle. But without the bye Rutgers' minds and legs wouldn't be as fresh for later rounds.

If the Scarlet Knights were seeded fourth, they would need to play three games in three days just to reach the championship game. They would need to win a fourth game in four nights to win the tournament.

With three other nationally ranked teams in the field, staying fresh was key.

Boston College had the advantage at that point in the season. With a 10–3 conference record, it had one fewer conference losses than Rutgers (9–4 in the Big East).

If Rutgers won, assuming neither team lost in their remaining conference games, it would get the higher seed by virtue of winning the head-to-head competition.

"This is a major game," Stringer said. "It backs us right up against the wall. It's nice, to be honest with you, for all this to be on the line and for this to be played in the final stretch of the year. We need to find out what we're made of. I wish that we were clearly in front, because then I'd be confident of everything we can do. In games we've demonstrated that we're capable of exploding, but I sort of like the idea of all the dramatics on the line. And I want to see if we come back the way we need to, which is in the spirit that it's going to take in order for us to win NCAA championship games."

Like Rutgers, Boston College lost to Villanova by a point. But it was riding a two-game winning streak. Rutgers was recovering from its loss to Notre Dame.

"Losing starts to wear on your confidence," Cunningham said. "No one wants to lose, but we see us as being just as good as the No. 1 and No. 5 teams. We were ahead in the games, we were down in the games and came back, and we fought with them. We can play with the best. We're among the best.

"The pressure is from within because we know we're capable of doing a lot more. We're capable of winning the big games, but we have to do it."

Senior Night

Shawnetta Stewart came off the court with less than two minutes to play, hugging the line of coaches standing along the Rutgers bench. She didn't want to get emotional, but she couldn't hide her pride.

In her last regular-season game at the Rutgers Athletic Center, Stewart had just played one of the best games of her career, scoring 27 points to lead Rutgers past Boston College 73–51 before 3,468 at Senior Night.

"'I just wanted to get the crowd going and make it a memorable night for the seniors," said Stewart, the first Rutgers player to commit to Stringer. "I didn't want to get too emotional because we had a job to do. Save the tears for later.

"This night kind of snuck up on me. I haven't had it on my mind. But I am just so proud of my teammates and how we established how we were going to play this game."

"This whole year was about positioning," Stringer said. "You play 27 games, do so many practices, and it's all to get position. Hopefully, we'll win the rest of our games and be third. Truthfully now, nothing else matters. Everything's up, and now you play as though you've never played."

In a move that fell somewhere between crazy and touching, Stringer started five of her six seniors in honor of Senior Night. It was a gesture of faith, similar to the one these players gave her five years earlier with their commitments to building this program.

"It was a big statement when Coach put us seniors out there," Stewart said. "Some of you may have been thinking she's crazy. But we had confidence in ourselves. We believed in the beginning and went out on the edge and got things going. This senior class has always had confidence, so I knew we would come out with heart, gunning for Boston College."

They did. The starting five—which included Stewart, Usha Gilmore, Coko Eggleston, LaTana Lillard, and Jen Clemente—secured the victory by setting a tempo Boston College couldn't match.

Rutgers built its lead to 28–12 with just under eight minutes left in the half.

"I was fired up," Stewart said. "I was so happy to see Jen playing well and Coko. You really don't see the talents that they have. Those two and LaTana work so hard in practice. I was so proud to see them come out and be composed and play well."

Boston College cut Rutgers lead to 33–24 at halftime, but never got closer than eight.

Rutgers held Boston College without a field goal for the final four and a half minutes. It ended the game with an 11–2 run, highlighted by an

NBA-length three-pointer by Stewart as the shot clock expired with 2:14 to play. It was her last basket of the game.

"Coming in (to college), I knew it wasn't going to be easy," Stewart said. "I struggled with everything. The transition from high school to college was difficult for me, from academics to getting myself where I was capable of playing Division I basketball. Right now, I'm in a nice position. Now we're all playing for the goal, playing for a national championship in my hometown."

Rutgers got the No. 3 seed.

chapter two

sacred heart

The Newcomer

Sixty miles south of Storrs, Connecticut, but well within the scope of the media spotlight that engulfs the UConn women's basketball team, sits one of the nation's newest Division I women's programs. Sacred Heart University, a small, independent, private Catholic school located in suburban Fairfield, made the quantum leap from Division II to Division I in 1999.

The Pioneers, as they are known, make no claims of supremacy, even within the confines of the Nutmeg State's narrow borders. Sacred Heart shares the state with UConn and five other Division I institutions—as well as the same tree-lined community on the shores of Long Island Sound with the more established Fairfield University.

"As I've said since we made the decision to go Division I, our goal is to become the second-best program in Connecticut," said Ed Swanson, the enthusiastic 34-year-old coach of the Pioneers, meaning he'll concede the number-one spot to UConn but that all other programs are fair game.

From the outset, Sacred Heart's new opponents in the Northeast Conference discovered a Pioneer program they barely knew existed even two years earlier was authentic. Swanson's squad, which featured four freshmen, a sophomore, two juniors, and two seniors, was far more talented and resilient than they had imagined. Picked to finish ninth in the NEC coaches' 1999–2000 preseason poll, Sacred Heart put an exclamation point on its debut as a Division I program with a surprising third-place finish. The Pioneers won 11 of 18 conference games and, overall, were a respectable 14–13.

"Our goal was to position ourselves to be competitive this year, not in three or four years," Swanson said. "Our players had high expectations; they expected to win now. They didn't want to hear anything about growing pains. As the year went on, the team kept improving, we kept getting better."

Founded as a commuter college in 1963, Sacred Heart reinvented itself during the final decade of the twentieth century. Seven residence halls were constructed and filled, dozens of new classrooms and laboratories were added, and new academic programs were introduced. Today, more than 70 percent of its 2,500 full-time undergraduates are residential.

To prepare for its transition into the major college ranks, Sacred Heart tested the waters during a two-year compliance cycle by scheduling 17 games against Division I women's teams. The Pioneers won seven of those contests, including four of five against future NEC opponents Long Island University, Fairleigh Dickinson, Central Connecticut, and Maryland-Baltimore County.

The opening of a new facility proved invaluable for recruiting. The university's $17.5 million William H. Pitt Health & Recreation Center came on line in the fall of 1997, providing a first-rank venue—with a seating capacity of 2,200—for basketball, volleyball, and wrestling, as well as needed office space for an intercollegiate athletic program that had expanded, seemingly overnight, from eight to 33 varsity teams. Pioneer basketball now had a "Pitt" of its own.

Yes, the scene had been set with care. But to anyone who had watched Sacred Heart women's teams even several years earlier, the transformation from Division II also-ran into a contender in a Division I conference boggled the mind.

Coach Swanson

Growing up on the streets and playgrounds in the Black Rock section of Bridgeport, Connecticut, Ed Swanson began to entertain thoughts about coaching even during his years at Kolbe Cathedral, a diocesan high school located in the inner city. He was a skillful swing player for the Cougars, tough enough and resourceful enough at 6'2" to challenge a scholastic All-American, Warren Harding's 6'8" Charles Smith (later a star at Pittsburgh and in the National Basketball Association), and other area standouts. As team captain, his leadership capabilities were in evidence.

"All of the coaches I had pointed me in the direction of coaching," Swanson said. "Dave Blagys and Dave Hennessey at Kolbe, and Tom McDonald, my grammar school coach."

On the collegiate level, Ed played a year of Division III ball at Plymouth State, but became homesick and decided to transfer closer to home at Sacred Heart. "I'm a city guy, and I missed the streets of Bridgeport," he noted.

Swanson's arrival on the SHU campus couldn't have been better timed; the men's team assembled by coach Dave Bike would win the 1985–86 NCAA Division II national championship. But instead of joining the squad, he opted to take a part-time assistant coaching position at Kolbe Cathedral, his alma mater, while continuing his college studies. "Sacred Heart had super guards, Roger Younger and Travis Smith, and I wouldn't have played a lot anyway," Ed reasoned.

Immediately after obtaining a bachelor's degree in business, Swanson joined Bike's coaching staff, and that's where he was when the Sacred Heart women's head coach resigned abruptly in September of 1990. The position was Ed's if he wanted it, but with the stipulation that he remain on the men's coaching staff. He would balance those dual responsibilities for the next three years.

"I was 24 years old and just happy to get a job as a head coach," recalled Swanson, who can afford to smile now. "We were tired of being a doormat and we were looking for respect. At that point"—he emits a small smile—"we didn't have many problems scheduling games."

Inheriting a Loser

The women's program that Swanson inherited had hit rock bottom. Talent was scarce, "crowds" could be tallied by head count on most evenings, and the team played its home games in an antiquated former high school gym known as the SHU Box (although the latter didn't seem to hamper the men's program). Underscoring its second-class status, the women's "media guide" consisted of two pages tucked away in the back of the men's book.

The Lady Pioneers were the undisputed doormat of the Division II New England Collegiate Conference. The program that Swanson was embracing had weathered 11 consecutive losing seasons and defeats by 40 and 50 points. One year even a single victory had been impossible to attain. "If we didn't have the worst women's program in New England, it was just a matter of semantics," remembered Rick Ferris, who worked as a statistician for both the Sacred Heart men's and women's teams during his undergraduate days.

Elizabeth "Bippy" Luckie, now the university's associate director of athletics and softball coach, led the women's team in scoring for two seasons during the mid-1980s, and she still holds the Sacred Heart single-game record with 42 points. But she was a softball player (an All-American shortstop with a line-drive bat) who dabbled in basketball, albeit well.

"In those years, just about everyone on the basketball team was a softball or a volleyball player," Luckie said. "Some of our teams were pretty bad. It wasn't until later, when the administration realized the impact women's basketball was going to have, that we made Ed our first full-time coach. Obviously he's a great recruiter and has done an outstanding job."

Swanson's first team, in 1990–91, won eight games and lost 19, which, although modest, represented a discernible improvement over the previous year's 4–21 record. "I became so frustrated that I think I resigned twice that first season because I didn't see us improving," he later admitted. His second team fared slightly better, at 11–16. His third, bolstered by the arrival of five recruits including a pair of transfers from the neighboring University of Bridgeport, produced a 16–13 record—the school's first winning season since 1978–79. That year was distinguished by a victory in the conference playoffs and a berth in the ECAC tournament.

Sacred Heart was a beneficiary of UB's decision to discontinue its intercollegiate athletic program (a move it later rescinded) with the infusion of transfers Melissa Jones, a 5'10" senior forward with a feathery shooting touch, and a 5'3" sophomore guard named Sarah Solinsky. Jones led the 1992–93 Pioneers in scoring, but Solinsky, although valuable as a playmaker, would achieve far greater success as an All-American shortstop in softball. A case of history repeating itself.

The team's second game of the season, a rousing come-from-behind 75–67 overtime triumph over nationally ranked Stonehill in the New England Tip-Off Tournament at Lowell, Massachusetts, provided conclusive proof that Pioneers women's basketball had turned the corner. In just her second game wearing Sacred Heart red and white, Jones scored 31, but it was senior Kim Filia's off-balance three-pointer at the buzzer that erased the last vestige of a 19-point deficit and sent the game into overtime. Then Sacred Heart breezed past the stunned Chieftains.

A Stumbling Block

Just when it appeared that Swanson had the Pioneer program heading in the right direction, a bona fide contender to the Bentleys, the Stonehills, and other Division II powers, there was a stumbling block. Sacred Heart made the decision to discontinue athletic scholarships. Instead, financial aid would be awarded based on need or academic prowess. Coaches grumbled. Some fans stayed away. Wondered more than one coach: "How the heck can we get blue-chippers when our opponents offer athletic scholarships?" How, indeed.

So, the blue-chippers went elsewhere, to the mid-level Division I programs and the Division II elite, and Swanson resigned himself to searching out the second tier of student-athletes. "It took a lot of hard work, but Ed was able to identify those need-based players," Luckie said. "Maybe they were a level lower, maybe they weren't blue-chippers, but they were pretty good. They kept us competitive."

Kim McCullion, who arrived on campus in 1992 from Nashua, New Hampshire, typified the Swanson recruit of the period. An angular 5'7", she was deemed too small (and too slow) to play power forward in Division I or for an upper-level Division II program, but she scrapped and she hustled and became an asset for four seasons.

"We wanted to prove those other teams wrong. We were playing just because we wanted to play," recalled McCullion, who returned to her alma mater last year as a graduate admissions counselor and an assistant on Swanson's staff. Prove them wrong she did. In her Sacred Heart debut, Kim merely pulled down 13 rebounds and scored 17 points to contribute to a victory over Merrimack.

As a senior tri-captain in 1995–96, McCullion became the catalyst in the program's first 20-victory season. In the span of one year, the Pioneers transformed themselves from conference also-rans into a 20–7 team capable of challenging—and defeating—the region's traditional Division II powers. They became a team that produced a 16–4 record within the New England Collegiate Conference, just one game behind champion Bridgeport and ahead of perennial contenders UMass-Lowell and Franklin Pierce.

"We understood team philosophy that year," McCullion said. "If you looked at the conference standings, we didn't have the leading scorer or the top rebounder. But on a given night, anyone was capable of having a big game."

"The players came back and created good chemistry," said Swanson, trying to explain the turnabout. "Coaches don't create chemistry. Players do."

Coaches create good coaching, though. For directing a team devoid of scholarship players to 20 victories in a scholarship conference, Swanson was voted Coach of the Year by his peers, both in District I and in the NECC.

Recruiting Winners

Shrewd recruiting within the state helped. In 1994, Sacred Heart landed its first high-profile player, Chrissie Perkins, an all-state guard from Waterford High School. Perkins became an instant hit at the college level, the NECC Rookie of the Year and four times a conference all-star. An intense competitor, she established a school record with 146 career three-pointers and accumulated 1,308 points, still third on the Pioneers' all-time list.

Then Swanson journeyed north on Route 8 to Naugatuck, where in successive years he signed a pair of all-state players from Naugatuck High School: Jennifer Rimkus, a lightning-quick guard, and 6'2" Heather Yablonski, an intimidating presence who had earned the nickname "Shaq" from overmatched Naugatuck Valley League opponents. Together with Perkins, they would comprise the nucleus of the 1997–98 Sacred Heart squad that produced a glossy 19–7 record and a second-place finish (13–3) in the New England Collegiate Conference.

From a long-range standpoint, however, the eight games that mattered most that year were those against Division I teams. After opening the season with successive losses to Bucknell, Colgate, and Monmouth, the Pioneers achieved their first victory over a Division I institution with an 87–77 thumping of NEC member LIU in Brooklyn, New York. For the record, the date was November 25, 1997. Rimkus, now a junior, blitzed the

Blackbirds with 31 points—a figure unmatched by any Sacred Heart player in the last seven years.

Four nights later, the Pioneers upset Fairleigh Dickinson 78–58. Later in the year, they would dispatch Central Connecticut and Maryland-Baltimore County, and lose to St. Peter's of the Metro Atlantic Athletic Conference. All in all, a 4–4 record on the road against Division I schools represented a promising start.

Yablonski, strong and quietly tenacious, quickly developed into a formidable post player. Most Division II centers lacked her height; few opponents on Division I teams would be a match for her power game. For three straight seasons, Heather ranked among the NECC leaders in rebounding and, on many nights, was capable of scoring 20 or more points against any caliber of competition. As a sophomore, she was selected to the NECC and ECAC all-star first teams, a feat unmatched by any Sacred Heart woman.

"When I was being recruited, I looked at both Division I and II schools," Yablonski explained. "I wanted to go where I fit in best, and it turned out I got to play both. Coach Swanson told me he was recruiting players who would help us when we made the move to Division I."

Equipped with the university's pending elevation to Division I as a selling point, and the restoration of athletic scholarships as bargaining power, Swanson continued to raise his sights in the recruiting vineyard. Heather Coonradt, a 6'0" forward from South Seneca High School in Interlaken, New York, and Abby Crotty, a 5'7" guard from Red Bank Catholic High School in Monmouth Beach, New Jersey, arrived in 1997. They were accompanied by Dawn Werner, a 5'8" transfer from Fairleigh Dickinson, where she had played for two seasons and made the NEC's All-Rookie Team.

"I was very excited about coming to Sacred Heart," Dawn said. "I knew they were going Division I, and I liked the enthusiasm. I also knew the (Northeast) Conference was so close and tight, and that we would have a chance."

Forced to sit out the 1997–98 season, Werner joined the squad the following fall along with another newcomer of note, Leslie Newhard, a 5'10" forward from Pennsylvania's Northampton High School. Leslie started slowly, then roared into high gear to lead Sacred Heart's final Division II squad to a 15–12 record, capped by highly satisfying wins over major college teams Hartford, Colgate, and Bucknell (the latter in overtime). Of the six defeats to Division I schools, three—Rhode Island, Harvard, and Lehigh—were by a scant three points. "A play here or there and we could have been 6–3 instead of 3–6 against Division I schools," observed Swanson.

Perhaps the most surprising aspect of the 1998–99 season was Newhard's rapid maturation. Consistency personified, she reached double figures in 20 of the final 24 games, topping the squad in scoring with a 14.1 average, in field goal percentage with 52.3, and in free throw percentage with 82.2. The latter eclipsed the Sacred Heart record. She also averaged 6.8 rebounds, just one-tenth of a point behind Yablonski's team-leading figure. "I knew Leslie would be a contributor, but I didn't think she'd do what she did so quickly," Swanson said.

Fittingly, it was Newhard who put the exclamation point on Sacred Heart's 25 seasons of women's basketball competition at the Division II level. With the score tied at 84–84 in the closing seconds of the finale against long-time rival Bridgeport, junior forward Katie Toole drove past a Purple Knight defender and lofted a soft pass to Leslie underneath the basket. The buzzer sounded as her shot dropped cleanly through the net in the Harvey Hubbell Gymnasium.

Moving Up

As Ed Swanson surveyed his roster at the start of preseason practice for Sacred Heart's debut season in Division I, he couldn't help but smile. For the first time in his career, the Pioneers' head coach had outrecruited a slew of Division I schools. On the roster were six freshmen, most of whom had been sought after by Northeast Conference opponents and other prominent institutions of higher learning.

Hard work had reaped dividends. "I spent an incredible amount of time on the road last year. In July I was away so much I slept in my own bed maybe four times," Swanson said.

"This is the first time we had to outrecruit Division I schools. The recruiting pressures were real. But for us, the whole scene has changed now that Sacred Heart is a Division I name. Years back we had to convince kids this was the place for them. Now, kids are recruiting us. We've had luck with the last two classes, getting kids with a passion for the game."

Swanson's travels took him to the national AAU tournament in Kingston, Tennessee, where he rubbed shoulders with Tennessee's Pat Summitt and UConn's Geno Auriemma. He also watched AAU tournaments in several states, went to the Blue Star Camp at Lehigh University in Pennsylvania, and crossed the border into Canada. Have scholarships, will travel.

When all was said and done, Swanson had attracted the finest class of recruits in the history of Sacred Heart women's basketball. "I struck gold with this class," he said. "The ceiling is high for these kids. I think they're hungry, and they want to get better. They listen."

From upstate New York, there was Brooke Rutnik, a hard-driving 6'0" forward from the Academy of Holy Names in Albany. Tara Brady, a 6'1" center who had been a high school rival of Leslie Newhard's, arrived from Wescosville, Pennsylvania. Brady's game was power. Averaging 19 points and 19 rebounds a game, she led Emmaus High School to the Eastern Pennsylvania Conference championship.

From New Hampshire came Ashley Durmer, a talented 5'7" point guard from Nashua High School who was chosen as the state's Player of the Year by the *Boston Globe,* and Meghan Farrell, a 5'9" swing guard from Manchester West High School.

Durmer was being recruited by Hofstra, Holy Cross, Fordham, and other notables, and hadn't even placed Sacred Heart among her possibilities. She knew of its existence only in the context that two earlier Nashua High athletes had matriculated there—Jessica Bresnahan, the point guard who captained Sacred Heart's 1998–99 squad, and Kim McCullion.

"Kim had been an assistant coach at my high school, and she called me after she returned to Sacred Heart to coach. I never would have even thought of going there if she hadn't called me," Durmer said. "Once I came to campus and met Coach Swanson, I saw how excited he was about going to Division I. I also liked the fact that I would be part of something from the beginning."

New Jersey, which has become a major source of talent for Sacred Heart in recent years, also contributed two players to the mix: Tara Gizzi, a 5'11" forward from Hazlet who had starred at Red Bank Catholic, Abby Crotty's alma mater; and Brooke Kelly, a 5'10" forward from Medford who played at Shawnee High School. Kelly was said to be a diamond in the rough.

Unlike Durmer, Brooke Kelly could speak volumes about Sacred Heart University. Both of her parents, LouAnn and Jim, were graduates, and her dad had been a valuable forward on strong Pioneer teams in the early 1970s, setting records for shot-blocking that still stand. In fact, Brooke spent her first 10 years in Monroe, just several miles removed from the university's Fairfield campus, before the family moved to New Jersey.

"When we lived around here, we would come here to watch a few games, and I used to read his old clippings and think how awesome that was," Brooke said.

Rather than live her father's life, Brooke had excluded Sacred Heart from her original list of colleges. But that was before Swanson was pointed in her direction by Wayne Stokes, a former SHU teammate of Jim Kelly's. At Stokes' urging, the Sacred Heart coach went to see her play in an AAU tournament at St. Joseph's University in Philadelphia in the summer of 1998. "It's funny," Swanson said, "but I had watched another kid play maybe 20 times in the recruiting period, and I saw Brooke Kelly play once.

"But from that point on, I knew she was the player I had to get. I trusted my instincts on it. I made some phone calls and got her to come up for a visit. She fell in love with the place."

The opening game in Sacred Heart's inaugural Division I season, against the University of Hartford, was made all the more auspicious by the identity of the opposing head coach. Jennifer Rizzotti, the spark plug behind UConn's 1994–95 national championship season and perhaps the best known female player reared in the state of Connecticut, was making her coaching debut with the Hawks.

Even with Rizzotti's presence on the Hartford sidelines, the Pioneers bolted to a 29–22 lead at halftime, but horrendous 25.8 percent shooting in the second half left Sacred Heart on the short end of a 57–54 score when it was over. Rutnik, the only freshman to crack the Sacred Heart starting lineup, and Rimkus scored 11 points apiece.

Three nights later, on November 23, the results were far more favorable. Playing its opening game of the season in the Pitt Center, Sacred Heart secured its first victory as a Division I entity with an 82–64 verdict over Lafayette of the Patriot League. Rutnik, although limited to 19 minutes playing time because of foul difficulties, led four Pioneers in double figures with 16 points. Newhard bounced back from a scoreless effort against Hartford with 15 points and a game-high 13 rebounds.

Apparently the Leopards never recovered from traffic delays on the Tappan Zee Bridge in New York and elsewhere that transformed their bus trip from Easton, Pennsylvania, into a six-hour marathon. They fell behind 13–2 in the opening four minutes and by 43–23 at halftime.

On the weekend after Thanksgiving, Sacred Heart found itself overmatched at the Harvard Invitational. In the opener, Ohio State, a mid-level team in the Big Ten, broke open a competitive game late in the first half and cruised to a 98–66 decision. The following day Harvard proved itself a less-than-congenial host by whipping the Pioneers 83–50.

Despite the lopsided final score, Swanson saw encouraging signs in the Pioneers' efforts against the Big Ten team. Sacred Heart shot 50 percent

Jennifer Rizzotti's success coaching the University of Hartford team wasn't enough to satisfy all of her basketball cravings. In the 2000–01 season, she would play a unique dual role.

Hey, she was the coach on the floor for four years at Connecticut, so the change was fairly natural to the Hartford bench.

Jennifer Rizzotti

Sometimes, Jennifer Rizzotti even sounded like the coach of the Huskies when the games were over.

Take, for instance, the 1996 Big East tournament semifinals in Storrs. UConn had just beaten Pittsburgh into submission, another dreadfully dull annihilation by a team that specialized in such endeavors.

What could the writers ask after the game that hadn't already been asked 2,100 times?

The *Hartford Courant*'s Bruce Berlet, in an attempt to break the ice, decided to lob an easy one out there, for Rizzotti to presumably hit over the fence.

Instead she hit Berlet with, "Is that a statement or a question?" Talk about a future coach.

Fast forward four years to 1999–2000 when Rizzotti, who could run for and be elected Connecticut's governor, coaches with the same passion at the University of Hartford.

Season tickets increased. Fans showed up. So did the media, presumably to ask questions and (gulp) not make statements.

Then Rizzotti and the university ended speculation that she'd give up her coaching career to play in the WNBA when it was decided in early February she'd do both.

She'll play for the three-time WNBA champion Houston Comets and coach the Hartford Hawks. Is her plate too full? As Comets coach Van Chancellor said, "We only practice two hours a day, so she's got 22 hours to do other things."

Like recruit. Thankfully, she should have plenty of energy as the youngest coach (at age 25) in women's college basketball.

"I'm not ready to give up my playing career," Rizzotti said, "and they're not ready to let me give up coaching here."

Never before has this happened in the women's game. There are seven WNBA players who are college assistants and a few high school head coaches, but none take on this much responsibility.

"She loves challenges," said Hartford athletic director Pat Meiser-McKnett. "She's a wild woman."

Two days before the February news conference to announce Rizzotti's intentions, the Hawks won their 10th game, two more than they won in 1998–99 under Allison Jones. Rizzotti, basically, had the same players.

But here's the rub: How does she get better players? The primary time to recruit for college coaches comes in the summer at various Amateur Athletic Union games and the Nike camp. Rizzotti will be busy playing basketball.

The WNBA plays a 32-game regular season. Sure, it would be nice to walk into a recruit's house and say, "See No. 21 there diving into the third row for the loose ball? That's going to be your coach."

But how does one get into the recruit's house?

Enter assistant coaches Brian Mik and Mimi Walters. Meiser-McKnett said the school would likely hire a third assistant to help the Hawks open doors, in the hope that Rizzotti can close deals, and in the summer of 2000 they hired Rizzotti's husband, Bill Sullivan.

Although knowing Rizzotti's passion, it's a little amusing to picture her during a game next year turning to one of the assistants and saying, "Hey, you recruited them, not me."

Fortunately, Hartford plans to fill only two scholarships for next season, likely making Mik and Walters focus on juniors. The state of Connecticut has been known to produce a decent player or two (Rizzotti and Nykesha Sales to name two) so perhaps they won't have far to look.

"The hardest part will be not being around here during the summer when the (existing) players are here taking classes," Rizzotti said. "I don't know whether we can recruit nationally right now, and so I think the positives outweigh the negatives."

If coaching and playing at the same time sounds a bit strange, consider the path Rizzotti took to coaching and playing. Meiser-McKnett hired her on September 17. A year earlier, she had been gearing up for another season with the New England Blizzard of the now defunct American Basketball League.

Rizzotti was just where she had always been: playing in Hartford, adored by the fans. Her trademark kneepads may have been a better fit for the ABL officials the day she signed a new contract in April of 1998. They'd at least have made getting on their knees begging her to stay a bit more comfortable. Rizzotti signed a three-year extension to stay with the Blizzard through the 2000–01 season. Terms of the contract weren't disclosed, but Rizzotti said she had been given "what we think is fair."

Rizzotti, then 24, decided to stay in the ABL one day after Dawn Staley, one of the league's most marketable players, jumped to the WNBA. Since Rizzotti led the Blizzard to the ABL playoffs, the league has lost Staley, the Long Beach franchise, and the best talent in the college class of 1998 to the WNBA.

"I don't know if I was ever on the brink of leaving," Rizzotti said. "When the season's over isn't a great time to make a rash decision. I took some time off. I needed that space. I wanted to weigh my options. I think every smart businessperson does that.

"I'm happy in New England, but from an economic standpoint, I had to see what's best for the future," she said. "The No. 1 factor was to be able to stay in Connecticut. Since high school, I've been playing in front of them for six years. I love our fans, I love our fan base. I didn't know if I wanted to start over."

Ironically, that's exactly what she did when she took over the Hartford program.

The America East has never been a national power in women's basketball. It's getting better, however. Maine beat Stanford in the 1998 99 NCAA Tournament, not long after current Boston College coach Cathy Inglese had undefeated seasons at Vermont.

Could it be Hartford's turn now?

The university is located in West Hartford, in a rather tranquil setting, far enough away from the city. The campus is highlighted by an inordinate number of speed bumps—a decent enough metaphor to illustrate what Rizzotti and men's coach Paul Brazeau face in efforts to make Hartford an America East contender.

Pre-Rizzotti, the most recognizable face on campus was Vin Baker, the All-American who became an NBA All-Star with the Bucks and Sonics. Even Baker's teams didn't come close to winning the league championship.

Hartford has a first-rate facility in the SportsCenter, which is reached after about 10 speed bumps.

"Recruiting has more to do with me and how long I'm here," she said. "It has to do with being sold on the school, the facility...things like that. The key is to get them here (to visit) and when they do, I'll be here."

from the field and made 23 of 28 free throw attempts against the taller Buckeyes. "We can win a lot of games with that kind of shooting," he said. Conversely, the only positive aspect of the Harvard loss was Rutnik's 16 points.

Building Confidence

A return to the Pitt Center provided the right antidote. Another venerable Ivy League institution, Yale, was no match for the Pioneers and bowed by a 72–62 score. On this evening freshmen Brooke Kelly and Tara Brady made their first significant contributions, coming in off the bench to score 15 and 14 points, respectively. Kelly also pulled down 12 rebounds, four more than anyone on either side.

Two of Sacred Heart's final three contests of the twentieth century could be viewed as an exercise in futility. Georgetown of the Big East prevailed in a one-sided game at its McDonough Arena 82–54, and Bucknell utilized 25-for-30 marksmanship at the foul line to hold off the visitors 70–60. In the latter game, the Pioneers shot themselves in the foot by missing 13 of 24 foul shots.

In between, the Pitt Center provided the backdrop for one of the finest efforts by any Sacred Heart team. Virginia Commonwealth, which had routed the Pioneers by 28 points in the previous year, found itself battling for its life against the youthful Pioneers. At the end of regulation, the score was tied at 64. After the first overtime period, the teams were deadlocked at 74. In the end, the Colonial Athletic Conference school capitalized on its experience and 27 points from junior guard Liz Remus to return home with a hard-earned 87–84 triumph.

Kelly was magnificent off the bench, soaring for a personal high of 21 points—including a trio of three-pointers and all ten of SHU's points in the first overtime. "That game was a good confidence-booster," she said.

"It was one of the most fun games to play, but one of our most upsetting losses. Everyone gave everything they had."

Brady contributed 13 points against VCU in a reserve role. Among the starters, Newhard netted 18 points and Rutnik took down 13 rebounds during her 45 minutes on the court.

Sacred Heart's 2–6 won-lost record entering the new millennium might have created self-doubt in some teams. Losing breeds losing. Swanson, however, knew it was just a matter of time before the Pioneers, with four freshmen beginning to assert themselves, would jell. Another plus: Two important seniors who had yet to log a minute of playing time because of injuries, tri-captain Dawn Werner and Katie Toole, were now healthy.

They opened the Northeast Conference portion of the season on the road, or literally just up the road against Quinnipiac in Hamden, Connecticut. The Braves had struggled in their transition to Division I a year earlier, closing the books with a 9–18 record. With Werner contributing 10 points and nary a turnover in 26 minutes and Rutnik scoring a game-high 14, the Pioneers prevailed by the narrowest of margins, 56–55. On the down side, Brooke Kelly incurred a broken nose during the second half and would miss one game.

A cad might suggest that all of the Pioneers were among the missing two days later when they faced Central Connecticut in New Britain. On this afternoon, they became the gang that couldn't shoot straight—19-for-64 from the field, one for 23 from three-point range, six for 17 at the foul line. Central, which had shot just 23.8 percent (5-for-21) itself during the desultory first half that ended with the home team on top 17–15, heated up after intermission and won handily 61–45.

Monmouth, which had been picked to finish third in the NEC coaches' preseason poll, was up next in the Pitt Center. If the Pioneers were intimidated, there was little evidence. They spurted to an insurmountable 45–21 lead at halftime and coasted to a 79–63 win. Kelly, fitted with a protective facemask, supplanted Rutnik in the starting lineup and contributed eight points in just 14 minutes.

Two days later, Leslie Newhard made the most of her 23 minutes on the court, generating a season-high 24 points en route to a 73–67 verdict over Fairleigh Dickinson. Kelly was continuing to demonstrate her prowess as a rebounder, pulling down a game-high 10. As Swanson would observe much later: "Brooke really has a nose for the ball. I have more confidence in her to get a rebound than anyone we've had since Karen Bell in my early years here."

A Woolworth Record

The emergence of the freshmen and Newhard's solid play were beginning to relegate the upperclassmen to lesser roles. Some accepted change, others did not.

Tri-captain Jennifer Rimkus, an all-NECC guard as a junior who had elected to redshirt the previous year so that she could play a full season of Division I basketball, was displeased with her diminishing playing time and left the squad after the Monmouth game. Toole, whose long-range marksmanship produced a 13.1 scoring average the previous season, never did become a factor. But Yablonski, twice an NECC all-star during the final two Division II seasons and a scorer of more than 1,000 points in a fine career, remained a productive force as the backup center to Tara Brady.

"I deserve to be coming off the bench because Tara has been playing better," Heather said. "I feel more comfortable coming off the bench anyway because I don't need to score all the points as in the past."

A 3–1 start in the conference offered promise, only to see the Pioneers go into a tailspin and lose their next three games. At home, they fell before Wagner 74–44. On a swing through Maryland, they lost to the NEC's defending regular-season champion, Mount St. Mary's, by a 67–55 count and then bowed to Maryland-Baltimore County 64–52. To pinpoint the reason, Swanson needed to look no further than the cold, hard facts of the box scores. The team shot a collective 28.2 percent—and an even more dismal 15.9 percent in three-pointers—in those three contests.

In another time it was known as the Woolworth record. Five and ten. And that's precisely where Sacred Heart found itself as January was drawing to a close. Five wins, ten losses. "Frankly, I thought we'd have a few more wins at this stage," Swanson said. "What we lack is a go-to player. Somebody who can score the big basket or make the big defensive play."

When the coach surveyed his roster, he found an abundance of "super kids" and exemplary students. The team's cumulative grade point average was a commendable 3.1, and no fewer than seven players had made the Dean's List during the fall. "If I had a daughter, I'd want her to be like our players," Swanson said.

Still, if the Pioneers expected to crack the upper echelon in Division I, the coach knew they would need to acquire "a bit of a swagger. You see it in UConn, Tennessee, La Tech, and the other top teams. They all have it," he said. Teams with swagger don't produce Woolworth records in late January.

A Winning Streak

Swanson's decision to utilize a rotation of nine players finally began to pay dividends.

January ended with a sweep of Long Island University on the road, 76–64, and St. Francis of New York in the Pitt Center, 68–28, the latter coming on Alumni Day. Sacred Heart's defensive tenacity was shutting down opponents, as evidenced by the Terriers' 22.9 percent shooting in the latter game. Four nights later, the Pioneers limited Quinnipiac to just

10 points in the second half and 24.1 percent shooting overall en route to a 57–34 triumph. The winning streak had reached a modest three games.

Rematches with St. Francis and LIU produced similar results. The Terriers fell by a 77–53 score in Brooklyn Heights, New York, and the Blackbirds came up short in the Pitt Center, 70–51, as Brady sparked the Pioneers to their fifth straight victory with a personal high of 18 points.

"Sacred Heart plays the best defense in the conference," said LIU coach Patty Delahanty. "They're scrappy and they're aggressive. He uses a lot of players, and they're always fresh."

For the first time since the second game of the season, the Pioneers' record stood at .500, at 10–10, and they had moved into a third-place tie in the NEC with an 8–4 mark. Was Sacred Heart really that good?

Lehigh, the final nonconference opponent of the year, provided one answer. The Patriot League team took charge in the opening moments and constructed an 11-point lead. The Pioneers pulled within two on several occasions, only to have the visitors reassert themselves to establish a 59–52 advantage with slightly more than four minutes remaining. The winning streak appeared over.

Two freshmen and a senior had other, brighter thoughts. Ashley Durmer, who would finish with a game-high 14 points, connected on her third three-pointer of the night, Heather Yablonski scored from in close, and Brooke Kelly deposited a pair of free throws. The score was tied. With 38 seconds left on the clock, Kelly's jumper from the left baseline put SHU in front, and then Yablonski capped the dramatic 11-point run with two foul shots of her own.

Not only did the Pioneers prevail, 64–61, but their sixth straight win tied the school record held by two earlier Swanson teams.

"I said to the coaches on the bench I feel like we're down twenty, but I had some faith we could stop them," said an emotionally drained Swanson. "At times our youth hurts us, but they're learning and they're improving. Ashley is a super player with a lot of confidence. She makes mistakes, but that's because she's a doer."

Filling a Void

Remarkably, the Pioneers had won the last three games without Leslie Newhard. The sophomore forward, who was leading the team in scoring (9.9) and rebounding (6.8), had injured her left knee against Quinnipiac. She rejoined the squad for the two-game trip to Pennsylvania.

In a game Swanson thought his team would win, Sacred Heart came up short against Robert Morris, 58–55. End of winning streak. And now the Pioneers would face St. Francis of Loretto, the conference leader with a 10–2 record and winner of the NEC's 1999 postseason tournament.

Swanson's team put up the good fight, trailing by just 44–43 when Yablonski hit a jumper at the 7:46 mark in the second half. At that juncture, a pair of free throws by senior center Jess Zinobile ignited a 19–2 Red Flash run to settle matters. St. Francis prevailed, 65–49, as Zinobile put up 20 points and 12 rebounds—numbers indicative of her status as the NEC's premier player.

Newhard appeared to lack her customary mobility in both games played in her home state. An MRI several days later revealed an injury far more serious than originally thought: a torn anterior cruciate ligament that would require surgery. She was lost for the balance of the season.

"I was ready to cry twice in the (doctor's) office," Leslie said. "I had never missed a game, even in high school. To sit out now is torture." A touch of irony: Laura Newhard, her older sister who played at La Salle, had incurred the identical injury a year earlier.

Who would step forward to fill the void? The fab freshmen? The seniors? Coonradt? Well, yes.

Within the span of 48 hours, Sacred Heart played inspired basketball to win a pair of overtime games, each as exhausting as it was memorable, in the Pitt Center. And, more than anyone else, it was the soft-spoken senior guard, Dawn Werner, who provided the spark.

Against Maryland-Baltimore County on February 19, Dawn scored 15 of her career-high 18 points in the first half to help the Pioneers overcome a 16–4 deficit. Four straight times she launched arching three-pointers that found nothing but net. "She's streaky, but today she was shooting with a lot of confidence. She looked like Reggie Miller out there," Swanson would say later.

Heather Coonradt and Tara Brady assumed the scoring load in the second half (each would finish with 15 points), while Werner's two defensive plays down the stretch—a steal and a forced jump ball that gave SHU possession—helped maintain precarious Pioneer leads. Alas, the resourceful Retrievers closed within a single point to 55–54, and then Dawn was whistled for a flagrant foul by referee Larry Savo with 1.8 seconds left in regulation.

Werner would later question the validity of the call—"I feel we just collided"—but that was academic as UMBC's leading scorer, sophomore Jami Lange, stepped to the foul line with the game in the balance. The Pioneers breathed a collective sign of relief when her first attempt went awry, but Lange made the second free throw to force overtime.

Given a reprieve, Sacred Heart then reeled off seven straight points to grab a 63–57 advantage, with Werner connecting on three of four free throw attempts. The final was 69–61.

"UMBC is a talented team. Athlete for athlete, they might have it over us, but we play with a team concept. We have the balance you need to win," Dawn said.

Brooke Kelly contributed to that balance by pulling down a game-high 17 rebounds, the most by a Pioneer since the 1993–94 season. Recalled Newhard: "Brooke said, 'I'm dedicating my rebounding to you.' I told her 'You had enough today for the both of us.'"

Coonradt, who was now putting up Newhard-like numbers as her replacement at forward, also heralded the freshmen. "At one point, we had four out there and Abby (Crotty). We rose with them," she said.

There was little time to savor the team's most dramatic NEC victory of the season. Mount St. Mary's, second in the conference with a 12–3 record and its defending regular-season champion, was a Pitt Center visitor two days later.

This time, the Pioneers bolted to a 12–4 lead, with Werner and Coonradt each registering five points, including a three-pointer. Soon, SHU increased its advantage to 22–13.

Regrouping behind Megan Gardiner, the NEC's 1999 Player of the Year, the Mount roared back to pull into a 30–30 tie at halftime, and then forged ahead 44–38. Gardiner would finish with 24 points. Enter Werner. For the second straight game, the senior from Port Monmouth, New Jersey, put forth a career performance, this time producing 21 points and four more treys—the last of which gave the Pioneers their first lead of the second half, 48–47.

In the furiously contested second half, there were 13 lead changes and five ties. From the Sacred Heart viewpoint, the most important deadlock occurred with 54 seconds remaining when Werner's pass to Coonradt on the baseline led to a layup and a 71–71 score. The Mountaineers missed two layups in the closing seconds.

In the overtime, Sacred Heart led by as many as four points, but the Mount pulled abreast at 82–82 on Kia Williams' layup with seven seconds to play. Ultimately, the game's outcome would hinge on a play that took place one millisecond later: nearly 80 feet from the Sacred Heart basket, Werner was fouled by Mountaineer senior Lauren Menichini. The least consistent of the Pioneers at the foul line, Dawn missed her first attempt. Her second rolled around the rim and dropped through.

When Werner corralled Gardiner's missed jumper with one second left, that was the signal for all but one of the Pioneers to erupt. And Swanson? "I thought it was tied until I looked back at the scoreboard and saw we were ahead," smiled the SHU coach.

"We've come a long way, even after losing our leading scorer. The kids have really responded," he said. "We could have left here with people saying, 'They can play with the good teams but they can't beat them.' But to tell the truth, I haven't walked out of any gym and said we can't beat that team."

Retribution and Reward

In the final two games of the regular season, Sacred Heart had an opportunity to avenge earlier losses. As was the case during the year on the road, the Pioneers fell behind early (16–5) against Wagner, and although they rallied to take the lead in the second half, the Seahawks prevailed by a 76–66 score. Once again Wagner held a significant advantage in rebounds (49–32) and once again SHU was unable to contain the quickness of senior guard Nia Ryan, who tallied 24 points.

So, a winning season and a potential No. 3 seed in the Northeast Conference tournament were on the line in the home finale against Central Connecticut on February 26.

It was Senior Day, which meant that Swanson awarded starting assignments to Werner, Yablonski, Toole, cocaptain Dora Clark, and Rachael Vierling.

Later, Toole would explain her rationale for remaining connected to the squad, despite her almost nonexistent playing time. "The rest of the team makes it easier (to accept). Winning games like today makes it worthwhile," she said.

In contrast to the emotional pregame ceremony honoring the five seniors and their parents, the Pioneers came out surprisingly flat. In a start reminiscent of their January meeting in New Britain, neither side was able to find the range. Central led throughout virtually all of the first half save for a Werner three-pointer that put SHU in front 24–21. The Blue Devils countered with a pair of baskets in the final moment to lead 25–24 at intermission.

With the score tied at 38–38 in the second half, Heather Coonradt's three-pointer from the top of the key triggered the decisive 13–2 spurt that placed Sacred Heart securely in front, 51–40, with 99 seconds to play. During that run, Rutnik hit a three-pointer from the same spot, and Werner drilled in a trey from the left corner. Coonradt completed the surge by converting a pair of free throws for her 19th and 20th points—a career high.

It may not have been artful, but the 55–49 outcome capped a season of indisputable proof that the Pioneers were a success in Year One of Division I. Swanson's all-for-one, one-for-all team concept had produced a 14–13 record (11–2 at home), a third-place finish in the conference, and a No. 3 seed in the NEC tournament.

No player ranked among the conference leaders in scoring or rebounding, but each took a turn in carrying the team.

"Ed's never had a superstar, but his teams have always been competitive," said Sacred Heart's athletic director, Don Cook. "He understands that to be a winning team, you have to play together. They did that exceptionally well this year."

"We don't have a prime-time player, but everyone takes their role and accents it," said Coonradt. "As a team, we're close on and off the court. In years to come, it will be nice to think that this season was the foundation for so many good seasons to come."

For the players who labored through the lackluster Division II seasons of the eighties and the gatherings of 50 to 100 who watched them in the SHU Box, the Pioneers' 1999–2000 season must have seemed surreal. If anyone had suggested back then that Sacred Heart would make a successful entry into Division I at the dawn of the next century, he or she would have been considered a wishful thinker. Or worse. In hindsight, "visionary" would have been the appropriate description.

chapter three

tennessee

A New Era

Could you call it a new era? What, exactly, do you call it when the best player to ever wear Orange—maybe the best one to ever play women's basketball—has graduated? What do you call it after three straight national championships, every individual honor you could conceive of, and as large a presence as ever set foot on the court?

So what do you call the start of a season without Chamique Holdsclaw?

A new era, sure. It's a natural conclusion. But is that truly accurate? "A new era" would imply that Tennessee's success, its power, its prestige, was unprecedented during Holdsclaw's tenure and that now, without her, they were entering new territory, a team without a superstar.

Was this correct? In a lot of ways, certainly. Never before had a player with Holdsclaw's talent passed through women's basketball, not even at Tennessee. But on the other hand, Tennessee had experienced plenty of success, had accumulated plenty of accolades, had won national titles— and all without Holdsclaw.

So what was so new here? What was the new era? Maybe, instead, it should have been labeled a return to an old era, a return to a time when Tennessee was *among* the top teams—rather than *the* top team—and boasted a slew of strong players rather than a mega-superstar surrounded by players in supporting roles.

Still, this situation remained: Whether you called it a new era or a return to an old one, three classes (sophomores, juniors, and seniors) had never played without Holdsclaw. And the freshmen, well, they're *freshmen*. One never knows exactly how they'll fit into the mix.

So, ladies and gentlemen, highlights of your post-Holdsclaw team: junior forward Tamika Catchings, an All-American. Catchings is a shy kid who feels a bit inhibited socially because of a hearing impairment which requires her to wear a hearing aid. She does much of her "talking" on the court. The question would be whether the lead-by-example player could add vocal leadership to her repertoire. Next: the passionate Semeka Randall. Could the highly emotional player control herself and her game enough to lead this team in a disciplined manner? At point guard: Kristen "Ace" Clement, a junior with a renewed work ethic. But would work ethic be enough to start at point guard and orchestrate winning drives that would inspire heroics from teammates?

Next, meet sophomore Michelle Snow, senior LaShonda Stephens, and sophomore Shalon Pillow, your inside players. Could they dominate the lane? Would they need to? And don't forget to say hello to freshmen Kara Lawson and April McDivitt, point guard possibilities to be sure, but still freshmen. Rounding out the team: seniors Niya Butts and Kyra Elzy, both talented players with the mantle of experience to pass along. Finally add freshman Gwen Jackson, a 6'2" center/forward; freshman Tasheika Morris, a 6'0" forward; and freshman 5'11" guard Sarah Edwards.

There it is: your new era team. Welcome to the 1999–2000 season. Welcome to quite a ride.

In a Foreign Land

So here they were, this new-era team, on foreign ground in more ways than one. No more Chamique Holdsclaw, who was off continuing her college success at the professional level in the WNBA. But foreign in a literal sense as well, as the team traveled to Europe in August for a 12-day tour, a series of games, and a strong bonding session.

Maybe the sentiment was best expressed by *Knoxville News-Sentinel* sports editor John Adams in an August 16 notebook: "Is a small gym in Namur, Belgium, any less familiar," Adams asked, "than a Tennessee lineup sans Chamique Holdsclaw?"

It was a rhetorical question, really.

And how about this for a foreign site: coach Pat Summitt, a fixture on the bench, instead sitting in the stands and handing over the reins to her assistant coaches. No stalking the sidelines. No passionate halftime speeches (well, okay, she would be offering some commentary here and there). No absolute control. But surprisingly, she loved it all.

"I think the biggest thing is emotionally, it was good for me and for them," Summitt said of sitting in the stands. "I wanted to allow Ace Clement to go and play and not coach her, but just see what she could bring to the team.

"I was really pleased....I think for me sometimes I expect too much too soon. I allowed the players to go and play; it seemed to work well."

An Opening Day Loss

This is how a rollercoaster ride begins. You start at some neutral point, then click your way up a large hill before getting flung down into the depths at what feels like 100 miles per hour. And then, of course, it is up again, down again, in split-second increments, with changes of direction whipping you around.

This is how the Lady Vols' season began. Start at neutral. Start in the preseason, when everything is new, when questions surround every aspect of the team. Start with possibilities.

They started uphill: 5–0 in Europe in August against solid competition. They had a healthy lineup. Although Semeka Randall was still recovering from offseason ankle surgery, she was playing and playing well, and Kyra Elzy was showing flashes of what she had been prior to knee surgery more than a season earlier.

They hit the top of the first hill: a win over the U.S. National Team on November 7. Then, exactly one week later, in the regular-season opener, they began the downhill ride. A 69–64 loss at home to Louisiana Tech. Gone was the 40-game home winning streak. The 17 straight opening-game victories? Gone. They shot just over 30 percent from the floor and demonstrated that the theories about needing a leader were valid.

"This is no way to start," read the headline in the *Knoxville News-Sentinel* the next day. "We were standing around, waiting for someone to make a play," Summitt told the paper. "I thought we dribbled too much. We didn't get open. We didn't set any screens to get someone open. We have to learn to play better together."

Instinctively, the team looked to its point guard, Clement, when it struggled. But what happened when Clement struggled? Again, no leader emerged. "When Ace was struggling, we didn't have anyone step up and help her," Summitt said. "It's a team game."

Specifically, Summitt pointed to sophomore Michelle Snow. At 6'5", Snow would be expected to contribute, at the very least in clogging the lane and grabbing rebounds. But Summitt had harsh words for her center, who scored two points and had six rebounds. "Michelle was a nonfactor today," Summitt said. "And until Michelle Snow becomes a force for us... She has to learn from this game. We can be a great team in March, but we're not a great team now."

Freshman Kara Lawson

The national media had been fascinated by her since she was eight years old and a youth football phenom. The national television shows *People Magazine* and *That's Incredible* did stories on her, the tough little girl with the ponytail swinging from behind the football helmet. You can find old clips of Lawson, ball tucked away, sprinting down the field, weaving through defenders and on to the end zone. This wasn't just a girl kicking extra points, this was a girl running the ball and scoring touchdowns. And that was incredible, certainly. No, national media has never bothered or distracted Lawson. Media attention has never rattled her, never diverted her attention from her main purpose in life: to win ballgames.

So Kara Lawson went to Tennessee, and you knew she would contribute to the Lady Vol's success—but who had any idea it would be to such an extent? How many freshmen are given the responsibility to run the team, and, even more impressive, how many are given the responsibility to add stability to a team of such stature as UT? Stability? From a freshman?

This is Kara Lawson, though. Cool-hand Luke.

Or Hot-hand. In November, she hit the game-winner against the U.S. Olympic team. History being made with a college team beating the Olympic squad? Ho-hum.

"Kara Lawson, I think, is mentally really tough," Summitt said early in the season. "You don't find many players, much less freshmen, with her focus, composure, and confidence. To tell you exactly how I feel about her: It went down to the last possession (against the Olympic team), and we put the ball in Lawson's hand. It was gonna be Lawson or Tamika Catchings taking the last shot. And because of the defense that occurred, Kara didn't flinch (and took it)."

On January 23, Summitt finally gave in to the idea that Kristen Clement was not the best player to run the team at the point. Clement was struggling with turnovers and with leading the team. In one four-game January stretch, she had 19 turnovers and just 9 points. Lawson was consistent, a coolheaded player in often frenetic surroundings. The swap was made: Lawson at point, Clement at shooting guard. And Clement handled it like a trouper.

The move was an instant success. In only Lawson's fourth game at the helm, UT defeated UConn at Gampel Pavilion in Storrs, Connecticut. Lawson's individual statistics weren't stellar—nine points in 27 minutes with one assist and two turnovers—but the team never lost its composure despite trailing by as many as 14 points in the first half. And you can at least partially credit the point guard for that.

On February 4, Lawson had a game-high 23 points in a 78–52 win over Vanderbilt. Much more significant was the fact that the fourth trey gave her 52 for the year, breaking the record held by Nikki Caldwell. Lawson already had six three-pointers in one game, tying another record held by Abby Conklin.

"It's been a much-needed dimension for our team," Summitt told the *News-Sentinel*. "We haven't had a player consistently be able to knock down three's."

Oddly enough, Lawson herself was surprised at the proliferation of long-range shots. "I've been surprised the number of times I've been on a roll," Lawson said. "I never had that type of a roll in high school."

By the end of the season, Lawson had firmly established herself not simply as an outstanding freshman player. She had earned a reputation as oustanding. And when the SEC awards were handed out, Lawson was named to the first team all-SEC (which has 10 members) as well as to the all-freshman team.

Turnabout

You just assumed every year that Tennessee would be one of the top two or three programs in the country, and you couldn't be blamed for believing as such. And with three national titles in a row, you got used to seeing Orange on national television a lot. You got used to hearing the name "Chamique Holdsclaw." Perhaps you even got a little sick of it. Opponents most certainly did. So much so that now, when those who had been kicked got a chance to do the kicking, it was something to savor.

Just such a payback was coming from Connecticut despite one Lady Vol's near epiphany.

Pat Summitt was watching Connecticut embarrass No. 3 Louisiana Tech when her phone rang. It was junior Semeka Randall on the line, the anchor of her No. 2 ranked Lady Vols' basketball team. Randall, who had been struggling with her defense, had an epiphany while watching the Huskies play defense en route to their convincing victory over Louisiana Tech.

"She said, 'Coach, I'm starting to understand how important it is to play defense, and what a difference it could make,'" Summitt said. "She knows she has to get better off the ball."

Randall's epiphany was supposed to come at that exact moment. The Lady Vols' best player was supposed to rededicate herself to her defense before hosting the top team in the country.

But the Huskies were having none of that. They beat the Lady Vols for the first time in four meetings to take a 5–4 edge in the series. Tennessee, which lost to No. 3 Louisiana Tech on November 14, had not lost two games at home since losing to Stanford and Georgia during the 1996–97 season.

"We didn't match their intensity," said Summitt, whose team led 25–24 early in the first half, but trailed 43–37 at halftime and never regained the lead. "They had a great game plan. We complained too much instead of just going after it. They kept their composure and made their shots in transition. They were more aggressive. They got us back on our heels. The list goes on and on."

Michelle Snow finished with a team-high 21 points on 8-for-20 shooting and 12 rebounds.

Randall was the only other double-figure scorer for Tennessee, which shot a season-low 28.6 percent from the field in the second half. Randall had 20 points, including 9-for-10 from the foul line.

"I wasn't frustrated," Snow said. "I was just trying to do anything I could to get the enthusiasm up and get the crowd into it."

But the Huskies had their own way of "getting the crowd into it." When they beat Tennessee—in Knoxville, no less, in front of over 20,000 fans—they pumped fists in the air, danced at half-court, and shouted to the UConn fans in the nosebleed sections.

UConn coach Geno Auriemma knew what it meant, to his team and to dozens of others. If there was finally going to be a chance to knock the Lady Vols down, every moment was to be savored. "I think it's 'Chamique Holdsclaw kicked our ass for four years, and now we're getting back at you,'" Auriemma said. This was turnabout. And to Auriemma it was fair play.

With the January 8 win the Huskies avenged their previous season's loss to the Lady Vols, which had snapped their 54-game home-winning streak at Gampel. That had been an emotional game, which featured the wrestling altercation between Randall and UConn's Svetlana Abrosimova that earned Randall her nickname. Following the incident, which both players say is behind them, the UConn fans booed Randall every time she touched the ball.

It stuck. To this day, Randall has adopted the nickname "Boo." Even her own fans affectionately call her Boo.

"We laugh about it now," said Randall, who flipped headfirst over Abrosimova during the incident. "I didn't mean any harm by it and there are no hard feelings. She wanted to win, I wanted to win. It's emotional, the heat of the moment. It's passion."

A Loss to Georgia

How much shock there must have been in Orangeville the morning of January 18, when anyone who had not watched the game on national television picked up the paper and saw the score of the January 17 game against Georgia.

Georgia 78, Tennessee 51.

Surely it was a typo. Surely it was reversed. For hadn't it been just two years since Tennessee had handed Georgia its worst-ever defeat, beating the Bulldogs 102–43 on January 28, 1998? How could two teams with much the same personnel swap scenarios so drastically, so that Tennessee instead had a "worst-ever" night? This was the Lady Vols' worst SEC loss ever (the worst loss overall was a 91–60 loss to Texas on December 12, 1984). Its second-lowest point total ever. Twenty-nine turnovers were the most so far this season.

Georgia's thrashing of the Lady Vols was another example of a turnabout. The memory of the Bulldogs' 102–43 loss to Tennessee two years earlier was fresh, the wound not yet healed. And when the Bulldogs had a chance to instill a similar hurt on the Lady Vols, they did so—and were not afraid to admit how good it felt. "We put it to them," said Georgia forward Angie Ball, "and it's sweet."

"This," Coach Pat Summitt said, "was an embarrassing loss." This was not Tennessee. And this certainly was not Summitt's style, this noncompetitive excuse for a game. "I don't know what our personality is," Summitt said. "It's certainly not what my personality is."

The first thing you notice about Pat Summitt, the first thing almost anyone notices about her, are the eyes. Intense is a word that almost doesn't provide enough emphasis. Enough oomph. But that's where to begin when describing the legendary coach. Everything you need to know is there. When *Sports Illustrated* magazine did a feature story on Summitt—one of those rare moments when it features a woman on its cover—what did it choose as its photo? The eyes, startling in the way they could pierce through a person, the way they could simultaneously intimidate you, yet refuse to let you lose hold of the gaze.

Her philosophy is simple: Be your best. That means practice the best, play the best, do everything the best. Ride the stationary bike like you're

Lance Armstrong in training; run sprints like Carl Lewis is your opponent; run each play in practice like it's the waning moments of the national championship game.

It's the way she always played. It's what she always expected from herself. Summitt told the *Knoxville News-Sentinel* this of her coaching philosophy: "Go in and be tough. You can always let up."

Some say she has let up after 26 years of coaching. But she hasn't let up in a way that has affected her success. Six national titles, over 700 wins, never a losing season, the title of Women's Coach of the Century—and, in the year 2000, induction into the Basketball Hall of Fame. She has mountains of honors, awards of the highest measure. Yet none of it happens without the drive, without the relentless pursuit of perfection and the unyielding desire to test limits. And you can see that—yes, all of it—in the eyes.

Tennessee's recent play, however, must have left her squinting. And don't even try to toss out some rah-rah cliché explanation about parity in women's basketball, for the Georgia game had nothing to do with that. Instead, it had everything to do with a lack of intensity. And how in the world does that happen with a team from Knoxville? How does that happen to Summitt? The fiery eyes, always ablaze during competition, instead bore bewilderment. And a certain amount of disgust. She accused her team of quitting at times and of not competing—which is always unacceptable.

"I have a hard time," Summitt said, "watching noncompetitive people go up and down the floor in Orange."

Yes, they capitalize the word "orange" here in Knoxville. The town is nearly painted with it, storefronts and displays boast it. Even the Women's Basketball Hall of Fame, located here, knows who it is marketing to. Try to find Blue and White at that gift shop. Not gonna happen, y'all. It's all Orange, all the time.

But against Georgia, it was orange pulp. Summitt wanted to rip the color off her players' backs and make them earn it back. Where did this weakness come from? Why was the *Knoxville News-Sentinel* describing the look in her players' eyes as "glazed"? Who taught them how to quit when the game got tough?

"I'm very concerned about mental toughness—or lack thereof," Summitt said. "We're too fragile, too fragile against physical teams."

Fragile? A Tennessee team? Again, it does not compute.

"They competed more, and they wanted it more," forward Tamika Catchings said in a postgame radio interview. "I don't know how that happened."

Halfway through the season, and that was just one of many questions the Lady Vols were struggling to find answers to.

Who was their go-to person when games got close? Who was their point guard, especially when starter Kristen Clement was demonstrating an unsettling knack for folding in big games. And who, in fact, would be moved to the shooting guard slot later that same week? Did they have depth in the post positions? Could a team with a different personality than Summitt's survive in her program? Could Summitt handle it?

Said Catchings, "We have a lot of work to do."

Some solace could be found in recent history, however. For it was as recently as the 1996–97 season that the Lady Vols suffered 10 losses and still won the NCAA championship. That included a lopsided loss to UConn and a late-season 18-point loss to Louisiana Tech.

That team quickly learned how to take defeat and transform it into victory. That was how the 1996–97 team had responded to the questions. But it was still up in the air for the 1999–2000 squad. Would they do the same? Or would they take a few defeats and transform them into a pity party?

"I think this game will be a game that will bring out the best or the worst," Summitt said. "It's all in how they handle it."

Questions with No Answers

Mid-January is when every team takes a hard look at itself and judges its progress. It is past the early-season stretching, where a team just tries to figure out how everyone fits together. You're a good way into the regular season and into conference play, and you have a glimpse of how that race

At the opposite end of the women's college basketball spectrum from Tennessee, at the end where teams lose most of their games instead of winning most of them, is the University of Rhode Island. But in the 1999–2000 season, that program had an asset unmatched by any other: the legendary KC Jones.

Go ahead. Start rolling off the names. Michael Jordan. Larry Bird. Magic Johnson. Elgin. Walton. Kareem. Want more? Mikan, Cousy, Oscar, McHale, Hawkins. Had enough yet? Shaq. Stockton. Malone.

KC Jones

And not even that esteemed list of Gentlemen of the Hardwood can equal the basketball success of KC Jones.

From the top, maestro: From 1955–66, Jones played on teams that won two NCAA titles, an Olympic gold medal, and eight NBA titles. After his playing days, he was head coach of two NBA championship teams and an assistant coach on two others.

Bill Russell, Jones' former Celtic and University of San Francisco teammate, might be the only player ever to have accomplished more.

So where could you have found KC Jones—THE KC Jones this past basketball season?

Kingston, Rhode Island, assisting his former assistant, Boe Pearman, coaching the University of Rhode Island women's basketball team.

And the one question most often asked: Why?

Jones says, "Why not?"

"It's what I enjoy," he said. "I'm like the hoot owl sitting on the bench, the old wise guy who can critique what's going on."

Jones did not travel with the Rams, who suffered through a 2–24 regular season. He did some community work and clinics, and, well, was the wise old guy who critiqued what went on.

"When they first hired him, my (high school) coach called and said, 'KC Jones! Can you

is shaping up. And you've played a few nonconference opponents—and, if you are Tennessee, have made sure they're nothing short of Top 10 caliber.

"A great deal of our success comes from playing great teams," Summitt said. "Immediately, all our weaknesses will be exposed."

get his autograph?'" freshman Lyrica Smith told the *Boston Globe*. "He's really calm and collected; I listen to everything he says."

Jones and the Celtics won the franchise's last two NBA championships in 1984 and 1986. He hadn't been seen much since, until he decided to give women's basketball a chance. He was named the New England Blizzard's head coach in 1997, during a news conference at the Hartford Civic Center that was better attended than many women's games.

Imagine the culture shock for players like Kara Wolters and Jennifer Rizzotti, who spent four years playing for the intense Geno Auriemma at Connecticut. Jones' coaching style with the Blizzard was similar to what you saw with the Celtics: observe, suggest, and never yell very much.

The American Basketball League, of which the Blizzard was a member, folded in December of 1998, leaving Jones to seek other employment.

If women's basketball offered more anonymity than his last head coaching job, that was perfectly all right with Jones, whose initial role with the Celtics was to back up Cousy. His first coaching job was at tiny Brandeis University in Waltham, Massachusetts, in 1968.

Jones joined the Celtics before the 1958–59 season after two years of military service and a brief tryout with the Los Angeles Rams. Finally, in 1963, Jones replaced Cousy and continued to play some of the best backcourt defense in NBA history. He nearly led the league in assists, too.

A perfect coaching candidate, he plays defense and gets everybody else involved. After Brandeis, Jones became an assistant under Bill Sharman with the 1971–72 Lakers, who, naturally, won the NBA championship.

From 1973–76, Jones was head coach of the Washington Bullets, who, naturally, won two division titles in three years.

Then after a few years as Bill Fitch's assistant with the Celts (where, naturally, they won the 1981 NBA title), Jones became the head coach in 1984 and won two more championships.

There is something of a checklist at this point. It is tune-up time. Check the list, gauge the progress, make a few changes if necessary. For the Lady Vols, many of the problems were still inexplicable. Many questions were being asked, and much searching was still going on.

First, there was still no answer as to who would take charge when needed. Who was the player you knew you would set up the last-second shot for? Who would draw the foul, get to the free throw line, and sink those shots? Would it be Tamika Catchings? Could it be Semeka Randall? Could it be a freshman like Kara Lawson? Did it even need to be one person? Summitt suggested that perhaps it didn't need to be.

"That's the biggest question mark about our basketball team right now," she said after the loss to UConn on January 8. "I don't think you have to have a person or two (be the leader). I think this basketball team could very well be led by committee, and they may very well have to."

Maybe this team had gotten too accustomed to Holdsclaw taking over. For years, they had stood and watched as Holdsclaw would keep the ball and make her own thing happen on the floor. They knew the ball was staying in her hands, and they knew they didn't really have to make a lot of moves off the ball. Just get in position to rebound in case she missed.

But now it was different. Now there were five players in the scheme of things. This was all about setting picks and making passes. And the players who were used to standing around and watching had to figure out who was going to be the one to make a move. Summitt pointed out that this was the way UT teams had always done things in the pre-superstar era.

"The rest of the (earlier) teams had to find a way to get the job done together on both ends of the floor," Summitt said.

The next big question surrounded the point guard position. This had been a position always dominated by one player, one strong, stable player. Michelle Marciniak, the mini-Pat. You knew what to do with Marciniak on the floor, and you didn't question it. Kellie Jolly, though maybe not a star, was consistent and could run the floor. But Kristen Clement was struggling. Ace was not living up to her nickname.

So in mid-January, it came down to this: Move Clement to shooting guard, put Lawson in as the starter at point, and sprinkle in appearances by freshman April McDivitt, though mainly for experience. You might think that point guard is a position held onto by one person, but Summitt disputed that notion.

"We don't just have to have a point guard," Summitt told the *Knoxville News-Sentinel*. "We can have a point guard by committee."

A risky idea, to be sure, especially on a team struggling to find its go-to person. So now, not only were the Vols lacking a take-charge player, they were lacking the play caller.

Next question: Where was the intensity? Why were quotes like these seen in newspapers the day after losses to UConn and Georgia? From Summitt after the UConn loss: "It was apparent from the beginning today that Connecticut was very confident and very aggressive both offensively and defensively. They caught us back on our heels. They were more confident and aggressive and mentally tougher. The list goes on and on." Also from Summitt after the UConn loss: "Their inside play overall was huge. They were physical, and we didn't match their intensity. We complained too much instead of going after it." And from Catchings after the Georgia loss: "They competed more, and they wanted it more. I don't know how that happened."

One theory could be that the team, inexperienced in such situations, was simply too eager to find answers and find them fast. Everyone knew they needed a go-to person. So everybody started trying to be that player.

"We're having a lot of individual stuff," senior forward Niya Butts told the *Knoxville News-Sentinel*. "That's kind of understandable when you're under pressure and you feel you have to step up, but we have too many people doing it."

And finally, what about depth at the post position? It was difficult to think about any recent Tennessee team and not think about its inside play. Opponents were always talking about the need to rebound, the need to be competitive inside, the need to match UT in toughness. But what of this year's post players?

The Rematch with UConn

Here it was, staring them in the face: a chance at redemption.

The loss to UConn on January 8 had sent the Lady Vols reeling, at least as much as the Lady Vols ever reel. They hadn't spiraled into a losing streak, but they had tripped, had lost their groove, and with it, lost a little confidence. For how much confidence can you have after you lose to UConn on your home court, win a pair of close ones that never should have been so close, and then get steamrolled by Georgia a few days later?

Even UConn coach Geno Auriemma admitted that the UT–UConn game did things to the teams that their coaches certainly wouldn't want: It sometimes sapped them of their strength. "Through the years," Auriemma said, "I've noticed this game does take its toll on both programs."

So here it was, February 2, nearly a month later, and the Lady Vols finally felt steady on their feet again. And here was UConn once again. Here was their chance. They were going to Gampel Pavilion, and wouldn't it be sweet to exact some revenge on the Huskies in their house?

From the looks of the first 20 minutes, it didn't seem they would get their chance. UConn jumped out to a 5–0 lead; Tennessee missed its first five shots. The Huskies built a 10-point lead, 19–9, then 21–11. Soon it was 14 points, 29–15, with 5:26 left in the first half.

But there is one thing you should know if you play Tennessee: Never get comfortable with your lead.

UConn did.

The Huskies were up by 14 points with 2:53 until the half, 34–20. They were even up 11 with 1:41 until halftime. But in the final 34 seconds of the half, Semeka Randall made a layup and Tamika Catchings hit a three-pointer, and it was only a six-point game.

Later, when looking at the tremendous momentum swing that run caused, UConn Coach Geno Auriemma was perplexed. "Why put the brakes on with three minutes left in the half?" he asked.

Why, indeed. Especially against the Lady Vols, so desperate to restore pride and confidence to the team. You simply don't do that when playing Tennessee. You simply don't relax.

Tennessee coach Pat Summitt, knowing full well what was happening, implored her team to continue the run out of the locker room. "You can be the best team the next 20 minutes," she said.

And they were. Just two minutes into the second half, and UT had taken the lead. They led most of the half, even stretching it to nine points with 7:17 left to play.

And then it was time for the final six minutes. Auriemma may have summed it up best when he spoke of how the game didn't feel like one game at all; it felt like three. "It really was kind of an odd game to be involved in, because it looked like there were a lot of games within the game," Auriemma said. "The first 17 minutes, the next 17 minutes, and then the last six minutes. It was hard for me to get a handle on the whole game. It just seemed like three different games."

At this point, this six-minute point, UConn came back with a run of its own. Tamika Williams and Svetlana Abrosimova vaulted the Huskies back into it, and with 3:45 to play, the game was tied at 65 points.

And if it could be divided into three separate entities, then the final third was certainly the most exciting. No more runs. This was the seesaw on the playground. At this point, neither team could wrestle the lead away and keep it.

But if we're talking wrestling, then Semeka Randall's name has to come up, for Randall had shown that she never shies away from a little wrestling. And who else could provide a more fitting ending for the game than Randall? Who else but the player who earned the nickname "Boo" after a tussle with Svetlana Abrosimova in this very same gymnasium had prompted a chorus of such from Husky fans? Who else could better plunge the dagger?

Forget the fact that Randall was 2-for-7 with four points at the half. These were the waning moments of a big game, with an ESPN audience watching it all.

So what did Randall do? She banked a shot in with 27 seconds left to play. And after UConn's Sue Bird helped the Huskies reclaim the lead, Randall answered. She took a shot off the dribble, one that Bird got her hand on on the way up, and she willed it in with 4.4 seconds to go for a 72–71 lead. Two timeouts and a foiled play later, Tennessee had its redemption. "I'm sure it was God who put the ball in the hole," Randall said, "because I did not know anything."

Auriemma knew what happened. Maybe it was God, maybe it wasn't. Maybe it was something called fate. "The shots Randall made are the kind of shots you make," he said, "when you're supposed to win."

And so they talked psychology after this one. Specifically, Tennessee's mental health. "I think psychologically (for) this team, this was a game which we felt we needed to come in and play aggressive," Summitt said. "And come in with attitude, and match their intensity."

It was also a chance, Summitt said, for the squad to get a better idea of what would define it. This had been a season of wondering who the go-to person was, who the point guard was, even who was in the starting lineup at times. And only the players could figure that one out.

"I think this team needed something good to happen," Summitt said. "They've worked hard, really tried to come together as a team. I've noticed they've tried to take some ownership here. It's their team. It's not the staff's team."

But the staff—namely, Summitt—noticed improvement. And once again, it was mind improvement. "I think we showed some signs of maturity," she said. "You don't get stronger, faster, quicker in February and March. But you have a chance to get smarter."

If you're UConn, you may have viewed this as opportunity lost. "I think we let the game get away from us," Auriemma said, "for long, long stretches of time."

But both teams knew it was not an opportunity lost forever. It was one moment in February, just as the first game was one moment in January. "We don't get the championship trophy today," said Randall, who had reminded everyone the first time that it wasn't March. "And neither did they in Knoxville."

Now, it was time to see what would happen to the team when it won a big game. "When we lost, I don't think we handled it very well," Summitt said. "Hopefully, we'll handle (winning this one) well. We've still got a long way to go."

Another Close Call

At least one thing would be clear to the Lady Vols this season: They had nothing to fear in close games. For how many times had they fallen behind in games—by 14 to UConn, by 18 to Louisiana Tech—and then fought back, putting themselves in the proverbial position to win? They also won close games on the road against Kentucky and Stanford, making it four wins decided in the waning moments of games (the upcoming February 24 squeaker at Vanderbilt would put the number at five). When you have Tamika Catchings, Semeka Randall, and Kara Lawson, you never worry about trailing in a game. Sure, you are concerned about the reasons why you fell behind; but you don't worry about your ability to come back and win. "We've done it before," Lawson said. "We know we've done it before."

And so it happened again at Mississippi on February 17. This time, though, UT could not blame the slim margin on poor play—for how in the world do you defend against 10 three-pointers? What do you do when your opponent hits seven of its first nine shots and makes 60 percent of its first-half shots?

You wait. After all, the Lady Vols were hitting 50 percent of their own shots. And a 12-point first-half deficit—why, that's only four Kara Lawson treys. And everyone knows how quickly she can sink those. In fact, it was Lawson who contributed to the comeback, sinking two free throws to pull within seven at halftime, and yes, hitting a three-pointer to pull within two early in the second half.

UT trailed by seven with 2:35 to play. Again, you must remember: There is no margin large enough when you play the Lady Vols. They fought back and regained the lead, thanks again to Lawson. And just in case anyone wondered if Mississippi would try for any heroics in the game's final moments, with 1.6 seconds to go and a one-point lead Lawson shot a three-pointer. Game sealed. Comeback complete. Final Lawson statistics: a game high 23 points, three three-pointers, and 8-for-8 shooting from the free throw line. Yes, she did it before. And she did indeed do it again.

Fair or Foul?

February 24. Five-tenths of a second left. Tie game. Semeka Randall grabs her own missed shot under the basket and goes back up with it. Vanderbilt's Jillian Danker goes for the block.

The shriek of a whistle pierces the air. Foul.

Two free throws and a desperation shot later, UT leaves the court with a 59–57 win.

There may be some argument as to whether or not Danker truly fouled Randall. It depends on whom you ask. And even opposing sides would likely agree that, had it occurred two minutes into the game, this call would have been forgotten.

But the argument that will linger the longest is whether or not referee Bob Trammell should have made the call. It's an eternal barroom discussion: Should a referee let those go? The common understanding is that they "swallow the whistle," let the final seconds of a game play out, then go into overtime. There's less controversy that way. If a player hits a game-winner from the floor, she gets the glory. If she hits them from the free throw line, you get eternal barroom discussions over whether or not she ever should have been at the line.

Vandy coach Jim Foster, of course, favored this theory: "Players should determine games."

Foster, and all Vanderbilt fans, were dismayed not only over the final call, but about the one at 28 seconds—the charge called on VU's Chavonne Hammond which turned the ball over to Tennessee and set up the final play. And in a home game for Vanderbilt, no less. Add insult to injury.

But Summitt, obviously, chose this theory: "It's a 40-minute game. The officials' job is to call what they see. It's not one possession only that determines it."

True. But it certainly was one possession that this game would be remembered for.

And it may have been a possession that would help determine the Lady Vols' position going into the postseason.

chapter four

uconn

European Tour

The last time a Connecticut women's basketball team went to Europe for a summer tour, they created a bond so great, it carried them to the program's first—and only—national championship in March.

It was 1994, and the Huskies were overseas without the player who four years later would become the school's all-time leading scorer. Nykesha Sales was an incoming freshman and thus ineligible to take the trip with the Huskies. Yet Sales had little problem assimilating into the lineup during the season.

The situation in August 1999 was similar. The Huskies were unable to take newcomer Kennitra Johnson to Europe. It's against NCAA rules.

The Huskies spent 12 days in Europe, visited four countries, and played five games. The Huskies lost their first two games, starting with a 69–59 loss to Valenciennes, France, on August 20. The following day, the Huskies lost a one-point (66–65) heartbreaker at Namur, Belgium.

UConn managed to win its final three games, however. The Huskies won 87–43 in Versailles, France, on August 22; they beat Vicenza, Italy,

103–66 on August 27; and they beat Familia Schio, another Italian team, 70–64 on August 28.

"The last three games, we played really, really good," said Connecticut coach Geno Auriemma, who isn't allowed by NCAA rules to start official practice until the Saturday after October 15, which in this year was October 16.

"We found out a lot about ourselves, and we found out in game situations, too, instead of practice situations," he said. "It gives more of a sense of purpose to your workouts when you get back. The 45 days will be really productive because they know what they have to work on."

The experience gave the players an opportunity to learn not only what their strengths and weaknesses were on the basketball court, but also who their teammates were.

Swin Cash found out that Kelly Schumacher is not Canadian, even though she lives in Quyon, Canada. Schumacher was born and raised in Cincinnati. Cash, who has 78 first cousins of her own, also learned more about Sue Bird's family.

A highly family-oriented native of McKeesport, Pennsylvania, Cash was eager to learn what kind of values her teammates live by. "It's all part of being a family," Cash said. "When stuff hits the fan on the court, it makes a difference when you know your teammate, how she thinks and feels. You can anticipate what move they'll make."

As hard as the Huskies rallied to come home with a winning record in Europe, it certainly wasn't all work.

In France, the Huskies climbed the historic Eiffel Tower. In Italy, they visited St. Peter's Square in the Vatican and watched the Pope say Mass. They climbed the famous steps in Rome's Piazza di Spagna, and they rode the gondolas in Venice. The Huskies went to Lake Maggiore, which is located in northern Italy, a short distance from Switzerland.

Some players even got the thrill of a lifetime—bumping into American actor Samuel L. Jackson in a museum in Venice.

Most of the players admitted they couldn't decide on their favorite part of the trip. "We started off in Paris, and I loved Paris, and then we went to Rome, and I loved Rome," senior Stacy Hansmeyer said. "I absolutely loved the entire trip."

Auriemma was also thrilled to be back in his native country. But it wasn't the touristy spots that enticed Auriemma. Instead, he enjoyed the quiet and beauty of Lake Maggiore.

What Auriemma loved the most, however, was the mature way in which the Huskies handled themselves. On this trip, there was no complaining, no homesickness, and no one asking, "What time are we going back to the bus?" Auriemma said the only kids complaining were his own.

"They handled it beautifully," he said. "They handled it like mature kids."

The 1999–2000 Schedule

Not long after the Huskies returned from Europe, the 1999–2000 schedule was finalized.

The fact it isn't released until late August makes UConn associate head coach Chris Dailey laugh. Dailey is quick to point out that right up until the Huskies won the 1995 national championship, she was still in charge of scheduling games. Because the television networks are now heavily involved, the schedule is juggled by Jeff Hathaway, UConn's senior associate director of athletics.

Auriemma got a kick out of mailing the season's schedule to his players. "We mailed out the schedule to our players, and they were shocked," Auriemma said with a wry smile. "I think it really opened up a lot of eyes. There are not a lot of easy wins in the nonconference schedule. I think we have our hands full, and I love it."

There was no question the out-of-conference regular-season schedule was one of the most competitive ever. Auriemma, who is not afraid to lose, could count 12 games on the schedule that the Huskies might lose.

UConn, which went 29–5 the previous year and advanced to the NCAA Sweet Sixteen for the sixth straight year, had a highly unusual home-and-away series scheduled with six-time national champion Tennessee. The Huskies would face the Lady Vols twice in the regular season for the first time, and there was a possibility of a third game down the road.

The Huskies also had games scheduled with Louisiana Tech, Illinois, UCLA, Penn State, and Kentucky. In the final game of the Coaches vs. Cancer Challenge, the Huskies would face either Clemson or Old Dominion.

The out-of-conference schedule complemented the Big East Conference schedule, which boasted three other Top 25 teams from the previous year in Notre Dame, Boston College, and Rutgers. The Scarlet Knights were a preseason No. 1 pick in at least one publication.

While Auriemma counted which games the Huskies could lose, junior redshirt Shea Ralph refused to. "I don't lose games before I play in them," Ralph said firmly. "As far as I'm concerned, I haven't lost any games yet."

The other players echoed Ralph's sentiment. Svetlana Abrosimova said she was really excited when she saw the schedule because she hates to play against teams she knows the Huskies will beat by 40 points. "I think it's going to make us better even if we lose a game," Abrosimova said. "It's a great situation even if we lose a game, but I hope we don't lose them."

The Connecticut program has never shied away from potential losses. Auriemma has always favored a tough schedule; he knows the experience —win or lose—can prove to be invaluable.

We're Number 1

When the preseason women's basketball polls were released, UConn was ranked No. 1 in four of five national polls. The Associated Press, Athlon

Sports, *Basketball News* and the *Women's Basketball Journal* all picked UConn to win the millennium's national title.

Did that affect the relatively young Huskies? No.

Being ranked No. 1 in the country means almost nothing to the Huskies, besides being an obvious honor. After having missed the Final Four in each of the past three seasons, each person associated with the team knew that it was finishing No. 1 that mattered, not starting there.

Besides, the Huskies didn't always hold on to their first preseason No. 1 ranking for very long. In their first game of the 1995–96 season, UConn lost in overtime to Louisiana Tech at the State Farm Tip-Off Classic in Knoxville. The loss bumped the Huskies to No. 4 when the first Associated Press regular season ranking came out.

It was a hard lesson Auriemma will never forget. That's why he's learned to avoid that situation. For the past five years, Auriemma has tried to keep the Huskies on an even keel so there is no letdown when it's time to win a big game.

At the start of the 1999–2000 season, Auriemma convinced his team that being ranked No. 1 is just part of doing business at UConn.

"I don't think it will affect this team at all," he said. "If we were picked 10th, they might feel slighted, but I don't think they feel a sense of euphoria because we're No. 1. I don't think that's going to enter into the big picture. Besides, with our schedule, we'll have a chance to prove whether we're No. 1 or not."

Preseason

October 16, 1999, was only the beginning of preseason, and Auriemma was confident the season was going to be a good one. He believed he had a good group. He liked the array of personality and character, not to mention talent.

The Fab Five of Keirsten Walters, Swin Cash, Asjha Jones, Sue Bird, and Tamika Williams were all sophomores with a year of experience under their belts. Bird was back at full strength after missing the majority of the last season. Bird started the first eight games of the previous season before tearing the anterior cruciate ligament in her left knee. Now she would resume the starting position.

Abrosimova and Ralph were already showing signs of more mature and unselfish competitive desires. Both were willing to surrender to Auriemma's wishes in order to get better.

Hansmeyer and Paige Sauer were seniors, their time at UConn now borrowed. If those two graduated having missed the NCAA Final Four, it would be the first class since 1990 to fall short of the Final Four. Everyone realized that from the moment the Huskies lost prematurely to Iowa State in March 1999.

There was a hotshot freshman coming in to back up Bird at point guard. Kennitra Johnson was a relative unknown in the basketball community, coming from a small school in New Albany, Indiana. From a physical standpoint at 5'7", Johnson appeared to be nonthreatening. She was quiet and shy, but confident. And Auriemma believed she was his trump card.

While there are always question marks entering preseason, unknowns like chemistry, depth, and talent, the biggest question mark for Auriemma entering the year was how the last year's NCAA loss to Iowa State in March would affect this year's team.

Auriemma had no idea at this juncture whether the loss would serve as motivation. Would it bind the team together and serve as a driving force? Would they remember the heartache they felt when the final buzzer sounded at Cincinnati's Shoemaker Center and Iowa State started celebrating? Would the young Huskies still feel the effects from their stunningly early exit in the NCAA Tournament?

Auriemma desperately wanted answers to these questions. But at that time he didn't know the answers; all he knew was that they would come soon enough.

Craig Ambrosio

A view of Gampel Pavilion in Storrs, Connecticut, as UConn battles Pepperdine.

Craig Ambrosio

Rutgers Coach C. Vivian Stringer reacts to a call during the Scarlet Knights' home game against UConn.

Craig Ambrosio

UConn's Kelly Schumacher, left, blocks a shot by Rutgers' Tammy Sutton-Brown en route to a UConn victory, 49–45.

Craig Ambrosio

Rutgers center Tasha Pointer shoots through Kelly Schumacher, left, and Kennitra Johnson, right, in Rutgers' home loss to UConn.

Chris Nicholson

Sacred Heart's Ed Swanson tries to rally his troops during a timeout.

Craig Ambrosio

The Fighting Irish's Monique Hernandez shoots against the Huskies as Notre Dame Coach Muffet McGraw looks on.

Craig Ambrosio

Notre Dame's Julie Henderson shoots over Kelly Schumacher in a game against the Huskies.

Craig Ambrosio

Photographers crowd the sideline at the Hartford Civic Center for UConn's game against Notre Dame.

Craig Ambrosio

Tennessee Lady Vols Coach Pat Summitt reacts to a call in the game at UConn.

UConn center Tamika Williams battles for the ball against the Lady Vols' Tamika Catchings and Michelle Snow, back.

Craig Ambrosio

Craig Ambrosio

Summit gives Sue Bird a pat on the wing.

Craig Ambrosio

Swin Cash, left, reaches high for the jump ball against Michelle Snow in UConn's home game against Tennessee.

Craig Ambrosio

Tamika Catchings drives to the hoop against Swin Cash.

Craig Ambrosio

Kristin Clement celebrates Tennessee's defeat of UConn at UConn.

Craig Ambrosio

During the UConn–Rutgers game in Piscataway, University of Connecticut Coach Geno Auriemma argues with the official as assistant head coach Chris Dailey attempts to restrain him.

Craig Ambrosio

UConn's Svetlana Abrosimova meets with Pepperdine resistance.

Craig Ambrosio

Sue Bird drives to the hoop through Tasha Pointer, left, and the Rutgers defense.

Craig Ambrosio

Svetlana Abrosimova shoots over
Tammy Sutton-Brown.

Craig Ambrosio

The Huskies' Asjha Jones
reacts after defeating the
Fighting Irish at the
Hartford Civic Center.

Craig Ambrosio

UConn's Shea Ralph dives for the ball in front of Pepperdine's Dee Braxton.

Ruth Riley attempts to shoot over Kelly
Schumacher and Swin Cash in Notre Dame's
losing effort again UConn.
Craig Ambrosio

Craig Ambrosio

Paige Sauer, middle, and the UConn bench cheer the team on in Philadelphia.

Christopher B. Carveth

UConn realizes it has a national championship in hand.

Christopher B. Carveth

Schumacher and Snow jump it up for the national championship.

Auriemma cuts down the net in Philadelphia.

Christopher B. Carveth

Of one thing he was certain, however: The Huskies' success in that season would rest on the shoulders of Abrosimova and Ralph. "The majority of the success of this team is going to come on their shoulders," he said. "And the better they perform, the more consistently they perform, the better the team's going to be."

Abrosimova, a 6'2" forward, was the team's only All-American. She garnered Big East Player of the Year honors after averaging 16.6 points and a team-leading 3.7 assists and 2.7 steals the year before. She was the only player to start every game in the prior season.

But in her two years at UConn, Abrosimova was also renowned for her quick, and sometimes bad, decisions. In the 1998–99 season, she averaged 3.8 turnovers per game.

A thorn in Auriemma's side at times, Abrosimova believed she was ready for a challenge. "This year, me and Shea are trying to tell our guys to just focus on everything," said Abrosimova, whose English now includes everyday slang. "I think I'm getting better at being patient because I'm trying not to force things."

Ralph, a 6'0" guard/forward, had long been the team's emotional leader, even when she was sitting on the bench. The top returning scorer from the previous season (16.8), Ralph twice overcame season-ending surgery to repair a torn ACL in her right knee. She had had minor surgery on the knee September 29, but was showing no ill effects.

In the previous year, Ralph had been named Big East tournament Most Valuable Player after leading the Huskies to their sixth straight championship.

But her sights were set beyond the Big East. She wanted a national championship; that was the reason she came to UConn in the first place. To attain that goal, Ralph was prepared to be the good guy, the bad guy, or the mediator off the court. She was willing to do whatever it would take, much the same way she was known for playing every minute of every game. For Ralph, it was the only way she knew.

"We know what Shea's personality is; it's to go 100 miles per hour all the time," Auriemma said. "We know what Svetlana's personality is; it's trying to do everything all the time. Now we need those two to also have a much more patient, much more understanding personality."

Supershow

Kennitra Johnson's phone calls home became less frequent, and her homesickness faded completely. Though she stayed in constant touch with her mother, Charlotte, and with New Albany High coach, Angie Hinton, she left her old life behind.

It had been two months since she left the nest in New Albany, Indiana, for Connecticut. In that time, she not only started to break away from her past, but she began to thrive in her new environment.

Johnson, the only freshman on the team, was fresh off her first week of practice. However, her progress from Day 1 to the end of Week 1 had been dramatic. She picked up the Huskies' schemes well and even grew accustomed to Auriemma's hard-nosed coaching style. "He yells at everybody," Johnson said. "You leave everything he says to you on the court because you know he's just trying to make you better."

Johnson, who dons a tattoo with her nickname "KJ" on her forearm, proved to her friends and family just how okay she really was in the Huskies' blue-white scrimmage, otherwise known as the Supershow, on October 23, 1999.

The scrimmage, held at Gampel Pavilion, is the team's annual official introduction to UConn's fanatical fans. Before the game, Johnson admitted she was nervous. But she did a pretty good job of hiding it in her first encounter with Huskymania.

A point guard who had never seen a UConn women's game live, Johnson stole the show. Representing the White team in the three-point shootout, Johnson hit 18 treys in the first round to beat Shea Ralph, who had 10 in one minute.

Three other pairs faced off to determine who would advance to the final round. Johnson, who hit more three-pointers than all seven of her participating teammates, squared off against Svetlana Abrosimova in the final round.

The two tied at 17 each, forcing a 30-second shootout. In the deciding round, Johnson beat Abrosimova 8–7 to win before a crowd of 4,500.

Not bad for an exhibition game.

After the game, Auriemma wasn't at all surprised. He knew Johnson was a great shooter, and he expected her to execute despite the nerves and anxiety.

"You can never have too many guards," Auriemma said. "I think that's something we found out last season, and no matter how much the game changes, it's still a guard game. You still have to be able to get the ball from one end to the other, you still have to be able to control the tempo and play good defense on the perimeter."

That Johnson could do those things, Auriemma was convinced. She had good instincts, she could shoot off the dribble, and she was competitive. It appeared that Johnson would log significant play early and be the first guard off the bench. Ready or not.

The First Hurdle

In the 1998–99 season, an array of injuries prevented UConn from achieving its goal of the Final Four. After 13 seasons without a serious injury to the lineup, the Huskies had been plagued for three seasons.

It started with Shea Ralph's first ACL injury in the 1997 NCAA Tournament, followed by Nykesha Sales' season-ending Achilles tendon injury at the end of the 1998 regular season. And it continued with Bird's season-ending injury eight games into her career in 1998–99.

The 1999–2000 season hadn't even begun yet, and the Huskies had already lost a guard.

After months of treatment and no results, Keirsten Walters took a medical redshirt, requiring surgery to repair her bad knees.

Her nightmare started during the 1999 Big East tournament, when a painful soreness crept into both knees. Walters, who averaged 3.5 points, 2.9 assists, and 20.7 minutes in 29 games that season, had surgery on both knees in April to shave bone fragments and remove inflamed tissue.

But further complications arose. In the left knee, an absence of fluid was causing a lack of support between the bones. She underwent a series of injections to lubricate the area, but all efforts failed.

Walters was initially expected to miss the first six weeks of the season, but the timetable quickly disappeared. The final diagnosis was osteo-arthritis. "It's an overuse thing," Walters said. "I guess I played too much when I was younger."

Despite having to forgo her sophomore season, the very sensitive Walters took the news well. She would be permitted to travel with the team and to attend practices. She would have surgery over the course of the season to repair the damage, first in the left knee, and after rehabilitation, she'd have the right knee done.

Walters, who hoped to be back on the court again by late spring, said she felt enormous support from her teammates, who scolded her if she tried to walk without crutches. "It's hard because I want to play," Walters said. "But I've had lots of time to adjust."

Beast of the Big East

UConn had had a chokehold on the Big East Conference for six years. And despite the competition, this year was expected to be no different.

The Huskies were picked to win the Big East by the league coaches, and no one was surprised. While the parity in the conference had indeed expanded—four nationally ranked teams would vie for the regular season and tournament titles—Connecticut remained the favorite.

UConn, which had won the past six straight regular season and tournament championships, received 10 out of 12 possible first-place votes and received 142 points at Big East Media Day in October. (Coaches cannot vote for their own teams.)

Rutgers, which reached the NCAA Midwest Regional final the year before and finished with a 29–6 record, was second. The Scarlet Knights garnered three first-place votes, and top fellow NCAA Tournament participants Notre Dame and Boston College finished third and fourth respectively.

Svetlana Abrosimova was chosen to repeat as Big East Player of the Year and Kennitra Johnson was picked to win the Big East Rookie of the Year award. The year before, Tamika Williams had won Rookie of the Year honors for UConn.

While coaches around the Big East gave their best company line about there being four teams that could win the conference that year, not one team had proven over the previous six years that it could consistently challenge UConn.

Auriemma, whose team was the center of attention at Media Day as usual, was flocked by newspaper reporters and television cameras, answering question after question about the parity in the league. While Notre Dame, Boston College, and Rutgers could give the Huskies a competitive game, the bottom line was: UConn continued to reign as the Beast of the Big East.

Even though the Fighting Irish (26–5) were coming off their best season and their fourth straight NCAA appearance, they had never beaten a UConn team in 10 tries.

Boston College, coming off a program-best 22–8 record and its first national ranking, had notched at least one win in the decade. The year before the Eagles beat an injury-depleted UConn team to record their first win over the Huskies in nine years.

Rutgers, a team ranked No. 1 in at least one preseason poll, hadn't fared much better. In eight meetings with the Huskies, the Scarlet Knights had won only once.

In fact, over the previous six years, UConn had lost only four Big East games. In the 1998–99 season, the Huskies were stunned by Boston College; the year before that, they lost to Rutgers; in 1995–96, they lost to Syracuse; and in 1993–94, they lost to Seton Hall.

Auriemma welcomed the growing parity. He welcomed the strides the Big East continued to make, and he welcomed the chance to play competitive games within the league. "I don't think there's anything bad about having more than one really good team in the league," Auriemma said. "We've been on top for so long that so many people probably feel like it's time for someone new. But right now, that's just talk."

Face Check

There was a distinct difference in the way sophomore forward Tamika Williams was practicing that October. With the Huskies still one week away from their first exhibition game, for the first time in her short career, Williams was consistent.

And she knew why. Williams had taken a face check from Auriemma earlier in the year. It was a lesson she won't soon forget.

In late August while the Huskies were in Europe playing against Vicenza in their fourth of five games overseas, they led by just 43–35 at halftime, but Auriemma decided he'd seen enough of a lack of effort from Williams. Even though she was one of the Huskies' most talented athletes, Auriemma benched her for the remainder of the game.

"I just thought Tamika was doing what she normally does, waiting for the light to go on before she decided to really turn it on," Auriemma said. "And I just thought it was a good opportunity to let her know that now that she's a sophomore, that's not acceptable anymore. The light needs to be on at the opening tap."

Auriemma didn't have to explain. In fact, he didn't say anything at all to Williams about why he benched her. He didn't have to. A 6'2" forward who averaged 13.5 points per game in her freshman year, Williams realized she wasn't playing with the enthusiasm, hustle, and drive that Auriemma expected.

"I got a face check from Coach in Europe," Williams said. "He taught me a big lesson when he sat me out, and the team was playing great without me. I really felt that was a changing point for me, mentally, that Coach expects us to show up. We're not freshmen anymore."

Williams learned she needed to constantly work on her mental approach to the game, while also being more aggressive and more consistent in her efforts. Otherwise, there would be consequences.

Shea Ralph could relate. Ralph, known for her hustle and emotion, had been benched during games by Auriemma for exactly the same reason. And she knew she had become a better player for it.

"With people like myself and Tamika, who are very aggressive, who want to play so bad, who can't stand to watch, can't stand to be on the bench and want to be a part of everything, putting us on the bench is the ultimate way to get us to see something," Ralph said.

"Once you realize you're not doing what he wants you to do, especially by getting benched, you don't take it for granted anymore. You know he's keeping you out there for a reason. And you know as soon as you don't get it done, he won't hesitate to (bench you) again."

It's a tactic Auriemma uses to get his players to strive for their fullest potential. And typically it works. The night after being benched, Williams had 14 points, including 11-for-12 from the free throw line, and 15 rebounds. She had three steals, one blocked shot, and no personal fouls in 30 minutes. Williams helped the Huskies beat a very good Italian team, Familia Schio, 70–64.

"One way Tamika leads on the court is being aggressive, getting out there and beating people up and saying 'I want to play, I want the ball now,'" Ralph said. "When you sit and you can't be a part of that, it eats you up. I can see the difference in Tamika and I know it has something to do with that day."

Over the years, Auriemma has been criticized for his tough-love tactics. Fans and even players, at times, don't understand what his motivation is. Some players have reportedly left the program because of his coaching tactics. Players like Marci Glenney, who had recently transferred to Clemson.

But Ralph understood. And she made an effort to support her teammates when it was their turn. After all, it's not supposed to be easy when you're a member of one of the most successful Division I college basketball programs in the country.

"It's tough to do what he does," Ralph said. "It's tough to do what we do. We practice for four hours, and we are not standing around. In high school, we didn't weight train. There were no 6 A.M. practices. It's a rude awakening and sometimes it gets into people's heads."

Ralph would quickly defend Auriemma, saying recruits were told from Day 1 what to expect. Players knew they must earn playing time, with no promises made.

The only guarantee? Auriemma challenged the best to get better.

"You have to give your complete trust," Ralph said. "There's no medium ground. Either you reach your potential or you don't. Those who don't, leave."

Growing Up

In all 34 games of her freshman year, Swin Cash tied her hair back with a white bow. The trademark hair clip served as a reminder from her mother to always act like a lady, even in her basketball uniform.

Those days were now over for Cash, at least on the basketball court. When she showed up more than an hour early for the Huskies' first exhibition game at Gampel Pavilion on November 7, 1999, the bow was gone.

She had a new attitude to go along with the new season. She believed she was a different player, a much-improved player, and she showed how it might influence her game in the Huskies' first exhibition.

Cash highlighted a group of seven Huskies in double-figure scoring in UConn's 96–64 victory over the Australian Institute of Sport before a sell-out crowd of 10,027. She scored 14 points, had three rebounds, three assists, one steal, and one blocked shot in 18 minutes.

"Last year, the bow symbolized me; it was my personality," Cash said. "This year, a lot of girls on the team were like, 'Swin, you're a sophomore now. Take the bow out and do something new.' And I started thinking what can I do to show my personality? I came down to nothing. Just be myself."

Cash was not the only player who appeared to come into her own. Her fellow sophomore classmates—point guard Sue Bird and forwards Tamika Williams and Asjha Jones—also showed signs of progress.

Bird had a stellar first game back from the injury. She scored 12 points on 5-for-5 from the field, including two three-pointers. She had a game-high seven assists and played a team-high 28 minutes.

"She's a vital part of our team, I think anyone would say that," said Cash, who is also Bird's roommate. "She's the one you want to control the ball and control the plays, be out there with her head on and get things done."

Williams and Jones were also productive. Jones had 11 points and five rebounds, and Williams had 13 points and five rebounds. The sophomore class lent support to Shea Ralph and Svetlana Abrosimova.

Ralph went 5-for-5 from the field and scored a team-high 15 points to go along with three assists and four steals. Abrosimova had 10 points, three assists, and three steals.

"Shea is playing fabulous basketball right now, and Svet played really, really well on the offensive end," Auriemma said. "The things I wanted to see, I saw. And I'm happy."

Perhaps the biggest surprise was the productivity of Kennitra Johnson. The freshman guard played 27 minutes, scored seven points on 3-for-7 from the field, and had five assists and two steals.

Australia coach Phil Brown, whose team also played Rutgers and beat

Boston College, said UConn was the best of the three. "Not just because of the point difference, but because of the way they play with a lot of maturity," Brown said. "They're physical and strong, they seem to be pretty together. I think they have a good season ahead of them."

The Sweet and the Sauer

Throughout most of her junior season, Paige Sauer experienced one disappointing game after another. She struggled while trying to make the transition from being a starter and scorer to a starter and role player.

This year, her final year, Sauer decided she needed to embrace a new role to make the season a success. Despite her capability to score as a 6'5" center, Sauer would no longer be relied upon for offense. Her role would be to provide experience and leadership instead.

Because of the depth at forward and the overall talent of the team, this season came down to positioning for Sauer. And Sauer, who averaged nine points and 20 minutes in her first two seasons, didn't need anyone to tell her that. She sat down by herself over the summer and reevaluated the talent on the team and her position on it.

"I was up here during the summer, but I focused more of it on basketball, whereas last year I focused on conditioning and being the strongest I could be. I was running for days," Sauer said. "This year, Coach Auriemma made a good point. He said, 'Paige, you can run as long as you want, but that's not what we do out there.'"

It was clear to Sauer that the talent of the sophomore post players, along with the emergence of junior center Kelly Schumacher, forced her to back away from a featured role. It prompted her to redefine her value to the team. She knew that each player had to assume a role, that a team didn't need five scorers. At least one person had to become the role player to set screens and pass the ball.

This was a big adjustment for Sauer, but she did not want to deemphasize the importance of the energetic Swin Cash, the incredibly athletic Asjha Jones, or the all-around game of Tamika Williams, the 1998–99 Big East Rookie of the Year.

Sauer respected all of her teammates and their abilities and wanted to support them, not fight them for playing time. "We have to jell as a team," Sauer said. "You're always going to need role players. We have plenty of stars out there. Now we need role players."

For Sauer, that meant setting an example by coming to practice prepared and with enthusiasm. She made a habit of going into the weight room before practice, and she worked every day with associate head coach Chris Dailey on developing an outside shot.

In game situations, her new role meant concentrating on the little things, such as denying second shots and playing help defense. And she was also not opposed to playing cheerleader.

"She has the experience factor," Auriemma said. "I'm going to keep going to her as long as she's productive."

Sauer's role may have changed, but she was not complaining. She didn't want to reflect back on the inconsistency that plagued her junior year, when she averaged 6.2 points and 13.5 minutes. Sauer left her junior season behind to focus instead on the precious time she had left in a Husky uniform.

"I'm in the best position on this team, I absolutely believe that," Sauer said. "As a senior, what more would I want? To have a junior class, a sophomore class, a freshman class that can take care of me. I have underclassmen that want to take me where I want to be, and I realize I can't do that without them."

A Battle of Wills

The eve of the Huskies' second exhibition game against Vologda Russia saw junior All-American Svetlana Abrosimova practicing with the white team—the second team. The season hadn't even started, and Auriemma was already disgusted with her practice tactics. He needed her to learn how to become more of a team player and take the SportsCenter highlights out of her game.

There were two specific plays—positive plays—that Auriemma remembered from the Europe trip. Abrosimova was at the center of both.

In the final game against Familia Schio, an Italian team, the Huskies were up by two in the final minute. They needed a basket to seal the game, and Abrosimova delivered. She rotated to the top of the key and stole a pass with 35 seconds left to help UConn notch a 70–64 win.

And in the game prior to that, which was a 103–66 victory over Vicenza, Italy, Abrosimova also made a play that stuck in Auriemma's mind. This time the Huskies didn't need the points.

"She has a one-on-three break, and we all know what she would've done in the past. She would've waited for the fourth guy to come down and gone one-on-four and tried to score," Auriemma said.

"This time, she got to the top of the key, realized what was going on, pulled it off to the side, and hit somebody cutting to the basket for a layup. That's what you want your kids to do, understand how the game grows and grow with it."

On the eve of the exhibition game, however, Auriemma was not convinced that Abrosimova would even be in the starting lineup. Apparently his hunch on how she would play was right on.

It didn't take long for her to revert to old form.

Just five minutes into the November 17 exhibition game, Abrosimova drove the lane, ran into three defenders, and made a layup. Because she made the basket, Abrosimova seemed pleased with the play. But Auriemma clearly wasn't. And it didn't take long for him to react. He yanked her almost immediately and punished her by benching her for the rest of the half.

"I do it to her because she hates to come out," Auriemma said. "She wants to play 40 minutes every game, so whenever I don't play her, she listens more closely."

The tactic worked, as Abrosimova came back to play 15 minutes of solid basketball in the second half. She played defense, set screens, grabbed rebounds, and yes, even scored a few points of her own. She finished with eight points and five rebounds as the Huskies rolled 94–47.

"I'm not sending Svet any more messages," Auriemma vowed after the game. "Generally speaking, when our offense becomes disjointed and crazy, Svet's usually at the root of it. I figured we would get some people in there who aren't very good one-on-one players who would move a little bit without the ball, and that's what happened."

A Leader Is Born

The Huskies headed to Iowa for their season opener on November 21 without team captains, even though Shea Ralph really wanted the job.

Ralph, who would have been a senior if not for missing the 1997–98 season with her second right knee injury, understood the potential of this team and the apprehensive nature of it. She realized that this team was comprised of good-natured girls who really didn't know how to be the bad guy. For example, senior Paige Sauer, the most daunting presence at 6'5", was probably one of the nicest individuals on the team. Sauer, Ralph's best friend and roommate, had found her own way to lead the team—with positive reinforcement.

But Ralph knew the Huskies needed a bad guy. They needed a player on the court, whom they respected, who would scream until she was red in the face to get her point across.

Auriemma didn't care whether or not the team had official captains. The team hadn't selected them because they hadn't been able to reach a consensus. They voted twice, and both times, Auriemma said, "They voted for everybody but Clinton."

Auriemma believes the only real purpose captains serve on game days is meeting with the referees before tip-off. But Ralph believed they are necessary, especially on a team full of young talent. Besides, it was some-thing Ralph had wanted since she came to UConn and a position she be-lieved she had earned.

A popular player with a dynamic personality, Ralph was accustomed to being everyone's friend, and she also knew how difficult it could be to try to get on others to play better when you're not playing well yourself.

"You have to look at our team, everybody who has come here has been a leader where they came from," Ralph said. "But it's different now. Some people have to realize that their role has changed. That's one of the biggest problems I've had in my four years is realizing I have to be a cer-tain way to be successful here. And no matter how hardheaded or stub-born I am, the way I do it isn't always right."

Ralph wouldn't always do things right, but she was determined to try. It showed during halftime against Iowa when one of Iowa's male cheer-leaders came charging out of the tunnel at Carver-Hawkeye Arena and onto the court with an oversized Iowa flag. In the process, he nearly knocked Ralph off her feet at midcourt. She glared at him with a scowl, probably embarrassed and probably contemplating saying something. But she didn't. She just pushed it away and concentrated on leading the team in the second half. UConn, which led just 30–22 at halftime, eventu-ally won the game 73–45, with 15 points from Ralph.

Ralph's heightened level of maturity continued to show in the postgame press conference. There, a reporter from Iowa asked Auriemma whether the Iowa State NCAA loss was motivating this year's team. Auriemma was blunt, as usual. He said probably not, since today's teenagers have short memories.

Ralph sat next to her coach and kept her mouth shut, even though she looked as if she were stewing inside. She patiently waited her turn, then said the opposite of her coach. With a soft voice, Ralph eloquently de-fended herself and the team.

"I haven't forgotten about it because it was probably the worst game I played last year," said Ralph, who shot 2-for-12 from the field against Iowa

State. "My team needed me to step up, and I didn't get the job done. So I'm not going to tell you that I carry that around with me and let it weigh me down, but it's definitely something I keep in the back of my mind as motivation. And it's something that I know I experienced, that I don't ever want to experience again."

A leader was born.

Coach Auriemma

Auriemma got to the podium at the Coaches vs. Cancer Challenge press conference, and unlike the coaches who preceded him there, Auriemma did not speak publicly about his personal experiences with cancer. Instead, Auriemma said he believes cancer is a very private experience for most people.

"There are a million reasons to play preseason exempt games. Some are trumped-up reasons to play," Auriemma said to the media audience. "This is an event that's long overdue, and there's no gimmick in playing for the American Cancer Society."

At the podium, that was about all he would say about the issue. Off to the side, however, the subject got Auriemma reflecting on his father Donato, who died of cancer in 1997, and on his humble beginnings.

He was born Luigi Auriemma in Montella, Italy, in 1954. When he was seven years old, his parents emigrated to the United States and joined relatives, who were already living in Philadelphia. As Geno went to school and learned English, his father got a job at a Norristown factory, and despite being in the country for decades, he never learned the American language.

At 45 years old, Auriemma was still frustrated by the fact his father never adapted to the American way of life. It built a gap between father and son. "One thing I've learned is there's a big difference between their culture and ours," Auriemma said. "Over there, they live to work. Over here, we work to live."

The cultural differences between old-school Italy, where his parents spent the majority of their lives, and progressive America can cause Auriemma to reflect on all that he has, feeling somewhat guilty.

Even though Auriemma worked as hard as anyone for what he has, he can't help but compare it to the lifestyle his father had. And comparatively, the younger Auriemma had an easier road. From his days spent coaching boys' high school basketball part-time at his alma mater, Norristown's Bishop Kenrick High School, to his first break as a full-time assistant at Virginia, Auriemma has always worked hard doing something he loves.

And his diligence at working hard brought him to his place at UConn.

Coming into the 1999–2000 basketball season, Auriemma was living a comfortable life in Manchester with his wife Kathy, two teenaged daughters, Jenna and Alysa, and son Michael, age 11. He found success on every basketball front since coming to Connecticut in 1985. On the court, he compiled a 357–94 record through 14 years and won nine Big East titles, making three trips to the Final Four and capturing the NCAA championship in 1995 to cap a remarkable undefeated season. His home arena was selling out before each season began, nearly every game was televised, and the university support was above average. He has his own radio show and his own TV show, making a base salary of $248,000 per year by doing what he loves the most.

Off the court, however, his lifestyle took a toll on his family life. Even though his wife stayed home to raise the children, Auriemma couldn't help but feel that he'd missed a few things along the way. "It's a real battle to connect with my kids," Auriemma said. "It's not easy. We are defined here by what we make. I was in second grade wearing clothes that my mother made me."

With a wardrobe now that includes expensive name-brand clothes, Auriemma will always be a product of his humble Pennsylvania upbringing, trying to instill those beliefs in his own family and in his "extended family" on the court.

That's why along with talent, Auriemma was notorious for recruiting kids with good character. The staff identified which kids fit the mold of the program by the questions they asked in recruiting visits. Were they interested in what kind of food the cafeteria served or how far the campus was from the mall? Or were they looking for a family atmosphere and a place to grow, both on and off the court?

Auriemma wasn't a great basketball player. He made the high school team as a sophomore and went on to play at Montgomery County Community College, where he met Kathy, before transferring to West Chester. So Auriemma prided himself on being a great teammate. And that's what, first and foremost, he asked his players to be.

"Times have changed, but you always want to hold on to certain things," Auriemma said. "At the core, you have to hold on to the things that are most important. You like to think you're brought up with the sense that you have to accomplish something in your life. I think, as little as they knew, my parents instilled that in me."

The Captain Comes Forward

As soon as referee Scott Yarborough blew his whistle, Geno Auriemma blew his top. About six minutes remained in the first half of UConn's November 24 first-round Coaches vs. Cancer Challenge game against Kentucky, and Yarborough called a hand-checking foul on freshman guard Kennitra Johnson. Seconds later, he was calling for Auriemma's departure.

In the second game of the 1999–2000 season, Auriemma got tossed, after two technical fouls, for the first time since December 29, 1992.

Auriemma ranted and raved, red-faced, with his arms flaying about. He was irate, and at that moment, he didn't care who knew it. While he eventually calmed down long enough to be quietly escorted out of the arena by the school's athletic director, Lew Perkins, and a security guard, he left the game in the hands of his associate head coach Chris Dailey, who had been by his side for 15 years.

It was probably the best thing that could've happened to this young team. Auriemma's absence forced the young Huskies to grow up quickly. It pushed them to look to one another for support as opposed to looking to the sideline for Auriemma's guidance. It was a lesson in maturity for the Huskies, who realized their talent, determination, and chemistry were something special.

The Huskies buckled down, dug deep within themselves, and came away with a hard-fought 68–62 victory over Kentucky. Shea Ralph grabbed the leadership reigns and Svetlana Abrosimova showed why she is an All-American.

With one minute remaining, Abrosimova hit the decisive three-point basket to spot the Huskies a five-point lead. When Kentucky missed a countering three-point attempt, Abrosimova grabbed the rebound and passed to Ralph, who was immediately fouled. Ralph hit both free throws to give the Huskies a 66–59 lead with 25 seconds left in the game.

Ralph finished with a team-high 17 points, including nine of 12 from the free throw line.

"We knew what he was doing, it's always about us responding," Ralph said. "He says we never respond to his challenges, and he's absolutely right. He doesn't play, we're the players on the floor, and he's the coach, he can only do so much. And I think that he just tried to prove to us what he's been talking about, the big picture, what we need to do to become a really good team and to beat good teams. Last year when we got challenged, we lost every one, every big game we played in."

After the game, the Huskies were so pleased they couldn't contain themselves in the postgame press conference. They celebrated like they'd just won the national championship. They were on a high, a high they hadn't felt in a long time.

For the first time since the Fab Five came to town, the Huskies pulled out a close game. And in doing so, they erased the memories of heartbreaking losses to Iowa State, Louisiana Tech, Tennessee, and Old Dominion.

And the captainless team did it without their only leader.

"We were challenged, and for once we stepped up and faced it," Ralph said. "We got punched and we punched back and we knocked them out instead."

Auriemma, who watched Dailey with her more passive coaching style improve her record as a head coach at UConn to 8–0, was just as satisfied with the outcome. It was the sign of maturity he was hoping to see. He forced the Huskies to face a situation they were afraid to be in, and they responded. Now he could expect that whenever adversity might arise again, his young team would be ready and confident.

And Auriemma believed Ralph was the main reason why. "Shea doesn't give herself enough credit," he said. "Last year, she took it to heart. She struggled in the Tennessee game, she struggled in the Old Dominion game, she struggled in the Iowa State game, and it somewhat clouded her view of what was an otherwise great season. She lives for certain games, like the rest of this program does, and in her mind she has to exorcise some of these demons."

Along with exorcising demons, Ralph also earned the title she had been working toward: captain.

"Shea's the sheriff," Auriemma said. "The players didn't know it before October 15 because she was a little reluctant to take on that role. They know it now."

Coaches vs. Cancer Challenge Championship

The top-ranked Huskies came out to win a championship.

On November 26, they used intensity, leadership, patience, accuracy, and execution to hand No. 14 Old Dominion its worst defeat in program history. The 109–66 decision gave the Huskies the inaugural championship in the Coaches vs. Cancer Challenge.

"I've never seen such intensity, I've never seen anyone execute the way they did," Old Dominion coach Wendy Larry said. "This team is better than last year's team. They're more experienced now, they're deeper. I think Sue Bird's leadership will take this team a long, long way."

Bird had a career- and game-high 10 assists. With seven points and two steals, she was one of three Huskies named to the all-tournament team. Earlier in the season, Auriemma had Bird practice against the likes of stellar former players Nykesha Sales and Rita Williams, and that tactic was starting to pay dividends.

Shea Ralph was voted tournament Most Valuable Player after scoring a game-high 23 points on 9-for-9 from the field. And Svetlana Abrosimova was the surprise recipient of Most Outstanding Defensive Player. Abrosimova had 13 points, seven rebounds, four assists, and two steals.

"I think it carried over from our win against Kentucky," Ralph said. "We really got a lot of confidence from that win, and we really showed it."

Ralph said they owed them one. Last year at ODU, UConn squandered a 14-point first-half lead en route to a stunning loss. This year, the Huskies prevented a repeat with a 21–6 run that gave them a 19-point lead with 12 minutes left in the first half.

UConn led 62–32 at halftime, shot 64 percent from the field, and had six players in double figures.

Kennitra Johnson came off the bench to score 17 points on 7-for-10 from the field. Tamika Williams scored 10 points on 5-for-5 shooting, Kelly Schumacher had 10 points and two blocked shots, and Asjha Jones had 12 points on 5-for-6 shooting and five rebounds.

"We've talked a lot about having some sort of an identity of what sort of team we want to be," Geno Auriemma said. "We showed a different side of ourselves against a team that wants to put a lot of pressure on us. We have a lot of talent. We have more good players than most people, and when they all play to their ability, we're going to be really good."

Friends Reunite

There has been much speculation over the years as to why Chris Dailey remains in Auriemma's shadow, even with the title of associate head coach. Dailey, who came in with Auriemma 15 years ago, is quite capable of leading her own team. She has turned down many attractive Division I offers.

But Dailey, or CD as she's known to her friends and players, is happy where she is. As far as she's concerned, this program is as much hers as it is his.

"Before it used to upset me when people suggested I leave," Dailey said. "Now I'm flattered. I feel comfortable, I feel very grateful, I've worked very hard. Why would I leave a job that has so much security?"

Dailey always planned to coach. Her original objective was to teach and coach at a high school. She studied education as an honors student and played basketball at Rutgers, but quickly changed her mind about the high school level after she completed her student teaching internship. "You couldn't get me near high school kids," she said. "I thought it was the worst experience of my life."

At the same time, however, Dailey was having a positive life-altering experience.

A four-year forward for the Scarlet Knights, Dailey decided to coach at the collegiate level based on her experience at Rutgers. And she caught her first break from her former coach, Theresa Grentz.

"I owe a lot to her," said Dailey, a New Brunswick, New Jersey, native who became Rutgers' first full-time assistant coach in 1983.

"I didn't really know anything, and she gave me a lot of freedom and a lot of responsibility. And I went with it, and that was the start of my coaching career."

Dailey shared the court with Grentz for just the second time since Dailey left Rutgers in 1985, and Grentz left 10 years later when top-ranked UConn faced No. 10 Illinois at Gampel Pavilion. The two friends also faced each other in the 1997 Midwest Regional semifinals in Carver-Hawkeye Arena in Iowa. The Huskies won both games.

When asked whether she thought Dailey would take a head coaching position one day, Grentz was adamant. "She could do anything she chose to do," Grentz said. "She could've been a head coach eons ago, but she is going to do what she's going to do, and that's what I love about her."

Dailey, the Huskies' recruiting coordinator, had been preparing for this type of coaching position since her playing days. Dailey said that during her senior year at Rutgers she would take the posted team practice sheets home with her to study game plans.

She still has them tucked away.

"I went through not playing at all, I went through starting, I was captain for two years (and) I got to be an All-American when I was on the scout team, so I went through it all," said Dailey, who won an AIAW Division I national championship in Philadelphia in 1982 and compiled a 108–23 (.824) record in four years as a player. "She taught me a lot about every aspect of the game. What it meant to be part of the team."

Grentz may not fully understand the magnitude of her impact on Dailey. She knows UConn has won a Division I national championship of its own, thanks to the caliber of players Dailey has been able to bring in. But she recently told Dailey that her program would like to mimic the tradition Dailey has helped build at UConn. Dailey said that it was the highest compliment she could have received.

"It's pretty amazing because why I even got into coaching and what I've done here all reflects back on what I did in college and her," Dailey said. "So in a way, she's already done it, without even knowing it, because that's why I'm here and why I like what I do."

An Unexpected Hurdle

Tamika Williams was shocked when her December 2 appointment at the UConn medical center in Farmington ended in surgery.

Williams had been experiencing pain in her left foot and went to have it examined. Three hours later, a screw was being inserted into her fifth metatarsal to repair a stress fracture.

Williams was expected to miss up to six weeks, her target date for return being January 2—the day UConn would play Louisiana Tech at Gampel Pavilion.

"It happened so quick," Williams said. "I'm pushing for four weeks. But (the doctors) said if I don't push it, if I stay off it, it can go between (five and six)."

Williams had been experiencing pain for days, but Dr. Jeff Anderson, UConn's director of sports medicine, said the injury did not occur on a single play in a particular game.

"This type of injury is cumulative in nature," he said. "And once our medical review was complete, it was appropriate to undertake the surgical procedure in order to allow Tamika to begin formal rehabilitation as soon as possible."

In UConn's first five games, Williams averaged 23.6 minutes as the first player off the bench. She was fourth on the team in scoring (10.6) and second in rebounding (5.8). And now she would do no more than watch from the sidelines.

Honda Elite 4 Classic

Geno Auriemma was happy to wear a microphone for ESPN's live broadcast of the Huskies' game against Penn State in the first game of the Honda Elite 4 Classic on December 5 at Disney's Wide World of Sports Fieldhouse.

However, Auriemma did say at least one thing he later regretted. Upset with Svetlana Abrosimova, Auriemma insulted her nationality.

"I had a momentary lapse," said Auriemma, whose wife told him afterwards that the blooper made the broadcast. "I said, 'Goddamn Europeans.' That's what I said. It was after two straight missed layups and she fouled a kid. People from ESPN apologized, but I think the damage was done. I'm sorry."

Auriemma, who himself hails from Europe, didn't seem to upset Abrosimova with his comment. The Russian native was just happy to play as well as she did while wearing a thermoplastic facemask to protect her broken nose. Abrosimova was largely uninhibited during the game, scoring 17 points and grabbing five rebounds to help the Huskies to an 87–74 victory over No. 14 Penn State, a team that would end up in the Final Four in March.

"I was excited to play here," Abrosimova said. "It was on ESPN. It's a great place, and I think the whole team felt excited."

Penn State junior Maren Walseth seemed anything but excited following the loss. Walseth, who played for two years at Simsbury High in Connecticut and was recruited by UConn, scored 20 points.

She felt little satisfaction however. "I wanted to play UConn," Walseth said. "I wanted to play the No. 1 team in the country. I didn't have any personal attachments to it."

Exceeding Expectations

Geno Auriemma was starting to realize that he probably wasn't giving his team the credit it deserved. Or maybe he was just a brilliant psychologist.

"Everybody keeps telling me we are really good," he said.

The Huskies had been ranked No. 1 in the nation all season. They were still undefeated and dominating opponents, including ranked teams. But it wasn't until the Huskies faced No. 6 UCLA at Gampel on December 23 that Auriemma started to really believe. UConn was really good.

Despite a 15-day break, the Huskies reverted to form and handled UCLA with relative ease to notch a 106–64 victory.

UConn won its eighth straight game, hit the 100-point mark for the fourth time that season, and got at least two points from every player but one. Five players scored in double figures for UConn, led by Abrosimova, who scored a game-high 19 points, had 13 rebounds, and was one assist shy of a triple-double.

Stacy Hansmeyer and Kennitra Johnson both came off the bench to score 17 points. Johnson went 5-for-5 from three-point land, and Hansmeyer was 6-for-6 from the field. Shea Ralph had 15 points, and Asjha Jones scored 10.

"We're probably a little better than I give us credit for, but I don't think we are as good as we could be," Auriemma said. "They kind of gave me a new perspective. We're probably a little better than I thought."

PAC 10 heavyweights Maylana Martin and Janae Hubbard were non-factors. Martin, a 6'3" senior forward, said she played probably her worst game. Martin was 0-for-7 from the field, had three rebounds, and finished with two points and four personal fouls.

Hubbard, a 6'4" senior center, got most of her 13 points from the free throw line. Hubbard was 0-for-6 from the field in the first half and 4-for-11 for the game.

Hubbard had scored 29 points against the Huskies the previous season.

"We exceeded our expectations from a coaching standpoint," said Auriemma, as he notched his 200th win at home to attain 200–26 (.884) at both the Hartford Civic Center and Gampel Pavilion in 15 years. "I thought they came out with a real mature approach to the game. They put everything behind them and kept everything that's ahead of them, ahead of them. I couldn't be happier."

Because he was pleased with the overall effort and because it was a blowout, even Auriemma laughed when UConn sophomore Swin Cash committed the most unusual and rarely seen blooper in the game.

She shot at the wrong basket.

It happened with 5:28 left in the game. Hubbard was on the foul line taking the second of two free throws. After she missed, Cash grabbed the rebound, and with no one anywhere near her, she aimed at UCLA's basket, shot, and scored two points for the opposing team.

The UConn bench erupted with laughter, and there were hundreds of gasps in the crowd. UConn senior Paige Sauer later said she had trouble inbounding the ball because she was laughing so hard.

Cash, who is often the butt of many jokes, may never live this one down. Even the UCLA players laughed.

"That was pretty funny," said Martin, a UCLA senior. "I think that was the funniest thing that happened all night."

Auriemma also poked fun. "I have two daughters that play basketball so I've seen it a lot, just not in front of 10,000 people," he said. "She looked great though. I thought her form was terrific, she was wide open, everything was just right, so I can't complain."

Hubbard was awarded the basket since she was the closest Bruin to Cash at the time.

Home Sweet Home

It had been almost five years, yet Oklahoma natives Paige Sauer and Stacy Hansmeyer remembered where they were when the Alfred P. Murrah Federal Building was bombed.

Sauer actually felt it.

A native of Midwest City, Sauer was sitting in first-period class at Carl Albert High School, about six miles from the downtown Oklahoma City site, when she heard and felt something.

"Everyone knew something wasn't right," said Sauer. "We had parents and former students who went there (for work). We were definitely affected by it. The whole state was. The whole nation was affected."

Hansmeyer, a native of Norman, was sitting in math class when she heard the announcement over the public address system.

"Someone said, 'No one panic; there's been a bombing in Oklahoma City,'" Hansmeyer said of the tragedy that killed 168 people, including 19 children. "Immediately people went home and started looking for their families."

UConn went to Oklahoma December 30, 1999, to play a homecoming game for Sauer and Hansmeyer. The game was played in front of a school-record crowd of 10,713—the largest to see a women's basketball game at the Lloyd Noble Center, which seats 11,100.

During the game, Shea Ralph became the 18th player in UConn history to reach the 1,000-point plateau, and Svetlana Abrosimova played without her thermoplastic facemask for the first time since breaking her nose in a game against Illinois on November 30. And while the Huskies took care of business with an 84–68 victory over the Sooners, they did something just as important as a team: They visited the Oklahoma City National Memorial.

Sauer, visiting the site for the third time, has followed the Memorial's progress, and she said the mood was the same that week as it was days after it happened. "There were tons of people other than us, and you never heard a word," Sauer said. "The mood was quiet. No one said a word, you just paid your respects."

Over the course of the months that followed the bombing, Hansmeyer said the community pulled together. They wore ribbons, lit candles, and drove all day with their headlights on as a sign of unity. That's why it's no surprise to her, or to Sauer, that the city is building a massive memorial on behalf of those dead and those left behind.

When it's finished, three components will make up the Oklahoma City National Memorial: the Outdoor Symbolic Site, the Institute for the Prevention of Terrorism, and the Memorial Center Museum.

Then under construction was the Outdoor Symbolic Site. The Huskies visited the awesome sight, which starts with a massive wall of granite that marks the front of what used to be the Murrah Building. It reads: "We come here to remember those who were killed, those who survived and those changed forever. May all who leave here know the impact of violence. May this memorial offer comfort, strength, peace, hope and serenity." It's dated April 19, 1995.

The memorial is being constructed partly so no one forgets those lives lost in the bombing. But Sauer said it was clear that four years later, the pain was still very real.

License plates, T-shirts, key chains, Christmas wreaths, and rosary beads are among the hundreds of items that line a barbed-wire fence surrounding the far side of the memorial.

"I saw the aftermath," said Sauer, who visited the site for the first time two weeks after it happened. "It was indescribable. Then to see in four years, the love—they haven't forgotten. There's still that compassion, that caring. I think what they're doing for the people and their families is very respectful. No one will forget it in this state."

The First Test

It wasn't supposed to be so easy.

The top-ranked Huskies had blown out their share of ranked opponents so far in the season. But the January 3, 2000, matchup against No. 3 Louisiana Tech was expected to be the first game that was decided in the final minutes, or even better, in overtime. Instead, it proved to be just another 20-point blowout when UConn won its 10th straight game in a 90–63 decision at Gampel Pavilion.

"It wasn't supposed to be that easy, and I don't know how easy it was," coach Geno Auriemma said. "It was harder than it looked maybe because it was pretty physical in there. But we're a good team, and we played pretty well."

Four players scored in double figures, led by Svetlana Abrosimova with

25. Shea Ralph had 15 points, seven rebounds, and eight assists to help the Huskies beat a ranked team soundly for the fifth time in the season.

"It's not easy to play against them, but I'm glad it looked easy," said Abrosimova, who also had six rebounds and four steals in 30 minutes. "We were really confident, and it's really hard to play against us because everyone can score. The way we played was great."

After taking a 2–0 lead, the Lady Techsters missed their next 12 shots from the field, including five from three-point range. And the Huskies took full advantage of the cold-shooting Lady Techsters, who came into the game with a 10–2 record. UConn hit three three-pointers during an early 16–0 run to even the series with Louisiana Tech at 2–2.

The Huskies avenged the previous year's 90–76 loss in Ruston, Louisiana, and denied Tech coach Leon Barmore his 500th career coaching victory.

"There's no question, we got beat and beat soundly," Barmore said. "I have a lot of pride and pride in our team, but there's no question that UConn was awesome. UConn deserves all the credit, they've got it all, they really do. It's one of the best basketball teams we've played against in a long time. We played hard. We kept trying, but we didn't have an answer for anything."

UConn beat Louisiana Tech in the three areas Auriemma believed to be the most crucial: defense, rebounding, and ballhandling.

Sue Bird led the stifling defense on Tech's powerful backcourt combination of Tamicha Jackson and Betty Lennox. The two regularly threw up errant shots and combined to shoot 9-for-29 in the first half. They took 48 of their team's 82 shots in the game and connected on just 18 attempts.

While Lennox led all players with 27 points, Jackson was the only other player in double-figure scoring for Tech with 14 points. "I was definitely impressed with Bird and Johnson," Jackson said. "I knew what was expected from them, and they did just that."

The Huskies out-rebounded Tech 36–27 on the defensive end. Swin Cash set the tone with five rebounds in the first five minutes. She finished with a team-high eight rebounds along with sophomore Asjha Jones, who came off the bench and played 22 minutes.

And the Huskies took care of the ball. They forced 11 turnovers in the first half, 19 for the game, and they tallied 26 assists in the game compared to Tech's 9.

"We did a lot of good things," Bird said. "It wasn't easy, but at the same time, practicing against Rita (Williams) and Nykesha (Sales), that's something that's really valuable to us. If you can keep control of the ball with them guarding you, you can keep control against anyone. We just had a lot of confidence going into the game."

The Huskies beat Tech in the paint 44–26, they beat them on the fast-break 17–6, and they got more second-chance points by one basket.

It was an effort Auriemma could not find fault in.

"We're a more mature team," said Auriemma, comparing the Huskies to their meeting with Tech the previous year. "We just seem to have a sense of when to and when not to. Sue and KJ, I just can't say enough about how they run the ballclub. And Shea and Svet, the way they've adapted...You take those four, and that's the difference in our team."

Connecticut sophomore Tamika Williams did reach her goal and played for the first time since breaking her left foot. She played two minutes and scored two points.

Taking Over

Shea Ralph stayed in step with Katie Smrcka-Duffy on January 5 as she sped down the sideline at Georgetown's McDonough Arena.

Smrcka-Duffy, perhaps the quickest and most talented of Georgetown's guards, was wearing a look of frustration as she grabbed a defensive rebound and crisscrossed downcourt heading for the Hoyas' basket.

But on this occasion, the Big East Conference's leading scorer, at

19.5 points per game, failed once again to sink her shot. Ralph simply wouldn't allow it to be easy.

"I've seen her play for a long time, and she's a good player," said Ralph, a native of Fayetteville, North Carolina, who played against Smrcka-Duffy in several AAU tournaments. Smrcka-Duffy, a junior who grew up in Sterling, Virginia, also played for NC State before leaving for Georgetown.

"I remember playing against her in AAU, and she scored like 40 points, but she took a lot of shots," Ralph said. "She took good shots (in UConn's 87–48 win), they just weren't falling. But at the same time, I think our guards all did a good job on her."

Particularly Ralph. The Huskies' dynamic junior had consistently played with the same intensity through the Huskies' first 11 games, bringing the leadership quality that the team desperately lacked the previous season. And she played every game as though it were her last.

Ralph was primarily responsible for holding Smrcka-Duffy to two points on 1-for-9 shooting. She constantly had a hand on Smrcka-Duffy, who wasn't made available for postgame interviews per coach Pat Knapp's request. And with her unrelenting energy, Ralph forced Smrcka-Duffy to rush her shots and play out of position.

"Shea has gotten to the point now that she understands what she has to do every game to be what we need her to be," coach Geno Auriemma said. "Sometimes it's to get 28 points, sometimes it's to get eight assists, sometimes it's to get a couple of steals to get something going. She's matured to the point where she understands what our team needs."

Ralph led four Huskies in double figures with a game-high 18 points on 7-for-9 shooting from the field. She also had six assists and five steals in 33 minutes.

But the enthusiasm and passion Ralph brought to the game doesn't show up in the box score. The Huskies played a team that hadn't beaten them in 12 straight meetings. The last time a Georgetown team beat UConn was the 1992–93 season. And the Huskies, who played at home before 10,000 fans every night, were playing in a small arena before a crowd of 1,175.

But none of those facts fazed Ralph. Whether the opponent was Georgetown or No. 2 Tennessee, to Ralph, it was a game and an excuse to play.

"I thought going into the game it was going to be hard because it's only natural, you're not going to be able to summon up the same energy for a game here that you would (for Louisiana Tech or Tennessee)," Auriemma said. "There's not the bigness of the venue, the national television, the name, so it has to come from within."

For Ralph it does. She has an appreciation for the game that supersedes that of a typical athlete. She has successfully returned from season-ending knee injuries twice in her career. And because there's never a guarantee she'll play again, Ralph relishes every second she gets on the court. No matter who the opponent.

"I'm very comfortable with my team and my role, and I'm very comfortable with my teammates," Ralph said. "I think we're all on the same page. It feels different this year than it has in the past. We're clicking on the floor, we know what we need to get done. We've gotten to that point this season, after what we've been through together last season, we've grown up a lot."

But no one, perhaps, more than Ralph.

National Showdown

None of the 1999–2000 UConn Huskies had experienced victory over Tennessee at Tennessee. Some classes get the burden of being the only ones not to win a national title. Some have the pressure of being the only class not to make it to the Final Four. This UConn senior class was in danger of graduating without ever beating the Lady Vols.

The crowd of 20,789 on hand for the January 8 contest at Tennessee didn't help the Lady Vols. Neither did the fireworks, the laser lights, the smoke show. For that matter, neither did Tennessee's chest bumping nor the arm waving. Not even the jock jams blaring from the announcer's table made a bit of difference.

When it came down to basketball, UConn simply won out.

The Huskies defied the hostile atmosphere and took the first of two regular season meetings, a rarity for nonconference opponents, with a 74–67 victory at Thompson Boling Arena. UConn upheld its No. 1 ranking, ending the Lady Vols' 11-game winning streak and handing them their second home loss of the season.

"I was not going to fly back to Connecticut not saying a word and disappointed. I refused," said Paige Sauer, who won for the first time at Tennessee. "So in the huddle before the game, I said, 'Guys, give it to me. I don't have a win here, give me one.'"

Sue Bird, who missed the Tennessee game the year before with a torn anterior cruciate ligament injury, scored a career-high 25 points. Svetlana Abrosimova had 14 points, and Shea Ralph had 13 points, eight rebounds, and five assists.

Bird was determined to make the most out of the hostile environment. In the team's huddles, she said the feeling was, "Can you believe they are booing us? Let's show them what we can do."

Bird's poise set the tone. She made the offense run, she hit basket after basket when she was left open, and she played with the confidence of a veteran.

Bird scored the second of three straight baskets in a 7–0 run to open the second half that gave UConn a 13-point lead (50–37), its largest of the game. And later in the half, she scored five straight points on back-to-back baskets to give UConn a 63–52 lead with 5:33 left.

"Sue Bird was the difference maker," Summitt said. "She hit the big shots, she controlled the tempo of the game, she stepped up and made the difference."

But the Huskies benefited as much from the 16 minutes they got from

6'5" center Kelly Schumacher and the 19 minutes they got from Sauer, also a 6'5" center.

"In games like this, so much pressure is on your best players," UConn coach Geno Auriemma said. "It is usually someone else that steps up and sneaks in there and makes a few huge plays."

Sauer was involved in the play that clinched the game.

With 2:57 left and UConn holding a three-point lead, Sauer fouled Tennessee sophomore center Michelle Snow under the basket. It was her fifth.

After the foul was called, Snow immediately spiked the ball in excitement. Before Sauer left the court, she pleaded for a technical foul on Snow. The officials, who didn't need Sauer's input, obliged.

Snow, who was clearly affected by the call, missed both of her free throws.

And Bird, who went to the foul line for the technical, made the second shot to give UConn a 64–60 lead and the confidence and momentum to finish off the Lady Vols.

"That possession cost us the game," said Snow.

Russians Unite

Perhaps no one was as excited to face West Virginia on January 12 as Svetlana Abrosimova. While the game was clearly not going to be a contest (the Huskies won 75–35), it gave Abrosimova a chance to see her childhood friend.

Abrosimova was reunited with her old teammate Darya Kydryavtseva, who grew up just minutes away from her in their native St. Petersburg, Russia. They both attended high school at Petrodradskoi N86, and they played together on the Russian Junior National team.

The close friends, who kept in touch weekly via e-mail, hadn't seen each other in three years.

"She watches on TV all the time," Abrosimova said. "And she's really excited for me."

Abrosimova was able to show her friend around campus, take her out to dinner, and speak Russian to her. While Abrosimova had a very close Russian friend on campus and spoke to her mother at least one a week, she said Kydryavtseva wasn't getting much chance to use her Russian anymore. Kydryavtseva had not been back to Russia since leaving for Seminole Junior College in Florida. After two years there, she transferred to West Virginia, the worst team in the Big East in the 1999–2000 season.

"She wasn't a really good player, so she didn't have a chance to play for the national team, so for her, it was a great opportunity to play college basketball," Abrosimova said. "For me, I had a choice."

After graduating from Seminole, Kydryavtseva was thrilled with the chance to play for West Virginia. The school was a perfect fit for Kydryavtseva, a serious student majoring in sport management.

"For her, (academics) is more important than basketball because she knows she's not going to be able to play in the WNBA," Abrosimova said. "She knows she's going to get some (playing) time. She doesn't want to sit on the bench."

Even though the two had known each other for 10 years, when they planned to leave Russia in 1997 for the United States, they kept their impending departures a secret.

"She left (one month) earlier, and everyone was like, 'Wow, she left this team and went to the United States?' But because she wasn't the best player, people didn't really care," Abrosimova said. "Then I left, it was like a huge deal."

A backup point guard for the Mountaineers, Kydryavtseva freely admitted she was not as good a player as Abrosimova, and not many people are.

"When we were practicing with the junior national team, she was already with the adults, the national team," Kydryavtseva said. "I told her how much I appreciate her effort. She doesn't only represent the school. She represents the nation."

A Constant Battle

Is she open? Am I open? Where is this person going? Am I in the right spot?

Those were a few of the many often paralyzing questions that plagued Asjha Jones' mind during each possession.

"I'm thinking too much out there," she said. "I don't think I'm seeing things well. It's taking me too long to make decisions. Going with the flow is my constant battle."

At the midway point of the season, it was clear that the extremely talented Jones had turned into an underachieving sophomore. Jones constantly fought the fear of making a mistake, and she second-guessed her own decisions. As a result, she was playing without confidence.

"I think the problem she has sometimes is she gets caught up in not wanting to mess it up more than just going out and playing," starting forward Swin Cash said. "Sometimes I have the same problem. I think it's understanding that when Coach is yelling about certain things, you just have to play through it. You're gonna make mistakes. Asjha wants to have everything down perfect. She doesn't want to make a mistake, and I don't blame her."

Jones' teammates didn't blame her for overthinking. It happens. But it wasn't something they could accept. As Cash said, Jones "has too much talent to be thinking too much." That's why Jones had become a project. Every player and the entire coaching staff got involved in trying to help her break through this mental barrier.

Cash tried to be subtle. She used positive reinforcement, complimenting Jones whenever possible. Cash knew her friend was a smart person and a smart player. She believed Jones would figure out the problem in time.

Junior captain Shea Ralph took quite a different approach, however. Probably the most outspoken and ambitious player on the court, Ralph didn't mince words. She told Jones what was working and what wasn't, and she let her know both in the moment and later, in the locker room.

"With Asjha, you just have to keep telling her, 'You got it, good move, take the shot,'" Ralph said. "You have to keep telling her what to do because she'll hesitate. You just have to let her know that her first thought, her instinctive thought, is the right one."

By the middle of January, Jones started to get it. She had had a solid game against West Virginia, leading the team in scoring with 14 points on 6-for-8 shooting and eight rebounds in 18 minutes. But it was a do-or-die game for Jones. Already in the doghouse once this season with Coach Geno Auriemma for her lack of hustle in practice, Jones knew she had to play better than the performance she gave at No. 2 Tennessee.

Against the Lady Vols, Jones had just six points and two rebounds in 12 minutes. She played tentatively, and she looked scared. "I don't think I'm scared, but Coach told me I played that way," Jones said. "Right now, I have to try to build my confidence up. Basically, I didn't play as well as Coach wanted me to."

Jones knew what she had to do. She was breaking down the game into simpler components to help her achieve her goal. Against West Virginia, she focused only on rebounding. Still, recognizing the problem and doing something about it were obviously two different things.

She had heart-to-heart talks with her teammates. She heard the motivational speeches by Auriemma. She had even been benched because of her lack of execution.

Now the only strategy left for Jones was to just play.

"Asjha's a thinker. What are you gonna do?" Auriemma said. "I think as each game goes on, she sees more and more what she can do and where she can be effective. As long as Asjha stays effective, she's a great player. The minute she gets tentative, she's just an okay player. So it's a matter of maintaining your aggressiveness. Whatever it is you decide to do, just make a decision and do it. Be aggressive and let's worry about it afterwards."

Depth Advantage

Auriemma was not privy to Rutgers' scouting report for its January 17 game with Connecticut at the Hartford Civic Center. But he had a pretty good idea about which of his players the Scarlet Knights would key in on. Leading scorer Shea Ralph, All-American Svetlana Abrosimova, and prolific point guard Sue Bird would get the most attention.

But there was a glaring weakness with that game plan, of course. Auriemma still had three dangerous players in his rotation: Swin Cash, Tamika Williams, and Asjha Jones.

And Rutgers, like the 14 defeated opponents before them, could not guard everyone. As a result, the No. 11 Scarlet Knights squandered a nine-point lead in the first half en route to a 65–50 loss. The Huskies scored the final 17 points of the first half and led 29–21 at halftime.

"Connecticut can take one out and put one in (and not lose a step)," Rutgers coach C. Vivian Stringer said. "Do you realize Williams is the (Big East Rookie) of the Year, and she's sitting on the bench? And we're not talking about a 5'2" midget, we're talking about a 6'3" giant. She's no slouch any way you shake it. And Jones is a lot of people's Player of the Year.

"Geno is one of the great masterminds. He does an excellent job with a lot of excellent talent and tremendous depth."

Williams had missed four games with a broken foot and had not been the same player since the surgery December 2. But she was on her way back, and she played through the pain against Rutgers. Williams missed all three shots she took from the field, but she had four rebounds and one block and made Rutgers center Tammy Sutton-Brown work hard for her shots.

Jones had proven lately why she was recruited. Jones put together a solid performance for the second straight game. She struggled on the offensive end, going 5-for-10 from the field, but Jones played solid defense.

"Coach expects a lot from me," said Jones, who finished with seven rebounds and three blocked shots in 27 minutes. "And I'm trying to give him what we wants."

Cash was one player Auriemma never had to motivate. Against Rutgers, she recorded her second double-double of the season with 11 points and 10 rebounds in 32 minutes.

More importantly, perhaps, Cash brought the same energy level and enthusiasm to every game, regardless of whether the Huskies were playing a ranked opponent or an overmatched team.

At times, her performance was overlooked and her accomplishments didn't always show up in the box score, but her efforts were never lost on Auriemma.

"This game is about so much more than how many points you score," Auriemma said. "Swin created so many points by the fact that every ball that came off the rim, she had a hand on it. She was doing things that no one else was doing."

Cash's effort and consistency were invaluable against Rutgers because they weren't getting enough contributions from the bench. Starting center Paige Sauer was yanked after four minutes, no points, one rebound, and one personal foul; and junior center Kelly Schumacher lasted only two minutes after a similarly unconvincing effort.

Ralph, Abrosimova, and Bird were already targeted in Rutgers' game plan. So it was up to the Huskies' three post players to take the reins.

"The things that Swin and Asjha and Tamika do, there's not one team in the country that can contend with all three of them when they all have their 'A' game going," Auriemma said.

Stringer agreed and went a step further. "Connecticut is the best (team in the country), no question about it," she said. "They have great balance, and they're extremely bright. It's Connecticut and everybody else, and they have a right to distinguish themselves."

A Close Call

Svetlana Abrosimova simply doesn't enjoy blowouts. She would rather play a tight game against a competitive opponent than score 25 points and beat a team by 40.

That's why UConn's last-minute 84–77 victory over No. 19 Boston College on January 26 was so special for Abrosimova. The Eagles came into Gampel Pavilion unbeaten in the Big East Conference, ranked nationally, and determined to give UConn a game. Abrosimova was counting on it.

So while the other Huskies struggled to handle the Eagles' intensity and the closeness of the game, Abrosimova thrived. She never faltered, even though the Eagles kept her team on its heels the entire game, leading 42–39 at halftime and trailing by just three points (80–77) with 45 seconds left. The game was not decided until the final 28 seconds when Boston College point guard Brianne Stepherson, who had verballed to UConn, made a costly mistake. She fouled UConn point guard Sue Bird.

"Svettie's a big-game player," said Bird, who scored 12 points, including two on free throws in the final seconds to seal the game. "She is a really competitive person, whether it's chess or running sprints in preseason practice. And she wants to be put in situations where she's forced to make something happen."

Abrosimova scored 20 points, hitting 8 of 9 field goals, including 2 of 2 from three-point range. She had six rebounds and five assists in 37 minutes. More importantly, she hit the big shot when the Huskies needed it most. And against BC, there were many of those instances. In fact, nearly every basket Abrosimova scored was an important one.

For example, trailing 11–6, she hit a three-pointer to stop the Eagles' momentum. And when the Huskies found themselves trailing by five again with 2:20 left in the first half, Abrosimova hit a jumper to cut the deficit to three and assisted on a basket by Asjha Jones on the next possession.

Abrosimova scored to tie the game on two occasions (6–6 and 18–18), and she hit three-pointers in an attempt to offset BC's prolific guards. And indeed, while the trio of Cal Bouchard, Brianne Stepherson, and Alissa Murphy combined to score 59 of the Eagles' 77 points and continually flustered the Huskies, Abrosimova's confidence never wavered.

"Svet has a real calmness about her right now that when she has the ball, she's dictating what she wants to do," Coach Geno Auriemma said. "She just had that look about her like, 'Don't worry about it,' and everyone else was in a panic. She gets bored by the blowouts. These games get her juices flowing. Me, I like the blowouts. But these games are more important than the blowouts. We can take more from this win, positive or negative, than you can from a 30-point win."

It was also a breakout game for Tamika Williams.

Since the surgery on her left foot December 2, the recovery and reemergence had been painfully slower than she expected. But it wasn't her physical health, rather the mental aspect of the game was inhibiting her. Williams finally put it all behind her. She scored 24 points on 11-for-14 shooting and had seven rebounds. Williams kept her poise down the stretch and played with confidence to lead UConn to its 18th straight win. The Huskies remained the only undefeated Division I women's team in the nation.

The Eagles, with a 16–4 overall record and 5–1 in the conference, were led by Bouchard's 25 points in 40 minutes. Stepherson scored 18 points and played 38 minutes, and Murphy had 16 points in 39 minutes. In spite of the gutsy performances from their guards, the Eagles saw their school-record win streak end at 12.

"I don't want them to be content," BC Coach Cathy Inglese said. "I want them to feel good, but not content. We were in this game."

UConn played the majority of the first half without starting forward Swin Cash, who picked up two fouls in the first two minutes. Shea Ralph, who finished with nine assists, committed two quick fouls and also sat on the bench for much of the first half. The two combined for two points in the first half. And without Cash and Ralph, two of the team's most dynamic leaders, the Huskies played one of their worst halves of the season.

A lack of urgency and 15 turnovers contributed to the Huskies' ineffectiveness in the first half. UConn shot 73 percent from the field, but the Huskies got embarrassed on the offensive boards.

Six players combined to grab 10 offensive rebounds for BC. UConn managed two, one from Kelly Schumacher and one from Abrosimova. And despite being down two post players—Becky Gottstein and Maureen Magarity—the Eagles matched the Huskies in the paint, scoring 16 points.

At the end of the half, the Huskies trailed for the first time since November 24 when they were down by four against Kentucky in the Coaches vs. Cancer Challenge. UConn also went on to win that game 68–62.

"Defensively, that was by far the most mentally unsound we've been," Auriemma said. "It was Svet in the first half, Tamika in the second half. Our two against their three. You gotta give BC a big, big hand in what happened."

The Streak Ends

There were no red or swollen eyes, no sniffles, and no excuses made.

Even Connecticut's emotional leader, Shea Ralph, didn't cry after the No. 4 Tennessee Lady Vols upset the top-ranked Huskies 72–71 at Gampel Pavilion on February 2, 2000, ending the Huskies 19-game winning streak.

"This isn't March," Ralph said. "We have a chance to be No. 1 at the end of the season, and that's what we are looking at."

Ralph shed a bucket of tears the year before after the Huskies lost games at Old Dominion and Louisiana Tech and at home against Boston College. She was particularly upset after the Huskies lost prematurely to Iowa State in the NCAA Sweet Sixteen.

She didn't beat herself up this time around, however. Ralph had grown up over the past year. She knew the difference between playing a good game and losing or playing poorly and losing. She wasn't disgusted in the Huskies' performance because she realized Tennessee happened to be better on one particular night.

"We're going to take this (loss) and learn from it," Ralph said. "I thought we fought back 'til the end. We almost stole the game in the last five minutes. Things just didn't go our way at the end."

Trailing 69–68 with 27 seconds remaining, Semeka Randall gave Tennessee the lead with a jump shot off the backboard in traffic. Sue Bird countered with a jumper of her own with 18.8 left, and after a Tennessee time-out, Randall hit the game winner to even the Tennessee–UConn series at 5–5.

After Randall's basket and two time-outs, UConn inbounded the ball to Svetlana Abrosimova for the last play of the game. Instead of taking the shot, Abrosimova passed the ball to Williams, who attempted a layup at the final buzzer and hit the bottom of the backboard instead.

"The plan was for Svet to get a layup but because she wasn't in the right mindset and she wasn't having a good game, she passed it," Coach Geno Auriemma said. "Today, Tennessee was better than us, but we also gave a little away."

The loss to Tennessee was a lesson Auriemma had secretly hoped he'd have a chance to teach all season. Auriemma doesn't really believe heading into the NCAA Tournament unbeaten is such a good idea for a young and relatively inexperienced team. Auriemma has led pressure-packed teams through undefeated seasons. He knows what kind of psychological toll being No. 1 and the only unbeaten Division I women's team in the country can take.

Now, his players knew too.

"I always worry more about wins than I do about losses," Auriemma said. "We have the appearance and the talent level of a great team, but we have the maturity level and the mindset of a team that isn't necessarily capable of handling where we are. Something like this puts it more in perspective for us."

Randall showed the Huskies exactly why details matter. Her game-winning shot showed why it's important to play the full 40 minutes. Thus far, UConn had gotten by everybody, including the Lady Vols once, on their talent and depth. Randall reminded UConn that there is more to the game than athleticism.

"You don't get physically stronger or quicker in February and March," was how Tennessee coach Pat Summitt put it. "You have a chance to get smarter and better."

The Huskies learned they can't relax when they're up by 14 points in the first half; Tennessee will come back. The Huskies also learned the value of offensive rebounding after the Lady Vols managed 20 points on second-chance shots. And they learned how important the first five minutes of the second half can be.

"It's not moving people around or changing starting positions," Auriemma said. "It's a collective growing and learning how this game is supposed to be played at this level."

After 19 straight wins, the Huskies were also reminded how it feels to lose. "It stinks, I'm not going to lie," Bird said. "But whenever you lose, you can take some positives. Now we know what we have to work on."

Nagging Injuries

Nagging foot injuries were disrupting Connecticut's practices.

Sophomore Swin Cash had been hampered by sore feet. She expected to continue starting at forward, but Auriemma said she would practice sparingly for the rest of the season.

"She's had a problem with her feet all along," Auriemma said of Cash, who also suffered from shin splits. "She's tried five different models of sneakers. We're going to give her the Sue Bird treatment."

Bird had also been limited in practice for two months due to a sore left foot. The injury didn't keep her out of games, but it did limit her practice time.

A foot problem had also been keeping Williams on the sidelines. Williams, who had surgery December 2 to repair a stress fracture in her left foot, had been slowed ever since. Williams practiced during the week of February 7 for the first time since the injury had been aggravated against Tennessee on February 2. Williams said the foot was stepped on twice. Yet she also expected to play out the season.

"It's just something I'm going to have to deal with until the end of the season," Williams said. "I hope and pray at night that no one steps on it."

Senior center Paige Sauer also suffered from a sore right foot. Like Cash and Bird, Sauer did not have a specific injury to her foot. However, she had been experiencing pain since stepping on it wrong while playing Seton Hall on February 5, and she would continue to rest it. Sauer was also willing to play through the pain because it was her last year at UConn.

Finding a Way to Win

Swin Cash watched her shot fall into the basket and screamed to her teammates, "Give me the ball!"

Cash was given one specific instruction before being substituted back into the Huskies' February 12 game against Rutgers: Make something happen.

And with the score tied at 40, that's exactly what she did. Cash called for the ball and sank the next two shots to ignite an 8–0 run and help the Huskies to an emotional 49–45 come-from-behind victory over No. 10 Rutgers.

Led by just one player in double-figure scoring, the Huskies, now boasting a 22–1 record, improved to 11–0 in the Big East. They ended the Scarlet Knights' win streak at five before a sellout crowd of 8,579—the largest ever to see a women's game at the Louis Brown Athletic Center.

The Huskies forced six shot-clock violations. And with their eight-point lead down to three in the game's final two minutes, they continued to play tenacious defense until, with 23 seconds left, Asjha Jones sealed the victory with a free throw.

"The only thing we might have done well is win the game," Coach Geno Auriemma said. "Rutgers played great. Their defense was really good. But I'm always amazed with the toughness of our guys. We figured out a way to win the game."

Unlike most UConn–Rutgers matchups—nine of the 10 UConn had won—this game was Rutgers' game to lose. The Huskies registered their lowest scoring output since January 27, 1993, when they lost to Villanova 50–44.

In the first half, they shot 31 percent. They didn't score a field goal for 9:19, they trailed by as many as 11 points, and they managed to score just 20 points before the break.

Svetlana Abrosimova was 1-for-7, Cash was 0-for-3, and leading scorer Shea Ralph was 0-for-2 for no points. However, the Huskies played one of their best defensive games of the season.

"We played great defense because we didn't have a choice," Abrosimova said. "When you're shooting and you can't make anything, that's all you can do."

Thanks to their defense, which canceled Rutgers' out, the Huskies rebounded from their offensively stagnant first half. They cut the deficit to six points just before halftime (26–20), and they regrouped at the break. They came out in the second half and took their first lead (38–37) since the game's opening minutes with 8:47 left in the game.

Kelly Schumacher, who started at center and had five blocks, gave the Huskies a three-point lead on a putback with 7:43 left. And after Rutgers tied it up on a three-pointer by Tasha Pointer, Cash was subbed in.

"I knew exactly what I was going in there for: to bring some energy to the game," Cash said. "My teammates were just feeding off that energy."

Abrosimova, who finished with 11 points and 10 rebounds, scored the next four points to give UConn an eight-point lead with 3:51 remaining.

Rutgers cut the deficit to three, but the Scarlet Knights, having come into the game at 16–5 and 8–3 in conference, were long deflated. They were forced to foul in the final minute just to get the ball back.

"It was a tight game from beginning to end," Rutgers coach C. Vivian Stringer said. "We were certainly pleased defensively, but we need to score more effectively offensively. I am real proud of my team. I feel like they worked every second of the game. Sometimes the shots fell, sometimes they didn't."

Rutgers controlled the tempo for the majority of the game. They out-rebounded the Huskies 22–12 in the first half and managed to frustrate them possession after possession with their methodical play. They took a five-point lead five minutes in and held onto the lead until UConn tied it at 34 with 13:38 remaining. But despite the gallant effort, it was not enough to beat UConn.

"I'm not sure that we did anything right but play good defense and win the game," Auriemma said. "But when it comes time to win, we usually know how to win."

Senior Night

Connecticut women's basketball fans got a special treat on February 19 before saying their final farewells to the Huskies' seniors, Paige Sauer and Stacy Hansmeyer, and then watching them dismantle Syracuse 100–74 at Gampel Pavilion.

Hansmeyer, also known to fans as "Bam Bam," stood at center court and sang the national anthem. Much the way she plays, Hansmeyer sang with a powerful confidence and moved some of her teammates to tears. The players held hands on the sidelines and swayed to the music. And as Hansmeyer finished the final verse, her teammates rushed out to give her a group bear hug.

"The singing is something my family has done for a long time, so it's natural, but I was pretty nervous," Hansmeyer said. "I wanted to do it for my teammates and my family. They've been bugging me to death. I was happy that I didn't mess up."

As for the game, the Huskies scored at least 100 points for the fourth time this season and won their 70th straight Big East game at home. The Huskies improved to 24–1 overall and 13–0 in the Big East Conference, and Hansmeyer and Sauer improved their overall record at UConn to 120–10.

The crowd was announced at 10,027, a sellout, but only about 7,000 fans actually braved the fierce Connecticut snowstorm to get here. Those who did, however, got a chance to show Sauer and Hansmeyer how much they'd be missed during Senior Night, the Huskies' final regular-season game at Gampel Pavilion.

No one perhaps will miss the two seniors more than Shea Ralph. Tears streamed down Ralph's face as Hansmeyer and Sauer received long ovations from the crowd. As Hansmeyer, wearing number 20, came to midcourt with her parents to receive her framed game jersey from Coach Geno Auriemma, Ralph hugged Swin Cash on the sidelines. Minutes later, when it was Sauer's turn to walk to midcourt with her folks and receive a replica number 41 jersey, Ralph embraced Svetlana Abrosimova.

Ralph came into the program with Hansmeyer and Sauer, and she was supposed to be walking out to midcourt to receive a jersey also. Instead, two surgeries on her right knee would keep Ralph at UConn for one more year.

"It was definitely hard for me because I was supposed to walk out there with them," Ralph said. "They are my two best friends in the whole world."

It was evident, however, that Ralph took an extra moment to relish when running out of the starting lineup circle at least one more time with Hansmeyer and Sauer. Ralph then wiped her face clean of tears with a towel and got down to official business.

She led four Huskies in double-figure scoring with 18 points on 7-for-7 shooting, including 12 in the second half. She also had nine assists. But perhaps her most memorable play was running down Syracuse sophomore Jaime James.

UConn won a recruiting tug-of-war with UCLA for the services of the top high school player in the country and a potential All-American, Diana Taurasi. The battle pitted Los Angeles, California, home of movie stars and Disneyland, against tiny Storrs, Connecticut, which doesn't even have a McDonald's in town. It even set mother against daughter. In the end, this battle only demonstrated that the rich get richer.

Diana Taurasi

The assembled media gathered in what one of them calls the "bomb shelter," a drab classroom that doubles as the interview room at the Harry A. Gampel Pavilion, the home, decorated in early concrete, of the Connecticut Huskies.

In the latter half of the nineties, the Huskies won them all at home, save two memorable instances. There was Martin Luther King Day, 1996, when Georgia's Saudia Roundtree pulled a Jordan and scored 28 points; and January 10, 1999, when Tennessee's Semeka Randall wrestled around the floor with beloved Svetlana Abrosimova in a one-point win for the Lady Vols. Randall became the state's biggest sports villain since Peter Karmanos dragged the hockey's "forever .500's," the Hartford Whalers, to North Carolina.

Normally, the assembled media waits for the opposing coach to enter the bomb shelter and asks the same question.

"Could you tell us how good UConn is?"

Most oblige. (There was Georgetown's Pat Knapp who stormed in one night and snorted, "You people think women's basketball began here. Well, I have news for you. It didn't.")

Today's subject was Pepperdine's Mark Trakh, the former wizard at Brea-Olinda High School in California—remember, for future reference, that the guy knows and has studied California high school basketball—where he built it into a national power.

Trakh, whose team was lunchmeat for Connecticut, sounded most impressed.

"It was good for our kids to see how hard they play," he said. "They're going at full speed, and they throw good, hard passes. It was good for them to see how smart a kid like (Sue) Bird is and how hard (Shea) Ralph plays. It was good for the kids to see up close what makes a great team and how well coached they are."

Not long after Trakh came Connecticut's Geno Auriemma, the reporter's dream. The repartee followed:

Auriemma: "I heard he said we were well coached. You should listen to that guy."

Reporter: "He also said that he's watched Diana since she was in junior high in California and that might be the best women's player ever, better than Cheryl Miller or Holdsclaw."

Auriemma: "Why the hell would you want to listen to him, anyway?"

Laughter followed.

The coach, who talks like he's paid by the word, just hates it when you tell him someone who has never played the college game is going to be the best ever.

But that's Auriemma's "problem."

What to do with Diana Taurasi?

Taurasi, a 5'10" guard from Don Lugo High in Chino, California, is considered by most recruiting analysts the best girls' high school basketball player in America. Joe Smith, who publishes the *Women's Basketball News Service,* calls her "the best player I've seen in 25 years."

In her junior year at Don Lugo, she should have caused tournament officials in Santa Barbara to rename the invitational to the Taurasi Tournament. She made last-second shots to win consecutive—yes, consecutive—games against Hanford, Ayala, Santa Barbara, and El Toro.

One college coach at Nike camp this summer said, "I swear Magic Johnson must be her illegitimate father."

And she's all Auriemma's.

It must have been culture shock for Taurasi on her visit to the Storrs campus in November. One writer, noting Storrs' rural character, likes to say "they called it 'Store' before they built another one." How would Ms. California function here in the Land That God Forgot?

Hey, to get her to visit was good news. Taurasi, once "99 percent sure" she wasn't leaving California, said the extensive travel to all the summer tournaments at least invited her to consider leaving.

Taurasi knew and liked Auriemma. She sat behind the Connecticut bench when the Huskies played at UCLA in November 1998, a 113–102 UConn win. If the Colonists had played defense like UConn and UCLA did this night, we'd all be sitting down to tea every day at 4 P.M.

It was, nonetheless, entertaining.

"Fifty goddamn points," he muttered, walking off the floor at halftime. "We just gave up 50 goddamn points."

Taurasi remembers giggling. "He certainly was intense," Taurasi said.

And so it would come down, essentially, to UConn and UCLA.

When the Connecticut media spent three days in Manhattan Beach before the UConn–UCLA game, it was noted more than once that Auriemma had to be a genius for being able to lure anybody to Storrs.

Walking around the UCLA campus the day before the game, Randy Smith, the outstanding columnist at the *Manchester Journal-Inquirer* mused, "Of course. Spend four years in Storrs than four years here in paradise? Of course. Why the hell not? The beach or Mansfield Depot? I pick Mansfield Depot. I mean, Holy Christ."

Taurasi, however, knew Storrs had its advantages. She knew Connecticut played in front of sellout crowds, while UCLA couldn't come close to filling the Los Angeles Sports Arena last March for the West Regional final against Louisiana Tech.

"I was disappointed they couldn't fill the bottom section," she said. "I was disappointed for Los Angeles....When you talk about playing in front of 18,000 or 2,000, it makes a difference."

But enough of a difference to offset the difference between Storrs and Los Angeles? Or her mother's desire to have her play closer to home?

Taurasi visited with her mother during an exhibition game against an Australian touring team. The Connecticut media, whose members called Taurasi regularly, wrote more extensively about the recruiting visit than about the game.

Two Connecticut writers went to the Nike camp over the summer—and two minutes with Taurasi revealed she'd flourish in the spotlight the UConn program offers. One called her a "cross between Shea Ralph's graciousness and Tamika Williams' magnetic personality."

Taurasi, no matter how many notebooks and microphones get shoved in her face, rarely breaks verbal stride.

"When people watch me, I want them to say, 'Boy, that kid has fun,'" Taurasi said. "I watch the WNBA and nobody ever smiles. I don't like that."

So the exhibition game starts, and the Connecticut faithful view the game as a sideshow to what really matters: Diana.

So one side of Gampel—9,000 of whose 10,000 seats are full on an NFL Sunday—began a "DIANA" chant. The other side yelled "TAURASI."

The cheer felt like some distant cousin of the Miller Lite "less filling/tastes great" ads, but the effect was palpable.

"People told me it was in the middle of the woods, without a McDonald's in sight," she said. "But it's not too bad. There are a couple of traffic lights....Really, I liked it a lot. Now I know why people come here. I've seen 10,000 people in an arena before, but I've never seen 10,000 screaming fans. I've seen 10,000 people before that didn't say a word."

Only two words were necessary: DIANA...TAURASI.

Taurasi visited with her mother, Lilly, who wasn't thrilled about her daughter leaving to attend school across the country. Taurasi felt the pressure to stay home.

Mother vs. daughter. Kid vs. community. Not easy, this recruiting stuff.

Taurasi decided on a Monday night that it would be Connecticut. While most of the northeast watched Bill Parcells and the Jets confound the Patriots once again, Taurasi decided she wanted to find out what would be in store...in Storrs.

"The coaches, the people, I just liked the environment," she said. "I just felt like it's where I needed to be."

It wasn't the first time Taurasi had taken a different path. She lives across the street from Don Lugo, her high school, but considered going to places like Brea-Olinda or Ayala, located in Chino Hills. "I'd have been doing that only because people were telling me I should," Taurasi said.

Auriemma is fond of shaking his head when he hears where high school athletes are "ranked" in the various scouting services. "You know how we'll know a kid is going to be good in college?" he says. "When they get to college."

He also knows that Taurasi has been saddled with outrageous expectations. Every time something went wrong during the 1999–2000 season, some of the wiseguy writers who follow the team would tell him, "Don't worry. Diana's coming." He'd roll his eyes.

Actually, Taurasi's "yes" encouraged a future teammate to hang around for her fifth year. Ralph, eligible to graduate that spring, decided to play next season. The wounded knee that caused Ralph such misery nearly two years earlier earned her an "extra" year of athletic eligibility—and Ralph decided to use it. Taurasi's decision to attend UConn cemented Ralph's re-

With 15:54 left, James was called for a technical foul after she intentionally shoved Abrosimova, who was en route to a breakaway layup. Abrosimova said she never saw it coming, but Ralph saw it coming from a mile away. And even before Abrosimova could get helped off the floor, Ralph was in Jaime James' face, giving her a piece of her mind.

turn for the 2000–01 season. "Especially since I've gotten to know Diana, I don't want to say I feel an obligation (to return), but I don't want to leave," Ralph said. "The extra year is a gift."

Taurasi mentioned during the recruiting process that she hoped Ralph would return. "Shea is awesome," said Taurasi, who befriended Ralph the previous summer at the Nike camp and stayed with Ralph during her recruiting visit.

"I want to be instrumental in Diana's transition from high school to college. I know how hard it is," Ralph said. "What you learn in your freshman and sophomore years defines you as a college player."

Maybe what Ralph learned in her first two years under Rita Williams, Nykesha Sales, and others has helped Ralph deal with her own life recently, too. Ralph made a "roller coaster" motion with her hands when describing her life before the first practice of the season. She says things are clearer to her now—and much of it is because of the college basketball program she chose.

"I didn't realize how important my decision to come here was," Ralph said. "No matter what happens in basketball, I know I have a support group behind me to make sure I get lifted off in life."

Ralph was a counselor at the Nike camp during the summer when Taurasi pared her college list to UConn, UCLA, North Carolina, and Arizona. If nothing else, Ralph and Taurasi share considerable basketball ability. Ralph was one of the most highly recruited players in the country four years earlier, and the *USA Today* National Player of the Year.

"Diana had a lot of questions. One thing I promised myself is that I wouldn't be the Connecticut saleswoman," Ralph said. "When people are so highly recruited, they're treated like objects. Some get fooled into thinking people care."

Taurasi is considered the most talented girls' high school basketball player in recent memory. Ralph agreed, saying, "By far. I've never seen anything like her. And you know what's cool about that? She's an even better person."

"I think that's part of my role," said Ralph, who sprinted downcourt to be the first to confront James. "These are my girls, and if you mess with them, I don't like that kind of stuff. I don't like it when people disrespect us, and I felt that's what she did."

Abrosimova, who finished two assists shy of a triple-double, missed the first free throw, but made the second. She scored a team-high 24 points, with 12 rebounds and eight assists.

Abrosimova, who had once tangled with Tennessee's Semeka Randall, said she was happy to see how Ralph reacted. "It was fine with me, she deserved it," Abrosimova said. "I don't like when people push me behind my back when I can't see them. I would want somebody to come to my face and push me to my face, but people push me to my back, I think it's real low."

Auriemma said he didn't see anything after the push, except for some of the Syracuse players giving high fives to each other.

"It was almost like there was more of an effort to foul rather than win the game," Auriemma said. "That got some of our guys in a foul mood. You gotta react the way you gotta react. This is a team, these are your teammates. You try to protect each other. No doubt that's the way Shea reacted, I'm not surprised."

Big East Champions

All Geno Auriemma could think was, "We let them off the hook."

On February 26 the Huskies had No. 5 Notre Dame flustered. The Fighting Irish were turning the ball over, missing easy shots, and having difficulty catching their breath against the Huskies' defensive press. But they managed to cut a double-digit UConn lead to six points with less than five minutes remaining.

"I'm thinking we could've blown them out in the first half if our offense was any good," Auriemma said. "When they cut it to six, I thought if they win this game, then this is a tremendous opportunity that we blew."

At that same moment, Sue Bird and Shea Ralph exchanged long stares. Both players knew full well the magnitude of the situation. On the line was the Big East regular season championship, and on the bench with five fouls was the Huskies' only All-American, Svetlana Abrosimova. Ralph and Bird reminded each other that it was time to bear down for a win. And they executed the game plan perfectly.

Bird scored nine points in a 19–7 game-ending run to give the Huskies a 77–59 win and at least a share of their seventh consecutive Big East regular season title before a sellout crowd of 16,294 at the Hartford Civic Center.

"We were only up by six, and it seemed like we were dribbling the ball with our knee, throwing it away. And we couldn't get anything to go," Ralph said. "All of a sudden Sue just came out, like she always does, and took over. She showed a great deal of leadership out there."

The Huskies, ending the season at 26–1, improved their Big East Conference record to 15–0 ensuring them a No. 1 seed in the Big East tournament. They ended Notre Dame's 20-game winning streak and beat the Irish for the 11th straight time.

"Obviously we're thrilled we won the game because anytime there's a championship at stake, we want to play as well as we are capable of," said Auriemma, whose team jumped out to an 8–0 lead, led 33–19 at halftime, and never trailed.

"When we needed a three-pointer, we got one. When we needed a foul shot, we got one. When we needed a steal, a rebound," he said. "Sue Bird didn't make a shot until it was time to win the game, then she made them all."

The Huskies improved to 10–1 against ranked opponents this season and won their 14th straight game at the Civic Center. The streak of conference wins at home, both at Harftford Civic Center and at Gampel Pavilion, was now 71 straight.

The Irish, who had never won a Big East championship, were now 0–11 against UConn. "They are definitely the No. 1 team in the country and they proved it," Notre Dame coach Muffet McGraw said.

Kelly Schumacher showed just how much she had grown up since being thrust into a starting role three weeks earlier. For the 6'5" junior center, her first start since UConn's season opener had come on February 8 when the Huskies beat Miami 93–46. She started that game in place of senior Paige Sauer, who was sidelined with a foot injury.

While Ralph or Abrosimova typically get the task of defending an opponent's No. 1 player, on February 26 that responsibility went to Schumacher. She was asked to contain Ruth Riley, Notre Dame's 6'5" junior center who was averaging 16.5 points and 7.2 rebounds and was an All-American and Naismith candidate. And thanks in part to Schumacher, the Irish never got their offense off the ground. Schumacher blocked shots, played smart defense, and called for the ball. When she was on the court, she had a hand in nearly every defensive play for the Huskies. And she never blinked.

"She played great," Bird said. "It's nice to know that when you get beat, there will be someone back there to clean up the mess. We've been looking for someone to do that all year, and she's stepped into that role."

Schumacher made it difficult for Auriemma to keep her out of the game, playing her for 26 minutes, a career high. She scored eight points, four of which came on putbacks, and she had eight rebounds and four blocks. Schumacher had two assists and committed no turnovers.

"I've been working on moving my feet more," Schumacher said. "I knew exactly where to turn, I didn't want to get in foul trouble. I knew that it was a big game and I knew exactly where the help was coming from."

Schumacher held Riley to four points on 1-for-4 shooting and five rebounds in 22 minutes. Riley, who battled foul trouble the entire game, fouled out with more than seven minutes remaining. Fouls were never an issue for Schumacher.

"Kelly was in the right place at the right time, she made all the right decisions," Auriemma said. "Shuey has come a long way in a short period of time. And she seems to play well in big games, and that's going to be really important going into (the NCAA Tournament)."

And the NCAA Tournament was just where the UConn women were headed following that final regular-season game against Notre Dame in late February 2000.

chapter five

postseason

The Tournament Schedule

The women's bracket announcements were scheduled to be aired on national television on March 12 at 5:00 P.M. on ESPN. Jay Bilas, the former Duke star and men's college basketball analyst, was in the studio along with veteran women's analysts Robin Roberts and Vera Jones.

The only team that could truly be characterized as a "bubble team" was Florida from the SEC, and it was quickly apparent to the Gators that they had been snubbed as the brackets were revealed to the nation.

Florida had an RPI ranking of 22 and played the fifth toughest schedule in the country. The committee noted that Florida's below .500 conference record affected the decision.

A number of SEC coaches were quite upset about the Florida snub despite the fact that six SEC schools did indeed get into the tournament. LSU coach Sue Gunter, whose own team had been left out of the tournament two years earlier under similar circumstances, said that "the snub basically sent a signal to schools to play soft out-of-conference schedules to bolster their number of wins."

Tennessee, UConn, Louisiana Tech, and Georgia claimed all of the No. 1 seeds. Connecticut was scheduled to stay home at Storrs, Connecticut, to host two opening-round games and then travel to the Eastern Regional in Richmond. Certainly a manageable trip for the massive UConn following.

The Lady Vols were tabbed as the top seed in the Mideast Regional and dealt the Furman Lady Paladins as their opening game at Thompson Boling Arena. The winner would play the winner of the intriguing Arizona–Kent (No. 8 vs. No. 9) game, on national television.

Rutgers would also host two first-round games, opening with Holy Cross and then on Sunday evening playing the winner of the Texas–St. Joseph's matchup, also before a national television audience.

The Rutgers team gathered to hear the announcement of the tournament schedule at the Hale Center, overlooking the Rutgers football stadium. When it was announced that Notre Dame would receive the No. 2 seed in the Mideast and most likely have to play Tennessee in the Regional Final in Tennessee, the team let out a collective sigh of relief. During the past two seasons Rutgers had faced the eventual national champions, Tennessee, and Purdue in the Sweet Sixteen and Elite Eight, respectively. This year the Rutgers team knew, despite the fact that head coach Stringer had expressed a desire not to travel out west to Oregon, that they would have their clearest path ever to the Final Four. Sure there were roadblocks. They would have to beat a tough Texas team at home, a team that they had beaten by only four points on the same floor in December. Then they would most likely have to defeat either Mississippi State or Oregon (almost at home) and then Georgia to make it to the Promised Land. It was still worth it for the Scarlet Knights because they knew that Georgia was an easier ultimate matchup than either Tennessee or Connecticut and most likely Louisiana Tech.

Right after the pairings were announced, much of the postseason hardware was handed out. Auriemma justifiably won the Naismith Award, handed out annually by the Atlanta Tip-Off Club to the top coach nationally. Tennessee's Catchings received the same organization's award as the College Player of the Year. Catchings had also been named a First Team All-American by the *Women's Basketball Journal*.

A Coach's Farewell

The biggest upset of the first weekend of the NCAA Tournament was not the Rice win over UC Santa Barbara nor NC State falling to Southern Methodist nor Alabama-Birmingham beating Oregon in Eugene, but instead it was Leon Barmore's announcement on the Thursday before the tournament started that he would resign after his team finished play. At the end of the traditional press conference, Barmore said, "I gave all I have, I have one more run at the National Championship and that is it." He made his tearful announcement in Ruston, Louisiana.

The crusty veteran was completing his 18th season at Louisiana Tech and had the best winning percentage (.872) in Division I men's or women's basketball. Louisiana Tech and Tennessee were the only women's teams to play in all 19 NCAA women's tournaments. The Techsters reached the Final Four nine times and won the national championship in 1988. He had told his players just before the news conference, and he refused to answer any questions about his reasoning until his team was either eliminated from or had won the national championship in Philadelphia.

The real reasons behind Barmore's decision related to two major factors. He hates to fly, and with Louisiana Tech now a member of the WAC, it would require many more plane rides, especially over mountains—something that Barmore really has a problem with. Also, his top assistant, Kim Mulkey-Robertson was always mentioned as a candidate for coaching vacancies. Barmore wanted to make every effort to ensure that she would end up with his job. Unfortunately for him, she took the Baylor job a few days after the Final Four.

First Round Highlights

Back to the games. No. 13 Rice scored perhaps the biggest upset of the first round of the tournament by defeating UCSB 67–64 on its home court. Kim Smallwood scored 16 of her 22 points in the second half to lead the Lady Owls before a capacity crowd of 5,824 at the Thunderdome.

Katie Remke hit a free throw with two seconds remaining as SMU upset No. 5 NC State 64–63 in Norfolk in the first round. SMU led by as many as 12 points in the second half, but NC State scored eight points to take its first lead of the game, 55–53, with a little over five minutes to go.

Rutgers had little trouble with Holy Cross on its home court. Tennessee easily whipped Furman, and UConn defeated Hampton by an incredible 71 points, 116–45. The Huskies set an NCAA Tournament record for points in a half (65) and set a school record for points in a tournament game. It was also the third largest margin of victory in an NCAA game, the third most points scored, and the second-best field goal percentage (71 percent) in an NCAA game.

The Second Round

The second round of play on Sunday, March 19, saw 11th-seeded UAB upset Mississippi State 78–72 in Eugene. LaToya Thomas, the nation's leading freshman scorer, scored 26 points for the losers but fouled out with 50 seconds left. The Lady Bulldogs from the SEC were bigger and faster but were hurt throughout the game by foul trouble. The victory set up a Sweet Sixteen matchup between Alabama-Birmingham and Rutgers in Oregon.

In what was truly a battle of Philadelphia, the Rutgers Scarlet Knights defeated a game but undermanned St. Joseph's team 59–39. Rutgers' stifling defense held St. Joseph's to its lowest game output since 1982 when, ironically, a Cheyney State team also coached by Stringer defeated St.

Joseph's and held them to under 40 points. St. Joseph's was held to 23 percent shooting by Rutgers' matchup zone defense, which Stringer had
learned from Temple's men's coach, John Chaney. Events of the day of
the game signaled the possibility of a St. Joseph's upset. In the men's tour-
ney, Chaney's Temple Owls, also a No. 2 seed like Rutgers, had fallen to
Seton Hall, a No. 10 seed like St. Joseph's. Stringer was certainly saddened
by her friend and mentor's loss. Rutgers led by only four points at the half,
but brought their "A" game to the court in the second half and blew past
the Philadelphia visitors to end St. Joseph's dream of reaching the Final
Four in their hometown.

Barmore's last game at home was almost his final game coaching for
the Techsters. Louisiana Tech narrowly defeated Vanderbilt 66–65 on a
disputed call at the end of the game to advance to the Sweet Sixteen in the
Midwest Regional. Freshman Katrina Frierson made two free throws with
2.5 seconds left to lift the home team to 30–2 and improve their all-time
NCAA Tournament game record at home to 32–0. The Lady Techsters
won despite shooting a paltry 31 percent and blowing an 11 point lead.
Vanderbilt coach Jim Foster said after the game, "I like to see players decide games."

Barmore received a standing ovation from the half-empty arena when
he walked onto the floor before the game, and after the game fans stayed
long after the last free throw and chanted his name until he returned to
the home court to acknowledge them with a wave.

On the same night that Barmore clinched his trip to the Sweet Sixteen, the nation knew that there would be a new national champion.
Defending national champion Purdue blew a 17-point lead and fell at
home to Oklahoma 76–74. Oklahoma took its first lead of the game with
63 seconds remaining.

Purdue's Katie Douglas, the Big 10 Player of the Year, scored just four
points in the game. Camille Cooper starred for Purdue with a career-high
34 points. The loss ended a seven-game NCAA Tournament winning
streak on its home court for Purdue.

UConn made it to the Sweet Sixteen with an easy 83–45 win over Clemson. The Lady Tigers shot just 10-for-49 for the game (20.4 percent). That set a new tournament mark for fewest field goals and tied a record for lowest shooting percentage.

Tennessee also had an easy ride to the Sweet Sixteen with a 75–60 win over a scrappy Arizona team. The game was most noteworthy for the fact that junior guard Kristen Clement unveiled some new writings on the tape wrapped around her ankles and lower leg. On the back of her lower leg was the phrase "THE NEW ME!" and on the left front was "AT-TITUDE" and on the right front "PHILLY." On the day of the victory, head coach Summitt was named women's college basketball coach of the twentieth century and Chamique Holdsclaw, who had led UT to three national championships, was named the century's top women's college player.

The Sweet Sixteen

In one dizzying 14.5-hour stretch captured on television by ESPN, the field of sixteen became eight. Depending on one's allegiance, the event also might have been characterized as the SEC/ACC challenge. Three SEC teams, Tennessee, LSU, and Georgia got the better of their ACC foes.

Perhaps the most compelling performance of the day was put on by No. 1 Connecticut in a 102–80 win over the Oklahoma Sooners in the East Regional semifinal. Connecticut was down by three points (9–6) a few minutes into the game and then went on an 18-point run to reach the 100-point plateau for the ninth time in the season. The Huskies came within one point of tying the East Regional record for most points in a game and set East Regional records for most points in a half (57), most steals (21), and forcing the most turnovers (33).

Even Auriemma and Ralph had to shake their heads after the game. Ralph said, "Jones stunned me with the way she played. She is just so talented." Auriemma noted, "We want to be the Microsoft of basketball. When we are investigated for having a monopoly, then I will worry."

Connecticut had so much depth that their second team, despite little depth at guard, could probably also be situated in the Elite Eight. Against Oklahoma, sophomore forwards Jones and Williams came off the bench to score a team-high 16 points each and they combined for 6 steals. Connecticut had eight players play 15 minutes or more in the romp. Even though the Huskies gave up 80 points, it was their relentless defense that led to most of their offensive scores.

The SEC's LSU was the come-from-behind 79–66 victor over the previous year's national runner-up, Duke. It would mark LSU's first Elite Eight berth in 14 years for veteran head coach Sue Gunter. Gunter was in her 36th season as a head coach and 18th at LSU. She was the fourth winningest active Division I coach but had never taken a team to the Final Four.

Tennessee overpowered Virginia 77–56 to reach its sixth straight regional championship and 16th in 19 years with its 18th consecutive victory. Seven of the previous nine games between the schools had been played in March, and Tennessee owned a 9–1 record.

The Lady Vols' lone loss to Virginia stuck out like a sore thumb to Summitt as it came in the 1990 regional finals in Tennessee's own gym and denied the Lady Vols a trip to the Final Four. Summitt called it "the toughest loss in my collegiate coaching career."

The 2000 tournament game was played at The Pyramid in Memphis, only 391 miles from Knoxville, and it seemed like the entire arena was clad in Orange—because it was.

The game was all about tempo, and Tennessee controlled it with their pressing defense, not letting Virginia force them into the Cavaliers' patented half-court game. Tennessee opened up with an 8–0 lead and ran out to a 30–13 advantage. Virginia cut the deficit to three with 13 minutes remaining in the game.

Tennessee could have collapsed as they did in the previous year's Elite Eight against Duke, but instead they played with a sense of urgency and went on a 14–2 run to earn a birth in the regional final on Monday night against Texas Tech, a surprise 69–65 winner over Notre Dame.

The Fighting Irish opened its Sweet Sixteen contest on a 17–0 run, but amazingly the Lady Raiders scored the next 17 points of the half to knot the score. Notre Dame led by as many as eight points in the second half, but couldn't overcome Riley fouling out or the lack of offensive fire power from Big East Freshman of the Year, Ratay. She only had two points, and they were scored in the last minute.

Barmore lived to see another day as his Techsters rolled past Old Dominion 86–74 in the Midwest Regional semifinals. Despite missing nine of her first 10 shots, Betty Lennox kept firing away and led her team to victory with 25 points on 10-for-32 shooting including four three-pointers.

Louisiana Tech would play Penn State in the regional finals for the right to go to the Final Four.

The Nittany Lions scored the day's most exciting victory, 66–65 over Iowa State in Kansas City. It was virtually a home game for the third-seeded Cyclones as thousands of fans made the three-hour trip from central Iowa.

Helen Darling kept Penn State in the race for its first national championship as the 5'7" guard scored the winning basket with 12 seconds remaining and finished with 21 points. Iowa State's Megan Taylor missed a jumper from inside the free throw line at the buzzer.

Georgia advanced to the West Regional final with an 83–57 thrashing of ACC foe North Carolina. The Bulldogs used an inside game led by 18 points from center Tawana McDonald. In the regional final Georgia would face Rutgers, the team on a mission to Philadelphia.

The second-seeded Scarlet Knights, who advanced to the Elite Eight for the second straight season, defeated Cinderella, Alabama-Birmingham, 60–45 for the right to face top-seeded Georgia. The Scarlet Knights had not faced an opponent seeded higher than 10th thus far in the tournament.

Rutgers opened up a 10-point lead early in the second half, but the

Blazers came within one at 44–43 with seven minutes remaining as the Scarlet Knights went cold offensively. Stewart then ignited a 16–2 run to nail down the victory. Rutgers' postseason offensive hero senior Gilmore was the star of the game, pouring in a game-high 18 points.

It was the 14th time that season that Rutgers held a team under 50 points. Defense and good guard plays win games in the postseason.

The Elite Eight

And soon there would be four.

Rutgers, UConn, Tennessee, and surprising Penn State all advanced to the Final Four in relatively easy fashion. Only Rutgers was really tested down the stretch.

The Scarlet Knights, the second-seeded team in the West, defeated top-seeded Georgia 59–51 in a game that ended after 2:00 A.M. eastern time, marking the first women's Final Four appearance for Rutgers.

The Scarlet Knights went on a 6–0 run in the second half to break a 39–39 tie and take the lead for good. They were led by Regional Most Outstanding Player, Stewart. It was really the defensive intensity of Rutgers in the first half that contributed to the victory. They held normally high-scoring Georgia to only 20 points en route to a 23 20 halftime lead.

UConn did have some first-half difficulties with LSU. With better than 70 percent shooting, the Tigers trailed by only six points after 20 minutes and closed to within two points in the second half, before Connecticut opened up its offensive machine and went on one of its patented runs to win 86–71 and advance to the Final Four. Auriemma was now 3-for-3 in Elite Eight games and feeling that it was the toughest game of all to win in the NCAA.

Tennessee throttled Texas Tech 57–44 in Memphis. Tennessee had some anxious moments in the middle of the first half when Player of the Year Catchings missed a jumper and turned her right foot after falling on an opposing player's foot. She collapsed on the floor, and it appeared that she would not return to the game.

She did return, though, and tied a career-high with 16 rebounds to lead Tennessee to the victory. Lawson had a team-high 13 points, and Snow and Randall each added 12. Texas Tech was outrebounded 47-31. That was the most telling statistic.

Penn State surprised many by trouncing Louisiana Tech 86–65, seemingly ending the coaching career of Barmore. Lisa Shepherd accounted for 20 first-half points in leading the Lions to a 45–29 halftime lead against the Techsters.

Penn State never looked back as the Techsters wouldn't get any closer than 15 points in the entire second half. Philadelphia native and center Andrea Garner led the Lions with 15 points and 12 rebounds.

The Championship Venue

The Final Four had the Philadelphia flavor which the organizing committee had coveted for over a year. Rutgers would trek to Philadelphia led by star Philadelphia high school sensation, Stewart. Stringer had head coached at nearby Cheyney State, and her best friend and mentor John Chaney was the men's coach at Temple.

One of the top cheese steak joints in Philly is Geno's, and if that wasn't enough, Auriemma hails from nearby Norristown and most of his buddies still lived in the Philly area.

Another top cheese steak hangout in Philly is Pat's, and that isn't the only Tennessee tie. Clement hails from Philly and desperately wanted an opportunity to play for the national championship in her hometown.

Penn State was led by, among others, Garner, and coach Rene Portland was a standout at the national powerhouse and Philadelphia school, Immaculata, in the 1970s.

The stage was set for perhaps the greatest weekend in women's college basketball history. Four teams, one destination: Philadelphia. Two national powerhouses in Connecticut and Tennessee. Seven national titles between them. Two programs with strong basketball heritages, but no prior trips to the Final Four, in Penn State and Rutgers.

All four programs had very strong ties to the city of Philadelphia. Connecticut's Auriemma grew up in a Philadelphia suburb, played high school basketball there, and served as an assistant coach at St. Joseph's. Summitt's team actually had traveled to Philadelphia in December to play St. Joseph's. Penn State's Rene Portland recruited heavily out of Philadelphia, and she also once coached at St. Joseph's. Her 6'3" center, Andrea Garner, was a graduate of Philadelphia's Masterman High. Rutgers' Stringer brought a Philadelphia school, Cheyney State, to the first national championship game in 1982, and her current star, Shawnetta Stewart, broke all of Wilt Chamberlain's schoolboy career scoring records in Philly at University City High. Temple men's coach John Chaney is Stringer's closest friend and her coaching mentor. She actually took her team to see the inside of the First Union Center in February.

A Brief History of Women's College Basketball

W. C. Fields notwithstanding, what better venue could there be for the 2000 Final Four than the city of Philadelphia? The city of brotherly love. The city that not only stands as the cradle of our democracy, but also as the cradle of women's coaching supremacy throughout the country.

Clearly when the NCAA committee chose Philadelphia over Orlando in 1995, it was done with a hint of tradition in mind. After all, it was the year 2000, the year of the millennium celebrations and a perfect year to recognize the impact of Philadelphia on the game.

In March 1969, the players wore skirts and six players played a half-court game as West Chester (outside of Philadelphia) defeated Western

Carolina 65–39 in the first women's national championship game. Current Kansas head coach Marian Washington was a forward for the West Chester team that day, and she noted, "We didn't know at the time what impact we were having on history."

In 1972 when Title IX became law, mandating that women receive equal treatment in amateur sports and forcing colleges to offer athletic scholarships to women, the first college championship with regional advancement was sponsored by the AIAW. Tiny Immaculata College in Philadelphia beat Pennsylvania's West Chester in the title game. Two influential national coaches played for Immaculata, Illinois' (and formerly Rutgers') Theresa Shank Grentz, who was also the 1992 Olympic coach, and Penn State's Rene Muth Portland.

In 1974, Immaculata achieved a rare threepeat as national champions, and Grentz succeeded Ellen Ryan as the women's coach at Philadelphia's St. Joseph's.

In 1981, Philadelphia player Linda Page scored 100 points in a game for Dobbins Tech, breaking Wilt Chamberlain's single-game public school record of 90. One year later Rutgers, coached by Grentz, won the last AIAW tournament championship game against Texas in no other place than Philly. The NCAA sponsored a competing national championship game, and Philadelphia's Vivian Stringer took Cheyney State to the first NCAA title game, losing to Louisiana Tech.

The semifinals and title game had never been played in a northeastern city and were originally scheduled to be played at the Spectrum. However, a new facility was built and opened in Philadelphia known as the First Union Center, and the NCAA Women's Basketball Committee quickly gave approval to the state-of-the-art 20,444-seat arena.

The 2000 Final Four

The ties between the 2000 event and the teams involved were unmistakable. UConn's Geno Auriemma grew up in tiny Norristown, Pennsylvania, a scant 30 miles from Philadelphia and played his high school basketball at West Chester College. He later coached Pennsylvania high school basketball under St. Joseph's head men's coach Phil Martelli and then served as an assistant women's coach at St. Joseph's.

Among NCAA championships, the women's Final Four is second in popularity only to the men's Final Four and ranks just behind the World Series and the Super Bowl among the great events in American sports.

The Final Four is not only three basketball games but also a weeklong convention of the women's basketball coaches association. The convention comprises numerous seminars and coaching job banks.

The games are played on Friday and Sunday, the same weekend as the men's Final Four, which was being held this year in Indianapolis. There is no attempt to compete with the men's games, though, as the women's semifinals are held on Friday evening and the championship game on Sunday night. All three games are played before an ESPN national television audience.

ESPN assumed the contract in 1996 and in 1999 the game between Purdue and Duke received a 4.3 rating, an ESPN record for a women's basketball game. The game was watched by an average 3.238 million homes, the second biggest audience for an ESPN college basketball game—men's or women's—ever. The rating was 16 percent higher than 1998's 3.7 for Tennessee–Louisiana Tech and bested the previous record of a 4.0 for the 1997 title game between Tennessee and Old Dominion. The most watched ESPN college basketball game remains the Princeton–Arkansas men's tournament contest on March 15, 1990, seen by an average of 3.4 million homes.

ESPN continues to contribute to broadening the exposure of the women's game by signing a contract with the NCAA to televise the tournament for the next seven years.

The 1981–82 season was the first year the NCAA held championships for women's sports, nine in all, including women's basketball. The women's Final Four has received much attention, appearing on national television and garnering overwhelming crowd support. The entire women's Final Four was televised live for the first time in 1991 by CBS.

The tournament's first advance ticket sellout occurred in 1993, and it has sold out every year since. 1998 marked the first ever ticket drawing, selling out in the first five minutes the day following the final game in Cincinnati in 1997. In 1998 the Final Four's economic impact to Kansas City was estimated at $17 million.

From Philadelphia's perspective, the weeklong event was expected to draw more than 40,000 visitors, many of them coaches, and to fill 15,000 hotel rooms and have at least a $25 million economic impact on the city.

Starting in 1996, organizers drew up an ambitious $2 million budget and much of the money involved was raised through an aggressive sponsorship campaign and fund-raising events.

The person running the 2000 event in Philadelphia was the energetic Cathy Andruzzi, whose passion for the women's game drives the event to another level. Andruzzi is a 46-year-old native of Staten Island, New York, who has been around college basketball for more than 25 years. She was a star guard at Queens College in 1973, and she and her team went all the way to the national championship with a loss to Philadelphia's Immaculata. She coached Wagner College from 1976 to 1978 before moving to East Carolina University.

Andruzzi is also no stranger to Philadelphia basketball, as she was the general manager of the Philadelphia Rage of the now-defunct American Basketball League. "Cathy is someone who I think is motivated by the desire to really excel and to make a difference in the world, especially in respect to girls and young women and their ability to participate fully and completely in sports," said Sharon Smith, chief executive officer of the Girl Scouts of Pennsylvania.

Every summer, Andruzzi sponsors a basketball camp for kids in New York. She notes, "Philly is much smaller than New York, but I love the city and the tightness of it."

Recently Tennessee's Pat Summitt noted that Andruzzi "has a great passion for what she does and has a vision for the sport that makes me fired up."

The Pretournament

The committee tried to make the event as user friendly as possible. Many clinics and fairs were held at such locales as Drexel and Temple universities and the Grand Hall at the Philadelphia Convention Center. All of those events were free to the public.

More than eight Philadelphia hotels served as hubs for the event with parties and coaching change rumors as prevalent as hotel lobby debates about which team would win the national championship or even who the five strongest teams would be in 2000–01.

The festivities really began on Wednesday when the four teams arrived from their different locales.

The sites of the team hotels are predetermined by the NCAA based on the regions from which they come. UConn was slated to stay at the Sheraton Society Hill, Tennessee at the Wyndham Franklin Plaza, Penn State at the Crown Plaza, and Rutgers at the Embassy Suites.

By the time the teams arrived, all of the hotel lobbies were decorated with balloons representing the team colors. The UConn hotel had signs everywhere, strategically placed by both the hotel and fans who had arrived a full two days before the national semifinals. The Huskies had the greatest fan gathering in Philadelphia, especially at the finals on Sunday when the fans swooped down from Hartford County, Connecticut, and purchased tickets from Rutgers and Penn State fans as well as from scalpers. It was reported that tickets were going for as much as $350 outside the arena.

When the Rutgers team arrived late Wednesday afternoon, Stringer was greeted by Chaney who presented her with a bouquet of pink flowers. The Kodak moment was not ignored by the local newspapers or television crews.

By late afternoon most of the national media had arrived. The NCAA had parceled out more than 600 media credentials, more than any previous women's basketball Final Four.

While Geno Auriemma was the recipient of Coach of the Year honors in 2000, he had his own favorite runner-up.

Traci Waites

It was in Traci Waites' first season, 1998–99, that she was asked what it would have meant to her Pittsburgh women's basketball program had Swin Cash stayed home. Cash, the dynamic Connecticut forward who catalyzes her team's pressure defense and runs the floor like Jerry Rice, is from nearby McKeesport, Pennsylvania.

Waites' look wasn't far from that of a kid on Christmas morning. "Oh, man," Waites said, her voice trailing off, and it couldn't have been clearer what Cash's impact would have been.

So before the 1999–2000 season, Waites did the next best thing: She got the top prep player in the area named Brooke Stewart of East Allegheny, who helped revitalize the Pittsburgh program. Stewart wasn't Pittsburgh's Rookie of the Week, either. Fellow freshman Mandy Wittenmyer was a third-time honoree.

The Panthers were one of the Big East's best stories in 1999–2000, a program clearly headed north in the Big East standings. They finished with seven conference victories. They had been 20–67 in the three previous seasons before Waites' arrival.

Waites even earned a Coach of the Year vote from a past Coach of the Year. "When you look at where they were a year ago to where they are now, it's night and day," Connecticut's Geno Auriemma said. "Traci is an outstanding young coach."

Auriemma voted for Waites, whom he said got the most out of the talent she had. "When you see them on film, you can see what they're trying to do, what they're trying to accomplish," one league assistant coach said. "That's not true of everyone. Some teams, it's confusing after one pass. Traci has done great things."

Waites came to Pittsburgh after an assistant coaching stint under Joan Bonvicini at Arizona. This was her second season. And while she achieved more victories, it was one of the toughest basketball seasons she ever endured.

In December, Waites coped with the death of her brother, James, from AIDS. She wore a red ribbon pin to the ensuing Pitt games. The Pittsburgh players also wore a black patch in honor of Mr. Waites.

Sometimes, according to a story written about Waites by JoAnne Klimovich Harrop in the *Pittsburgh Tribune Review,* Waites had trouble with her pregame speeches to her team because "it was too painful." There was a game against Campbell in late December, for instance. "I told them, forgive me for crying, again," Waites told the *Tribune Review.* "I also told them when things seem to get hard or you don't understand what we are going through on the court, just grab your jersey, and realize that my brother fought for his life very, very hard. When things get tough, know that you can grab your jersey, and you can fight too, no matter what."

The Panthers were playing Campbell at a tournament in Atlanta. They won it, en route to an 11–3 start. The lesson the players learned along the way is that while you can't last an entire season on emotion, there is some value in playing with it.

"Coach talked to us about her brother," Stewart said. "We knew she took it hard. The team captains pulled us together and said, 'Let's go. We can do this.' We can win this season."

Stewart knew what her coach had experienced in recent times. Not only had Waites lost her brother, but also an aunt and her grandfather earlier in 1999. "I knew my brother was going to die, but when it happened, I wasn't ready for it," Waites said. "I cry every single day. But I am grateful my team has been there for me. My players could see I was hurting, and they wanted to help me. They asked me what they could do. I told them to play hard, and they did.

"I am going to wear this ribbon every single game that I coach, in his honor. My brother would always tell people I was a player. He knew I coached, but if he could have one wish, he always wanted me to play again. I know I could never do that. But if I could go back and relive my playing days, I would want to play on this team."

And for this program. Things figure to only get better once the Panthers move into a new on-campus arena, replacing the venerable but dingy Fitzgerald Field House. In a city with no pro basketball and the National Hockey League's Penguins who nearly went bankrupt, there's room for some college basketball headlines—of both genders.

The Ikon/WBCA Coach of the Year banquet was held Wednesday evening at the Philadelphia Marriott. Auriemma picked up his second Coach of the Year award. He had previously won in 1997. Unbelievably enough, he did not win in 1995 when the Huskies won the national championship and went undefeated. Some speculate that there was still a bias against male coaches as late as that season. Summitt had won the award three times. Also honored at the banquet with the President's Citation was Cathy Rush, former coach of Philadelphia national powerhouse Immaculata. Rush was humbled by the award and talked at length about all of the Philadelphia ties to the growth of women's basketball.

Thursday opened up with an ESPN news briefing, analysis of the state of the game, and the analysts' picks. UConn was the consensus choice. The network is in its sixth year of a $19 million contract with the NCAA which also calls for ESPN to televise other women's collegiate events.

The main topic of discussion was whether or not the Final Four should be held on the same weekend as the men's tournament. The consensus of the panel was that the event should be moved either to the week before or the week after. The only possible conflict the following weekend would be with the Masters Golf Tournament on CBS, but it seems clear that a far different audience views the Masters than would watch the women's tournament. Doris Burke, ESPN analyst and former Providence star, is in favor of moving the weekend and spoke very passionately about not competing with the men's tournament, especially for the missing male audience aged 18 to 34.

There was also much speculation about the wisdom of holding the first two rounds on campus sites. In 2000 the No. 1 and No. 2 seeds in each regional were 8–0 in the second round and won their games by an average of greater than 20 points. In 1999 they were also 8–0, and in the past seven years that the tournament has involved 64 teams, the top two seeds are a combined 53–3 in the second round.

Some even suggested trying to mimic the lead of Val Ackerman of the WNBA and make a wholesale change in the season. Play the regular season from some time in October through January with the Final Four weekend taking place the week before the Super Bowl. It worked for the WNBA. Why not for college basketball?

The afternoon was an opportunity for coaches to mingle both at seminars and at the giant expo in the Convention Center. It was also the time for all four teams to hold open practices, autograph sessions, and news conferences.

The expo was highlighted by new product displays, newly created recruiting websites, and the ever-present bulletin board where prospective coaches placed their resumes and teams openly advertised game slots for next season. Maryland was looking for a home game along with Mississippi State, and Dartmouth was looking for teams to fill out its December tournament. The more prominent teams usually provide a guarantee of $2,500 along with free hotel rooms for visiting teams. It is an opportunity for some of the smaller Division I programs to get some national exposure and beef up their coffers. There was also the normal convention buzz about coaching openings such as Temple, Indiana, and Louisiana Tech and at California to replace Marianne Stanley who reportedly stepped down to take an assistant's job with the WNBA's Los Angeles Sparks. With respect to Temple and Indiana the speculation related in part to whether or not those universities would be devoting more resources to the women's game.

Some 4,500 fans watched the open practices, and most people were there to either greet Tennessee's Philadelphia native Clement, a former beauty queen, or to cheer wildly for the Huskies. Rutgers and Connecticut actually ran some plays while Tennessee and Penn State conducted glorified shoot-arounds.

The late afternoon was capped off by the Kodak All-American announcement at the NCAA Hoop City at the Convention Center. Catchings, Ralph, and Abrosimova highlighted the announcement, regaled in their team uniforms.

The evening belonged to the WBCA All-Star game. The East beat the West 73–58 behind Shaka Massey's (Louisiana Tech) 18 points. Iowa State's

Stacey Frese defeated Boston College's Cal Bouchard 19–16 in the entertaining three-point shooting contest. WNBA scouts and player agents were sprinkled throughout the crowd of 2,351 at the University of Pennsylvania's storied Palestra.

Friday at noon Catchings picked up the Rawlings/WBCA Player of the Year Award at a luncheon at the Marriott, and then all four teams huddled with their coaches at their respective hotels for both academic study halls and film preparation for the evening games.

The Semifinals

Saturday afternoon belonged to the media and the players. There were a plethora of Tennessee and UConn press conferences, and both teams conducted closed practices. The evening saw a VIP party at the Franklin Institute. Food stations were abundant and attendees got an opportunity to watch the men's national semifinal games from Indianapolis in the Omni Theater. Philadelphia's own Bobby Rydell entertained.

Auriemma held his own annual Final Four bash that same evening. He does it every year for about 250 of his closest friends and relatives. His "bouncers" were former players. He picked up the tab himself and seemed thoroughly relaxed, even at 2:30 A.M. with the national championship encounter with Tennessee on Sunday evening a scant 18.5 hours away.

In a game in which the tempo was very much to the liking of the UConn Huskies, Connecticut put points on the scoreboard at a feverish pace, defeating the Lions 89–67 in the second national semifinal clash before a sellout crowd of 20,060 at the First Union Center.

The Huskies had a relatively cold-shooting first half in taking a 37–29 lead. They only shot 38 percent from the field but warmed up considerably in the second half, as did Penn State.

The Lions connected on 10 of their first 15 shots in the second half and bumped the deficit to 57–53 with just over 10 minutes to play. Connecticut then went on one of its patented runs (20–6) to open up an 18-point lead and put the game out of reach.

Connecticut shot 64 percent from the field in the second half, led by Bird's game-high 19 points. Still, Auriemma, a perfectionist, wasn't happy, stating after the game, "Our defense at times was lousy."

Garner had 19 for Penn State and Shepherd 15, but star point guard and national 5'8" and under Player of the Year Darling was held by Bird to zero points, despite the fact that she had a game-high nine assists.

Tennessee sprinted away from Rutgers in the final six minutes to defeat the Scarlet Knights 69–54 in the other semifinal, setting up the championship game everyone anticipated.

Freshman Kara Lawson scored 19 points, 14 in the second half, to lead the Volunteers, who went on a 13–3 run midway through the second half to break open a close game. The loss ended Rutgers' season one game short of their goal, but at 26–8, the Scarlet Knights still posted one of their most successful years in school history. Shawnetta Stewart, Linda Miles, and Tasha Pointer all scored 11 points to lead the Scarlet Knights.

The Final Game

It was supposed to be a game for the ages. A game, by virtue of its sheer competitiveness, that would propel women's basketball to yet another level. It was supposed to grab the attention of the male fan, especially those aged 18–34, the average Joe that the sport has yet to capture.

Instead, it was a blowout. Connecticut, which split with Tennessee in the regular season, won the rubber match at the First Union Center in the biggest game of the season. If there was a question in anyone's mind whether the 1999–2000 Connecticut women were the No. 1 team in the nation, it was officially answered. Thanks to a swarming defense, the top-ranked Huskies got out to a commanding start against No. 2 Tennessee and won the national championship 71–52 by never relenting.

They put on a convincing display of confidence, poise, and determination from the opening tap. Led defensively by center Kelly Schumacher's nine blocked shots and by a balanced offensive attack, the Huskies took the reins and never relinquished them.

"This team was intent on proving tonight they were the best team in the country," UConn Coach Geno Auriemma said. "I've told these kids all year long that every pass we make in practice, every cut, every rebound, pretend it's like the one that's going to win the national championship. And the night they had to do it, they did it better than any other time in the season."

The favored Huskies executed their game plan to perfection to capture the school's second national championship—the first in five years to the day—with a lopsided victory before another crowd of 20,060. They were the largest crowd ever to see a basketball game—men's or women's—in the state of Pennsylvania.

"Obviously they just schooled us, even some of our veteran players," said Tennessee coach Pat Summitt, who has won an unprecedented six national titles. "They were awesome," Summitt said. "I was frustrated, my team was frustrated. Everything they did, we scouted, we knew it. Semeka Randall, she just got lost defensively more than anyone."

UConn junior Shea Ralph was named Final Four Most Valuable Player after scoring a team-high 15 points and getting seven assists and six steals. Sue Bird, Svetlana Abrosimova, and Asjha Jones were also named to the all-tournament team. Jones came off the bench to score 12 points and grab eight rebounds. Abrosimova scored 14 points and had five rebounds. Tamika Catchings, the Associated Press Player of the Year, was the only player named to the all-tournament team for Tennessee. She was the only Tennessee player in double-figure scoring with 16 points.

"I don't know if I've seen us play this well all year," Ralph said. "And we got the ultimate prize." The Huskies (36–1) capped their season with a 17-game winning streak while snapping Tennessee's winning streak at 20 games.

The Lady Vols (33–4) played without junior starter Kristen Clement, who apparently sprained her right ankle in the team's morning walk-through. Summitt said she wasn't sure if Clement would have made a difference in the game since the Lady Vols committed 26 turnovers and were never able to handle the Huskies' attack. The 26 turnovers tied the most by one team in an NCAA title game. "I don't think that any of us expected this quite to this extent," Summitt said. "When you go against a team that plays as aggressive and physical and as intense, you have to have great guard play. I thought they came out with a great plan to really take us out of some things we wanted to do."

Although she didn't receive any accolades, the Huskies' leader in the first half was the most unlikely of heroes—Kelly Schumacher. The 6'5" junior, who lost the starting position in the season opener and won it back at the end of the season, blocked six shots and grabbed five rebounds in the first half alone. She finished with a career-high nine blocks, an NCAA championship record. "She was a huge factor," said Randall, who was limited to six points on 1-for-11 shooting from the field. "Most of the time, I drove to the key and I got rejected. Her blocked shots were very important to their winning the basketball game."

UConn won its first national title since the 1995 team went 35–0. Many former players from that team were in attendance, including Kara Wolters, Jen Rizzotti, and Rebecca Lobo. Even superstar comedian and actor Bill Cosby was on hand. And the popular band Boyz II Men was there to sing the national anthem.

It might not have been the game ESPN was hoping for, but the lopsided score wasn't a complete surprise. The Huskies showed all year that they were capable of blowing out ranked teams. They went 12–1 against ranked teams in the regular season. The Huskies maintained their No. 1 ranking, which they held for all 19 weeks, despite a one-point loss to Tennessee in the regular season. They had proven they could score quickly and in bunches, and their runs did the Lady Vols in.

Ahead by five early in the first half, UConn scored 10 straight points to take a 21–6 lead with 7:50 left in the first half. The Lady Vols managed to get themselves in double figures on a pair of free throws from Shalon Pillow and April McDivitt, but they couldn't buy a basket from the field. The Lady Vols went 1-for-15 to open the game and shot just 18.5 percent in the first half. Combine that with the 13 turnovers and the Lady Vols were fortunate to be down by just nine points with 1:33 remaining in the first half.

However, while the Lady Vols threatened, the Huskies went on yet another run. Thanks to baskets by Swin Cash and Bird, UConn put together a 4–0 run to take a 32–19 halftime lead.

The scoring spurts didn't end there, however. Coming out of halftime, the Huskies reiterated how valuable the first five minutes of the second half can be. Thanks to two blocks from Schumacher, the Huskies opened with an 8–0 run to take a 21-point lead (40–19) with 16:58 remaining in the game.

"I think that coming in, we knew that transition defense was going to be a key for us to be successful against them," said Tennessee freshman point guard Kara Lawson, who had six points on 3-for-13 shooting. "And a lot of times, we took quick shots, and we weren't able to set up our defense. We really wanted to make them play in the half-court offense, and we weren't really able to do that."

The game between the longtime rivals was not without its heated moments. The first incident came with 8:51 left in the first half and UConn ahead 19–6. Randall and Kennitra Johnson were both chasing a loose ball and ended up on the ground wrestling for it. Both got up quickly, and Randall put her hands high in the air as if to signify an innocent surrender.

The second near-altercation came between Tennessee sophomore Michelle Snow and Asjha Jones. Snow was called for fouling Jones with 9:35 remaining and the Huskies ahead by 22 points. Words were exchanged, and the two had to be restrained by their respective teammates.

And the final heated moment also involved Randall. As she attempted to bounce the ball off Abrosimova and send it out of bounds, Randall hit Abrosimova square on the head.

But none of these incidents took away from the obvious: Connecticut was simply the better team this season. "Obviously they are a great team and obviously they have great players and great coaching and great tradition," Auriemma said. "And you don't take anybody like that lightly, not one bit. And we certainly didn't."

Now with the 2000 women's college basketball national championship decided, it was time to look forward to the 2000–01 season and to see which programs would reap the greatest rewards from the crop of high school players.

chapter six

recruiting

Media Influence

The quote did not go unnoticed.

The quote came from Iowa State Coach Bill Fennelly.

"Now everyone knows who Iowa State is," he told the *Women's Basketball Journal* before the season began. "That's what happens when you beat UConn on their network."

He was referring to ESPN.

Iowa State beat Connecticut in the NCAA Tournament in the 1998–99 season, the program's most significant win ever. It came on ESPN for anyone interested in such matters to see.

ESPN, Fennelly says, is UConn's network.

He was being funny, one surmises, but there's an element of cynicism there, too.

Most of the Big East coaches, in marveling at Connecticut's 1999–2000 team, normally don't escape Gampel Pavilion without saying, "I see them on TV all the time."

The same could be said of Tennessee, Connecticut's alter ego, and part of the made-for-TV rivalry of the nation's two preeminent programs.

Yes, this is how far women's basketball has come, and where it still has to go. There is more media exposure now than ever—it's just that the heavyweights are the ones being exposed.

But in the classic chicken-and-egg argument, there's the "Tennessee and UConn deserve it for all they do to promote the game" theory versus the "What's so good about them?" comments.

Jeff Jacobs, the sports columnist for the *Hartford Courant,* decided to do a little research in recruitment success before the February 2 UConn–Tennessee rematch at Gampel. He found that an examination of the 25 rated high school seniors in the Blue Star Index over the past five years reveals 21 percent (25 of 121) went to UConn and Tennessee and one-third (40 of 121) ended up at four schools, including Stanford and Duke. Sixty percent (72 of 121) landed on just 11 campuses. Jacobs' list included women from the 1999–2000 college senior class down to senior year in high school. It's short four names because not everyone has decided on a college.

Twenty-one percent have gone to two programs. Is it because ESPN is "UConn's network"?

"One thing I think is a problem in women's basketball is not enough teams are televised," Auriemma said. "Kids get brainwashed with only certain schools. Another problem is we have too many scholarships. You can horde players. It's like the old days when UCLA [men] had the top three teams in the country: their varsity, their JV, and their freshmen. We could effect change quicker by cutting back to 13 scholarships, like the guys are."

Television has allowed UConn and Tennessee to recruit nationally. The star player in California has seen them play on television…and not many others.

In 1998–99, Nina Smith, the consensus No. 1 high school player in the country, decided to attend Wisconsin. Some coaches believe that's Step One in getting the best players to look somewhere else besides Storrs or Knoxville.

Of course, the top two prep players from this past season, Diana Taurasi (California) and Ashley Robinson (Texas) are going to, yep, UConn and Tennessee.

"It wasn't always that way, I assure you," Auriemma said. "We got to the Final Four in 1991 with no high school All-Americans on our team. None. Not first, second, or third team. What did it for us was doing it with regular guys and then saying, 'Look, if we can do it with guys who work really hard, think what we could do with you?'

"The hardest sell I ever made was Lobo. Not Rebecca. Rebecca's mother. She was the most difficult one. The program wasn't what it is now.

"Tennessee got a much earlier jump on the movement. They bought Yahoo when it was $3 and rode the wave. Them, La Tech, Old Dominion. Some dot.coms went away. Immaculata, Delta State, Wayland Baptist. Great teams. They couldn't sustain it, because they didn't have the money. When big schools started pouring money into programs, everything changed."

And people notice. An ESPN.com poll in February asked Internet surfers to choose the nation's best college basketball rivalry after the Duke–Carolina men. Thirty-two percent picked the UConn–Tennessee women.

UConn–Tennessee added a second regular season game to the rivalry, too, becoming the first-ever women's basketball regular-season game to be shown in February prime time (7 P.M., ESPN).

It became the highest-rated women's game ever. It was even discussed the following day on New York all-sports talk radio WFAN, by popular afternoon drive hosts Mike Francesa and Chris Russo, two sports guys who have very little regard for women's hoops.

Will You Play?

So how does the rest of the country get what UConn and Tennessee have? Well, they can't get ALL the best players.

Recruit, recruit, recruit.

And then ask them the question: If you go there, will you play?

Take the case of current Nebraska forward Stephanie Jones, from the Nike camp two summers ago. Jones, a young woman from Omaha who said it was her dream since she was eight years old to play women's basketball at UConn, had just finished playing another game and plopped down on the bench. No time for water or a towel. No, Jones' eyes were too busy darting across the gym like projectiles.

"Look," a coach says. "Look at her eyes. She's looking for him. She wants to see if he's here."

The "he" in this case is Auriemma. Jones says of him, "I always watch him. He looks so big on TV. I think, 'Wow, this is the guy I admire so much.' My heart beats really fast."

Quotes like that from a prospective recruit would likely make other coaches here lose their lunch. Other coaches probably did after Auriemma landed the top-rated recruiting class in the country from 1998 (Tamika Williams, Swin Cash, Keirsten Walters, Sue Bird, and Asjha Jones).

Stephanie Jones' eyes told a significant story: The idea here is to be seen.

That's why coaches, representatives from virtually every Division I program in the country, wear the logo of their school on shirts, pants, sweaters, and hats. That's why they carry cell phones. After basketballs and sneakers, cell phones are the third most popular inanimate objects seen here. You figure there's the rush provided by winning a game at the buzzer—but for a recruit to catch your eye while you're on a cell phone with a look of self-importance rivaling Anna Kournikova, well, that's just positively delicious.

"I swear they call each other from across the gym just so they can be seen talking to each other," a coach says.

Coaches are not permitted, under NCAA rules, to talk publicly about prospective recruits. The Nike camp occurs during a "dead" period, meaning coaches may not even speak to the players. The best they can hope for is a look, or even better, an acknowledgment.

Yet as sure as Auriemma's hair doesn't move, you should know what every other coach is telling prospective UConn recruits for this season: "If you go there, where are you going to play? Look at the freshmen they have."

Tennessee, too.

Listen more to Jones, whose parents paid for her to attend Auriemma's camp in June: "Since I was eight it's been my dream to play for UConn. My parents finally gave me the opportunity to go," said Jones, who even has pictures of UConn players on her bedroom walls. "I liked the way (Auriemma) talked to me, and I like the way he talks to his players. It's a real family atmosphere. The players even asked me to play in their staff games. Shea (Ralph) passed me the ball and everything."

A kid couldn't like a coach and a program more.

Jones went to Nebraska.

Indeed, conversations with different players made you think of an old Yogi Berra line, "Nobody goes to that restaurant anymore because it's too crowded."

For UConn, it might be, "nobody wants to go there. There's too many good players."

"Connecticut is a top-player's school," said Schuye LaRue, a 6'1" guard/forward from Washington, D.C., who would go to Virginia. "It's not that it's too far away for me, and I like to play with good players. But I'm not sure how much I'd play."

"Sometimes, kids go to schools for the wrong reasons," said LaToya Turner, a 6'4" forward from Ohio, likely the nation's second-ranked high school player. "A lot of kids go, 'They're winning so I'm going to go there.' Do you want to play and help out or just sit there?"

Auriemma isn't alone. Tennessee's Pat Summitt hears the same thing.

"Clearly, our success has opened doors for us," Summitt said. "But we know we have to battle some perceptions: You have all these great players, is there room for us, there won't be enough minutes, there won't be enough basketballs. You have to stick with your system. You can't forget how you got to where you are."

At UConn, it's been pretty simple: The coaches are as honest with them as they can be, they never trash another school, and they look for kids who understand "we" is more important than "I." Rebecca Lobo and Nykesha Sales are examples 1 and 1A.

At Tennessee, you needn't look any further than Tamika Catchings, one of the most respectful, unselfish, multitalented players ever.

"You have to want to be a part of it, not everything there is," Chris Dailey said. "Last year, we found five great players who want to be a part. We were very lucky. Don't get me wrong, we worked hard to get them, but we were lucky to find them.

"Across the country, coaches and players know where the good players go. You hope that's viewed as a positive. But if another school brings up the point (too many good players, not enough playing time), then it certainly will become an issue. We want them to understand the kind of people they'll be playing with. We have a shot to bring in good kids, but it's probably not going to be easy. But then, it's not easy any year."

epilogue

What did the 1999–2000 season and specifically the postseason really tell us about the state of women's basketball? Well, for one thing, UConn is clearly the dominant program, having surpassed Tennessee in both quality of recruiting, execution on the court, and depth. It's not that the Tennessee program has collapsed; it is simply that the Huskies have gotten that much better.

We also know that the ratings for the 2000 championship game were down from the 1999 championship game between Duke and Purdue on ESPN, and for yet another season the championship game did nothing to capture the more expansive audience it so desperately coveted, men between the ages of 18 and 34. If they tuned into the game, they saw a blowout and probably turned it off after five minutes.

So where is the game headed not only in 2001, but further down the road? There are problems lurking around the bend that need to be addressed. Sooner rather than later.

There are simply not enough competitive teams on the national level. Realistically there are only three or four teams that are positioned to challenge the Huskies over the next few seasons. Georgia, Tennessee, Louisiana Tech, and Rutgers all look relatively healthy, but there are a plethora of programs at universities with rich athletic heritages that simply cannot compete.

Take the Big East for example. Football and basketball powerhouses such as Syracuse, West Virginia, and Miami are not only fodder for the Huskies but they also have virtually no chance of playing competitively with the likes of Boston College.

This is an epidemic, which crisscrosses the country and strikes virtually every major conference, with the possible exception of the SEC. Indiana, Washington, Michigan State, and Arizona State all stick out like sore thumbs in this regard. Athletic administrators at these schools and many more must make a conceptual decision if they are going to pour more resources into their women's basketball programs, specifically into the recruitment of better athletes to better market their programs to students, alumni, and members of the communities in which the universities are located. The women's game needs to reach a level where at least 20 teams can realistically compete for the national championship year-in and year-out.

The wisdom of playing the Final Four on the same weekend as the men's tournament must be reevaluated. As presently constituted, the women's Final Four is relegated to pages 3 and 4 of most national newspapers not in a Final Four team or site city. One very simple solution would be to play the event on the following weekend. Executives at ESPN fear competition with the Masters Golf Tournament, but the audiences for the two events are far different. Basketball-hungry junkies would get their season extended by another week, and it is hypothesized that even the male-dominated audience which watched the men's tournament the weekend before would tune in for the women's Final Four if for no other reason than to get more hoops.

A more radical alternative would be to dramatically change the women's season. Practice could start towards the end of September, and the season could begin in early to mid October and culminate with the national championship during the first week of February. In early

February, there is really very little going on nationally. Men's college basketball is in its dog days. Football is over, and baseball and hockey have not really revved up enough to capture a national stir.

The interest in girls' basketball on a local AAU level has increased dramatically over the years, and it is no longer the case that Mike Flynn's Liberty Belles is the only nationally recognized AAU program. Still more resources have to be pumped into AAU programs to ensure that there is enough talent nationally so as to enable 20 teams to compete for the national championship and 50 to 60 teams to compete regionally. The flip side of such a suggestion is that the sneaker money from the Nike's of the world may end up creating or replicating the evils of the well-documented boys' AAU programs nationally. Devils such as street runners and street agents could be hired by sneaker companies to influence 13- and 14-year-old girls with respect to not only which shoes they should wear, but which colleges they should attend and which agents they should hire in order to play in either the WNBA or in Europe. Right now there probably isn't enough money in the women's game to believe that this concern is a reality, but in time, and as the dollars increase, there certainly could be reason for concern.

Tennessee's Holdsclaw was heavily courted after graduation by both Adidas and Nike and ended up signing with Nike. In the men's game this courting process often takes place five or six years earlier and specifically with respect to whether or not the top 100 or 200 high school players are going to attend a Nike-sponsored summer camp or an Adidas-sponsored summer camp. Somehow the girls' AAU programs must maintain their purity and not be influenced by the sneaker giants. Auriemma has a lot of friends in the men's game, and while he certainly wants the quality of the women's game to improve, he is fearful that in the process its purity could be sacrificed.

The quality of the officiating must improve in many of the major conferences. No less of an expert than Joe Smith, national high school and college basketball guru, has advocated that officials in conferences officiate both men's and women's games. He feels that officiating has worsened over the past five years and cites the fact that games in many conferences are called much too closely with touch fouls in the pivot slowing down the game and fouling out many star players.

The national television and radio exposure must increase. Television executives need to be persuaded that there is an audience for the women's game not only at the end of March but also in December, January, and February. The men's game grew dramatically when ESPN made the decision in the 1980s to televise two or three games a night every Monday through Thursday throughout the season. It is far too difficult, even with Direct TV, to locate a women's game on television before the tournament starts in March. Conference matchups such as Rutgers–Connecticut, Tennessee–Georgia, and UCLA–Stanford should be televised nationally, and intersectional clashes such as Connecticut–Tennessee are made for Saturday afternoon television viewing. Some of those games have already been shown on national television with decent viewing results but until more sponsors step up to the plate and pay the money necessary to fund such a broadcast, these games will not become a reality on television nor increase dramatically the national audience which pays attention to women's basketball.

Lastly, an admonition to the NCAA: Do not alter the July recruiting rules so as to shorten the time frame in which coaches can observe and evaluate players at summer camps and programs. All that would accomplish in the women's game would be to further lessen the ability of the mid-level and smaller programs to observe and locate players. Once again, the rich would get richer and the poor would get poorer. That is certainly not in the best interests of the women's game. That legislation, currently in its infancy stage, should be stopped by the athletic directors and conference leaders.

ncaa women's tournament

Individual Statistics

Scoring (Totals)

Rank	Player Name	School	Points	Games
1	Tamika Catchings	Tennessee	99	6
2	Svetlana Abrosimova	UConn	88	6
3	Shea Ralph	UConn	84	6
4	Lisa Shepherd	Penn St.	79	5
5	Semeka Randall	Tennessee	78	6
6	Sue Bird	UConn	77	6
7	Marie Ferdinand	LSU	72	4
8	Tamicha Jackson	LA Tech	71	4
9	LaNeishea Caufield	Oklahoma	71	3
10	Asjha Jones	UConn	71	6
11	Andrea Garner	Penn St.	71	5
12	April Brown	LSU	70	4
13	Deanna Jackson	UAB	69	3
14	Phylesha Waley	Oklahoma	68	3
15	Coco Miller	Georgia	67	4
16	Maren Walseth	Penn St.	66	5
17	Kara Lawson	Tennessee	66	6
18	Aleah Johnson	Texas Tech	64	4
19	Lucienne Berthieu	Old Dominion	60	3
20	Plenette Pierson	Texas Tech	60	4
21	Helen Darling	Penn St.	58	5
22	Catrina Frierson	LA Tech	58	4
23	Shawnetta Stewart	Rutgers	57	5
24	Detrina White	LSU	57	4
25	Swintayla Cash	UConn	57	6
26	Tamika Williams	UConn	56	6
27	LaQuanda Barksdale	North Carolina	55	3
28	Hamchetou Maiga	Old Dominion	55	3
29	Camille Cooper	Purdue	55	2
30	Usha Gilmore	Rutgers	54	5

Assists (Totals)

Rank	Player Name	School	Assists	Games
1	Helen Darling	Penn St.	44	5
2	Tasha Pointer	Rutgers	33	5
3	Melinda Schmucker	Texas Tech	29	4
4	Svetlana Abrosimova	UConn	27	6
5	Shea Ralph	UConn	26	6
6	Sue Bird	UConn	25	6
7	Nikki Teasley	North Carolina	23	3
8	Marie Ferdinand	LSU	23	4

9	Deana Nolan	Georgia	22	4
10	Stacey Dales	Oklahoma	21	3
11	Katrina Hibbert	LSU	19	4
12	Tamika Catchings	Tennessee	18	6
13	Angela Harris	Miss. St.	18	2
14	Keitha Dickerson	Texas Tech	17	4
15	April Brown	LSU	17	4
16	Katrisa O'Neal	Texas Tech	17	4
17	Betty Lennox	LA Tech	16	4
18	Felicia Jackson	UAB	15	3
19	Stacy Frese	Iowa St.	14	3
20	Kristen Clement	Tennessee	14	5
21	Kara Lawson	Tennessee	14	6
22	Renee Robinson	Virginia	13	3
23	Natalie Diaz	Old Dominion	13	3
24	Kennitra Johnson	UConn	13	6
25	Ashley McElhiney	Vanderbilt	13	2
26	Tiffany Krantz	Auburn	12	2
27	Lisa Shepherd	Penn St.	12	5
28	Kelly Miller	Georgia	12	4
29	Andrea Garner	Penn St.	12	5
30	Alli Spence	Old Dominion	12	3

Rebounds (Totals)

Rank	Player Name	School	Rebounds	Games
1	Tamika Catchings	Tennessee	59	6
2	Andrea Garner	Penn St.	44	5
3	Tammy Sutton-Brown	Rutgers	38	5
4	Helen Darling	Penn St.	38	5
5	Semeka Randall	Tennessee	37	6
6	Hamchetou Maiga	Old Dominion	37	3
7	Svetlana Abrosimova	UConn	36	6
8	Michelle Snow	Tennessee	36	6
9	Keitha Dickerson	Texas Tech	35	4
10	Detrina White	LSU	34	4
11	Tawna McDonald	Georgia	32	4
12	Plenette Pierson	Texas Tech	32	4
13	Maren Walseth	Penn St.	32	5
14	Takeisha Lewis	LA Tech	31	4
15	Ayana Walker	LA Tech	31	4
16	LaQuanda Barksdale	North Carolina	29	3
17	Asjha Jones	UConn	29	6
18	Shawnetta Stewart	Rutgers	28	5
19	Megan Taylor	Iowa St.	28	3
20	Kelly Shumacher	UConn	28	6
21	Deanna Jackson	UAB	28	3
22	Angie Welle	Iowa St.	27	3
23	Schuye LaRue	Virginia	26	3
24	Linda Miles	Rutgers	26	5
25	Gwen Jackson	Tennessee	26	6
26	Caton Hill	Oklahoma	26	3
27	Tasha Pointer	Rutgers	25	5
28	Shea Ralph	UConn	25	6
29	Zuzana Klimesova	Vanderbilt	24	2
30	Tamika Williams	UConn	24	6

Field Goal Percentage

Rank	Player Name	School	FG	FGA	FG%	Games
1	Charlie Rogers	Nebraska	5	5	100	1
2	Carlin Chesick	St. Francis (PA)	5	5	100	1
3	Marie Philman	UCLA	3	3	100	1
4	Daneesh McIntosh	Rice	3	3	100	2
5	Rachel Bryan	Vermont	2	2	100	1
6	Monica Vicarel	Youngstown St.	2	2	100	1
7	Lindsey Ryan	Texas	2	2	100	1
8	Katie Wulf	W. Kentucky	2	2	100	2
9	Karen Swanson	Notre Dame	2	2	100	2
10	Barbora Kuklova	St. Joe's	2	2	100	2
11	Vanita Krouch	SMU	1	1	100	1
12	Taresha Coleman	Alcorn St.	1	1	100	1
13	Shavonda Willis	Georgia	1	1	100	2
14	Queriston Haynes	Alcorn St.	1	1	100	1
15	Michelle Duhart	Purdue	1	1	100	1
16	Meaghan Leahy	Notre Dame	1	1	100	2
17	Lello Gebisa	Duke	1	1	100	1
18	Kenisha Walker	Michigan	1	1	100	1
19	Kaisha Lymon	LSU	1	1	100	4
20	Jen Horner	Youngstown St.	1	1	100	1
21	Jana Wright	W. Kentucky	1	1	100	1
22	Lesha Jones	Tennessee Tech	1	1	100	1
23	Ebony Williams	Marquette	1	1	100	1
24	Desiree Taylor	Oklahoma	1	1	100	3
25	Cristi Carbone	St. Peter's	1	1	100	1
26	Carla Littleton	Texas	1	1	100	1
27	Angela Burnham	Youngstown St.	1	1	100	1
28	Amy Phillips	Montana	1	1	100	1
29	Allyson Glazebrook	Drake	1	1	100	1
30	Tracy Guerrette	Maine	0	0	100	1

Three-Point Shooting Percentage

Rank	Player Name	School	P3	P3A	P3%	Games
1	Paige Sauer	UConn	2	2	100	6
2	Monica Vicarel	Youngstown St.	2	2	100	1
3	Michele Matyasovsky	Duke	2	2	100	3
4	Marie Philman	UCLA	2	2	100	1
5	Felicia Harris	St. Peter's	2	2	100	1
6	Elizabeth Dudley	Wisc. Green Bay	2	2	100	1
7	Vanita Krouch	SMU	1	1	100	1
8	Taryn Turnbell	Tulane	1	1	100	2
9	Taresha Coleman	Alcorn St.	1	1	100	1
10	Tamara McDonald	Pepperdine	1	1	100	1
11	Stacy Krueger	Wisc. Green Bay	1	1	100	1
12	Semeka Randall	Tennessee	1	1	100	6
13	Selena Scott	Kansas	1	1	100	1
14	Megan Isom	Tennessee Tech	1	1	100	1
15	Liz O'Connor	Holy Cross	1	1	100	1
16	Liz Martin	Dartmouth	1	1	100	1
17	LaKeisha Johnson	Auburn	1	1	100	2
18	Kizzy Lopez	Maine	1	1	100	1
19	Karalyn Church	Vermont	1	1	100	1
20	Jenniffer Leitner	Brigham Young	1	1	100	1
21	Jennifer Jackson	Kansas	1	1	100	1
22	Jana Wright	W. Kentucky	1	1	100	1
23	Ivy Gardner	NC State	1	1	100	1
24	Andrea Garner	Penn St.	1	1	100	5
25	Alyson Vogrin	Youngstown St.	1	1	100	1

26	Allyson Glazebrook	Drake	1	1	100	1
27	Aja Wellington	Alcorn St.	1	1	100	1
28	Adrianna Spears	Boston College	0	0	100	1
29	Abbie Willenborg	Marquette	0	0	100	1
30	Aarika Florus	Rice	0	0	100	1

Free Throw Percentage

Rank	Player Name	School	FT	FTA	FT%	Games
1	Sheana Mosch	Duke	13	13	100	3
2	Lori Nero	Auburn	13	13	100	2
3	Allison Curtin	Illinois	10	10	100	2
4	Jamie Cassidy	Maine	9	9	100	1
5	Alissa Murphy	Boston College	9	9	100	2
6	Sharon Wilkerson	Liberty	8	8	100	1
7	Kylie Martin	Illinois	8	8	100	2
8	Diane Seng	Tennessee Tech	8	8	100	1
9	Okeisha Howard	Old Dominion	6	6	100	3
10	Maria Perez-Barris	San Diego	6	6	100	1
11	Katie Griggs	Xavier	6	6	100	1
12	Jamie Carey	Stanford	6	6	100	2
13	Felicia Jackson	UAB	6	6	100	3
14	Conswella Sparrow	Auburn	6	6	100	2
15	Angela Zamplella	St. Joe's	6	6	100	2
16	Nadja Morgan	Pepperdine	5	5	100	1
17	Carrie Nance	Kent	5	5	100	1
18	Tynesha Lewis	NC State	4	4	100	1
19	Tawnee Cooper	Santa Barbara	4	4	100	1
20	Stacy Jensen	Brigham Young	4	4	100	1
21	Mercy Aghedo	St. Peter's	4	4	100	1
22	Megan Isom	Tennessee Tech	4	4	100	1
23	Lisa Hosac	Virginia	4	4	100	3
24	Lisa Griffith	Arizona	4	4	100	2
25	Kristin Santa	Drake	4	4	100	1
26	Keisha Brown	Georgia	4	4	100	4
27	Jenniffer Leitner	Brigham Young	4	4	100	1
28	Erin Richards	Drake	4	4	100	1
29	Datishella Byrd	Clemson	4	4	100	2
30	Coko Eggleston	Rutgers	4	4	100	1

Team Statistics

Scoring Offense (Avg.)

Rank	School	Offense	Games
1	UConn	91	6
2	Old Dominion	90	3
3	Wisc. Green Bay	85	1
4	Miss. St.	83	2
5	Notre Dame	82	3
6	Boston College	81	2
7	Brigham Young	80	1
8	Oklahoma	80	3
9	Oregon	79	1
10	LA Tech	78	4
11	Iowa St.	78	3

12	SW Missouri St.	77	1
13	Nebraska	76	1
14	Duke	75	3
15	Penn St.	75	5
16	Michigan	74	1
17	UCLA	72	1
18	Stanford	72	2
19	Georgia	72	4
20	Xavier	72	1
21	Purdue	72	2
22	Auburn	72	2
23	LSU	71	4
24	SMU	70	2
25	Illinois	70	2
26	Holy Cross	70	1
27	Youngstown St.	70	1
28	Kansas	69	1
29	George Washington	69	2
30	Tennessee	69	6
31	W. Kentucky	69	2
32	Vanderbilt	68	2
33	Texas Tech	68	4
34	Virginia	68	3
35	UAB	67	3
36	North Carolina	67	3
37	Arizona	66	2
38	Dartmouth	66	1
39	Marquette	65	1
40	Santa Barbara	64	1
41	Rutgers	64	5
42	St. Francis (Pa.)	63	1
43	Pepperdine	62	1
44	Tulane	62	2
45	Kent	61	1
46	NC State	61	1
47	San Diego	61	1
48	Vermont	60	1
49	St. Peter's	60	1
50	Rice	59	2
51	Stephen F. Austin	59	2
52	Utah	58	1
53	Maine	57	1
54	Liberty	54	1
55	Tennessee Tech	54	1
56	St. Joe's	54	2
57	Clemson	54	2
58	Alcorn St.	53	1
59	Drake	50	1
60	Texas	48	1
61	Montana	46	1
62	Hampton	45	1
63	Campbell	42	1
64	Furman	38	1

Scoring Defense (Avg.)

Rank	School	Defense	Games
1	Tennessee	53	6
2	St. Joe's	53	2
3	Rutgers	53	5
4	Georgia	56	4
5	Texas Tech	58	4

6	UConn	60	6
7	Maine	62	1
8	LSU	62	4
9	Notre Dame	63	3
10	North Carolina	63	3
11	Duke	63	3
12	Drake	64	1
13	NC State	64	1
14	Stephen F. Austin	64	2
15	Iowa St.	65	3
16	Vermont	65	1
17	Clemson	66	2
18	Vanderbilt	67	2
19	Santa Barbara	67	1
20	Marquette	68	1
21	Arizona	68	2
22	Illinois	68	2
23	Tulane	68	2
24	Virginia	69	3
25	Miss. St.	69	2
26	LA Tech	69	4
27	Texas	69	1
28	Dartmouth	70	1
29	UAB	70	3
30	Kansas	71	1
31	Purdue	71	2
32	Penn St.	71	5
33	Campbell	71	1
34	Xavier	73	1
35	Rice	73	2
36	Utah	73	1
37	Kent	73	1
38	Montana	74	1
39	Pepperdine	74	1
40	Boston College	75	2
41	Auburn	76	2
42	SW Missouri St.	76	1
43	W. Kentucky	77	2
44	Liberty	77	1
45	Stanford	78	2
46	UCLA	79	1
47	Oregon	80	1
48	SMU	81	2
49	Michigan	81	1
50	Old Dominion	82	3
51	George Washington	83	2
52	Tennessee Tech	83	1
53	Youngstown St.	83	1
54	Oklahoma	85	3
55	Brigham Young	86	1
56	San Diego	87	1
57	Furman	90	1
58	Holy Cross	91	1
59	St. Francis (PA)	92	1
60	Nebraska	93	1
61	Wisc. Green Bay	94	1
62	St. Peter's	94	1
63	Alcorn St.	95	1
64	Hampton	116	1

Scoring Margin (Avg.)

Rank	School	Margin	Games
1	UConn	31	6
2	Notre Dame	19	3
3	Georgia	16	4
4	Tennessee	15	6
5	Miss. St.	14	2
6	Iowa St.	13	3
7	Duke	12	3
8	Rutgers	10	5
9	Texas Tech	9	4
10	LA Tech	8	4
11	LSU	8	4
12	Old Dominion	7	3
13	Boston College	6	2
14	Penn St.	3	5
15	North Carolina	3	3
16	Illinois	2	2
17	Purdue	1	2
18	SW Missouri St.	1	1
19	St. Joe's	0	2
20	Vanderbilt	0	2
21	Xavier	-1	1
22	Virginia	-1	3
23	Oregon	-1	1
24	Arizona	-1	2
25	UAB	-2	3
26	Kansas	-2	1
27	NC State	-3	1
28	Auburn	-3	2
29	Santa Barbara	-3	1
30	Marquette	-3	1
31	Dartmouth	-4	1
32	Oklahoma	-4	3
33	Maine	-5	1
34	Vermont	-5	1
35	Stephen F. Austin	-5	2
36	Stanford	-6	2
37	Brigham Young	-6	1
38	Tulane	-6	2
39	Michigan	-7	1
40	UCLA	-7	1
41	W. Kentucky	-8	2
42	Wisc. Green Bay	-9	1
43	SMU	-11	2
44	Clemson	-12	2
45	Kent	-12	1
46	Pepperdine	-12	1
47	Youngstown St.	-13	1
48	George Washington	-14	2
49	Rice	-14	2
50	Drake	-14	1
51	Utah	-15	1
52	Nebraska	-17	1
53	Holy Cross	-21	1
54	Texas	-21	1
55	Liberty	-23	1
56	San Diego	-26	1
57	Montana	-28	1
58	St. Francis (Pa.)	-29	1
59	Campbell	-29	1

60	Tennessee Tech	-29	1
61	St. Peter's	-34	1
62	Alcorn St.	-42	1
63	Furman	-52	1
64	Hampton	-71	1

Three-Point Field Goals (Avg.)

Rank	School	P3ERS	Games
1	UConn	36	6
2	Iowa St.	32	3
3	Penn St.	28	5
4	Tennessee	24	6
5	Virginia	20	3
6	Duke	19	3
7	LA Tech	18	4
8	Georgia	17	4
9	Texas Tech	16	4
10	George Washington	16	2
11	Old Dominion	15	3
12	Oklahoma	15	3
13	Miss St.	15	2
14	UAB	13	3
15	Youngstown St.	13	1
16	SMU	13	2
17	Rutgers	12	5
18	W. Kentucky	12	2
19	Brigham Young	12	1
20	Boston College	11	2
21	Arizona	11	2
22	Stanford	11	2
23	Tulane	10	2
24	Notre Dame	10	3
25	LSU	10	4
26	Holy Cross	10	1
27	Auburn	9	2
28	Wisc. Green Bay	9	1
29	Utah	9	1
30	North Carolina	9	3
31	Clemson	9	2
32	Stephen F. Austin	8	2
33	Marquette	8	1
34	Vanderbilt	8	2
35	Xavier	8	1
36	St. Francis (Pa.)	8	1
37	San Diego	8	1
38	UCLA	7	1
39	St. Joe's	7	2
40	SW Missouri St.	6	1
41	Oregon	6	1
42	Maine	5	1
43	Santa Barbara	5	1
44	Dartmouth	5	1
45	Pepperdine	5	1
46	Kansas	5	1
47	Michigan	5	1
48	Vermont	5	1
49	Campbell	4	1
50	Purdue	4	2
51	Alcorn St.	4	1
52	Montana	4	1
53	Liberty	4	1

54	Drake	4	1	
55	Nebraska	4	1	
56	Illinois	4	2	
57	Hampton	3	1	
58	St. Peter's	2	1	
59	Furman	2	1	
60	Tennessee Tech	2	1	
61	Texas	1	1	
62	Kent	1	1	
63	Rice	1	2	
64	NC State	1	1	

Field Goal Percentage

Rank	School	FG	FGA	FG%	Games
1	Wisc. Green Bay	30	51	58.82	1
2	UConn	203	355	57.18	6
3	Xavier	23	42	54.76	1
4	Notre Dame	80	148	54.05	3
5	LSU	117	220	53.18	4
6	Old Dominion	97	186	52.15	3
7	Holy Cross	23	45	51.11	1
8	SW Missouri St.	29	57	50.88	1
9	Nebraska	29	57	50.88	1
10	Illinois	51	102	50.00	2
11	Boston College	56	114	49.12	2
12	Kansas	27	55	49.09	1
13	Iowa St.	88	180	48.89	3
14	Rice	50	103	48.54	2
15	Oregon	30	62	48.39	1
16	Oklahoma	84	174	48.28	3
17	Auburn	50	105	47.62	2
18	Maine	20	42	47.62	2
19	UAB	75	158	47.47	3
20	Brigham Young	26	55	47.27	1
21	Kent	25	53	47.17	1
22	Miss. St.	65	138	47.10	2
23	St. Peter's	24	51	47.06	1
24	Stanford	50	107	46.73	2
25	Georgia	110	237	46.41	4
26	Texas	19	41	46.34	1
27	Purdue	52	113	46.02	2
28	Utah	22	48	45.83	1
29	Rutgers	126	276	45.65	5
30	Vanderbilt	51	113	45.13	2
31	Stephen F. Austin	54	120	45.00	2
32	George Washington	44	98	44.90	2
33	Duke	79	176	44.89	3
34	Vermont	25	56	44.64	1
35	Penn St.	134	301	44.52	5
36	Tennessee	141	317	44.48	6
37	NC State	24	54	44.44	1
38	North Carolina	76	172	44.19	3
39	Tulane	40	92	43.48	2
40	Tennessee Tech	19	44	43.18	1
41	Virginia	69	160	43.12	3
42	UCLA	26	61	42.62	1
43	Marquette	23	54	42.59	1
44	San Diego	19	45	42.22	1
45	Texas Tech	108	256	42.19	4
46	LA Tech	121	288	42.01	4
47	Arizona	47	112	41.96	2

48	Michigan	30	73	41.10	1
49	Drake	16	40	40.00	1
50	W. Kentucky	50	126	36.68	2
51	SMU	50	127	39.37	2
52	St. Joe's	39	101	38.61	2
53	Youngstown St.	26	69	37.68	1
54	Dartmouth	21	56	37.50	1
55	Santa Barbara	18	49	36.73	1
56	St. Francis (Pa.)	26	71	36.62	1
57	Alcorn St.	19	54	35.19	1
58	Clemson	36	104	34.65	2
59	Pepperdine	24	70	34.29	1
60	Campbell	14	44	31.82	1
61	Liberty	17	54	31.48	1
62	Hampton	18	60	30.00	1
63	Montana	17	58	29.31	1
64	Furman	13	55	23.64	1

Free Throw Percentage

Rank	School	FT	FTA	FT%	Games
1	Tennessee Tech	14	14	100.00	1
2	Montana	8	8	100.00	1
3	Auburn	36	37	97.30	2
4	Maine	12	13	92.31	1
5	Alcorn St.	11	12	91.67	1
6	Liberty	16	18	88.89	1
7	Drake	14	16	87.50	1
8	Arizona	28	33	84.85	2
9	Brigham Young	16	19	84.21	1
10	Duke	50	60	83.33	3
11	Kansas	10	12	83.33	1
12	Utah	5	6	83.33	1
13	Clemson	28	34	82.35	2
14	Xavier	18	22	81.82	1
15	Pepperdine	9	11	81.82	1
16	Illinois	35	43	81.40	2
17	W. Kentucky	26	32	81.25	2
18	Iowa St.	28	35	80.00	3
19	NC State	12	15	80.00	1
20	Penn St.	81	102	79.41	5
21	Dartmouth	19	24	79.17	1
22	San Diego	15	19	78.95	1
23	North Carolina	41	52	78.85	3
24	Oklahoma	59	76	77.63	3
25	Tulane	34	44	77.27	2
26	Kent	10	13	76.92	1
27	UCLA	13	17	76.47	1
28	Oregon	13	17	76.47	1
29	Notre Dame	77	101	76.24	3
30	Wisc. Green Bay	16	21	76.19	1
31	Stanford	34	45	75.56	2
32	Boston College	40	53	75.47	2
33	Georgia	54	72	75.00	4
34	St. Francis	3	4	75.00	1
35	Rutgers	59	79	74.68	5
36	Santa Barbara	23	31	74.19	1
37	UAB	40	54	74.07	3
38	Nebraska	14	19	73.68	1
39	LSU	40	55	72.73	4
40	SW Missouri St.	13	18	72.22	1
41	Tennessee	109	151	72.19	6

42	UConn	105	146	71.92	6
43	St. Joe's	23	32	71.88	2
44	Old Dominion	61	85	71.76	3
45	Furman	10	14	71.43	1
46	LA Tech	52	73	71.23	4
47	SMU	27	38	71.05	2
48	Virginia	46	65	70.77	3
49	George Washington	35	50	70.00	2
50	Purdue	36	53	67.92	2
51	Texas Tech	40	60	66.67	4
52	Holy Cross	14	21	66.67	1
53	St. Peter's	10	15	66.67	1
54	Hampton	6	9	66.67	1
55	Miss. St.	21	32	65.62	2
56	Vanderbilt	26	40	65.00	2
57	Marquette	11	17	64.71	1
58	Michigan	9	14	64.29	1
59	Texas	9	14	64.29	1
60	Rice	17	29	58.62	2
61	Vermont	5	9	55.56	1
62	Campbell	10	19	52.63	1
63	Youngstown St.	3	6	50.00	1
64	Stephen F. Austin	2	4	50.00	2

Three-Point Shooting Percentage

Rank	School	P3	P3A	P3T%	Games
1	St. Peter's	2	2	100.00	1
2	Rice	1	1	100.00	2
3	NC State	1	1	100.00	1
4	Maine	5	7	71.43	1
5	Tennessee Tech	2	3	66.67	1
6	Xavier	8	13	61.54	1
7	UConn	36	60	60.00	6
8	Holy Cross	10	17	58.82	1
9	Arizona	11	19	57.89	2
10	Montana	4	7	57.14	1
11	Wisc. Green Bay	9	16	56.25	1
12	North Carolina	9	16	56.25	3
13	Brigham Young	12	22	54.55	1
14	Auburn	9	17	52.94	2
15	Youngstown St.	13	25	52.00	1
16	Tennessee	24	48	50.00	6
17	Texas Tech	16	32	50.00	4
18	George Washington	16	32	50.00	2
19	Kansas	5	10	50.00	1
20	Campbell	4	8	50.00	1
21	Kent	1	2	50.00	1
22	Old Dominion	15	31	48.39	3
23	SMU	13	27	48.15	2
24	Boston College	11	23	47.83	2
25	Stanford	11	23	47.83	2
26	Tulane	10	21	47.62	2
27	LSU	10	21	47.62	4
28	Utah	9	19	47.37	1
29	Vanderbilt	8	17	47.06	2
30	Penn St.	28	60	46.67	5
31	UCLA	7	15	46.67	1
32	Rutgers	12	26	46.15	5
33	SW Missouri St.	6	13	46.15	1
34	Oregon	6	13	46.15	1
35	Notre Dame	10	22	45.45	3

36	Pepperdine	5	11	45.45	1
37	Georgia	17	38	44.74	4
38	Virginia	20	45	44.44	3
39	Marquette	8	18	44.44	1
40	Purdue	4	9	44.44	2
41	Alcorn St.	4	9	44.44	1
42	Miss. St.	15	34	44.12	2
43	Iowa St.	32	73	43.84	3
44	Santa Barbara	5	12	41.67	1
45	Oklahoma	15	37	40.54	3
46	Liberty	4	10	40.00	1
47	Drake	4	10	40.00	1
48	W. Kentucky	12	31	38.71	2
49	San Diego	8	21	38.10	1
50	Illinois	4	11	36.36	2
51	UAB	13	37	35.14	3
52	Stephen F. Austin	8	23	34.78	2
53	Clemson	9	26	34.62	2
54	Duke	19	55	34.55	3
55	LA Tech	18	54	33.33	4
56	St. Francis	8	24	33.33	1
57	Dartmouth	5	15	33.33	1
58	Nebraska	4	12	33.33	1
59	Texas	1	3	33.33	1
60	St. Joe's	7	25	28.00	2
61	Vermont	5	18	27.78	1
62	Furman	2	8	25.00	1
63	Michigan	5	21	23.81	1
64	Hampton	3	13	23.08	1

Index

796.323
Ken   Kent, Richard
         Inside women's college
         basketball : anatomy
         of a season

DISCARDED

                    12/2000

DISCARDED

ANDOVER PUBLIC LIBRARY
       ANDOVER, CT